THE
LAST IRISH
QUESTION

Glenn Patterson was born in Belfast. The author of
fifteen previous works of fiction and non-fiction, he
co-wrote the screenplay of the film *Good Vibrations*.
He is currently Director of the Seamus Heaney
Centre at Queen's University.

ALSO BY GLENN PATTERSON

NON-FICTION

Lapsed Protestant
Once Upon a Hill: Love in Troubled Times
Here's Me Here
Backstop Land

NOVELS

Burning Your Own
Fat Lad
Black Night at Big Thunder Mountain
The International
Number 5
That Which Was
The Third Party
The Mill for Grinding Old People Young
The Rest Just Follows
Gull
Where Are We Now?

THE LAST IRISH QUESTION

WILL SIX INTO TWENTY-SIX EVER GO?

GLENN PATTERSON

An Apollo Book

First published in the UK in 2021 by Head of Zeus
This paperback edition first published in 2023 by Head of Zeus,
part of Bloomsbury Publishing Plc

9 7 5 3 1 2 4 6 8

A catalogue record for this book is available from
the British Library.

Lines from *Little Gidding* on page 245 by permission of T. S. Eliot estate

ISBN (PB): 9781800245464
ISBN (E): 9781800245457

Typeset by www.benstudios.co.uk

Printed and bound in Great Britain by
CPI Group (UK) Ltd, Croydon CR0 4YY

Head of Zeus Ltd
5–8 Hardwick Street
London EC1R 4RG

WWW.HEADOFZEUS.COM

Contents

Thank you to everyone who stopped to talk.

A note on terminology

Ireland is an island.

Ireland is the preferred name of the United Nations member state officially described as the Republic of Ireland.

Many republicans won't thank you for the Republic of Ireland, or the Republic, or the Irish Republic.

Éire is its preferred name in Irish. If you do not speak Irish, and most of all if you are English, you should not say Éire.

Poblacht na hÉireann is the official name in Irish. If you do not speak Irish and most of all if you are English, you are maybe better off sticking to getting stick for Éire.

Northern Ireland is that bit of the first definition of Ireland that is not the second definition of Ireland.

Northern Ireland is still the preferred name of that bit of Ireland for the majority who live in it.

Which does not seem to stop many who object to other people using Éire or the Republic going out of their way to avoid saying it. It is the North of Ireland to them or just the North.

The North is geographically inexact.

The South ditto.

Don't even talk to me about Ulster.

Northern Ireland occupies the north-east corner only of Ireland Mark 1.

Donegal is north of the rest of the South and north of some of the North, and west of all of it.

Island Ireland is divided into thirty-two counties.

United Nations Ireland contains twenty-six of them.

Northern Ireland contains six.

In this book I use all the above names and terms promiscuously (though I am probably lighter on Éire than any other, beyond these pages, obviously) and possibly one or two others.

United Ireland is the term for island Ireland under a single jurisdiction. It is usually preceded by the indefinite article. Which, article-wise, for now, seems about right.

Right, is that us? Then let's go …

Although...

Where to begin?

1921? 1916? 1801? 1690? 1542? 1169? Partition, the Easter Rising, the Act of Union, the Battle of the Boyne, the Plantation, the arrival in Waterford of Richard, Earl of Pembroke, aka Strongbow?

If you know the answer, or do not care overmuch, go straight to the next chapter.

No one sprang from here. They – we – all arrived from somewhere else, sometime else. Robert Kee, in *Ireland: A Television History*, goes for 8000 BC, the first arrivals crossing the land bridge from Scotland, not that they knew that that was only a land bridge they were walking across or indeed that that was Scotland they were walking across from. Eventually the waves of migration and invasion – seaborne latterly, the land bridge having become a channel (the North Channel) – stopped long enough for the people who were on the island, as it had become, to think of it fairly, and Viking raids notwithstanding, as theirs, even if they did still dispute among themselves which bits were really theirs, and nobody else's on the island.

In the closing decades of the twelfth century, a deposed king of these people invited the step-grandson of the last invaders of the island next door to help him regain his crown, by taking the Viking-settlement-turned-city of Dublin, which the step-grandson, the French-born Henry II, duly did, first through the offices of Richard de Clere, Earl of Pembroke, the aforementioned Strongbow, then when Strongbow appeared to be establishing a powerbase of his own, in person. (Diarmaid Mac Murchadha, who had issued the invitation, had quietly died before its outworkings could be seen.) Henry became Lord of Ireland* in the way that kings then tended to do, by telling everyone to call him that and killing anyone who refused, although after an initial period of expansion his heirs and successors controlled only a few hundred square miles of the Ireland he had tried to Lord it over, an area, centred on Dublin, known as the Pale. Five more Henrys came and went, interspersed with Richards and Edwards, until Henry VIII broke with the Roman Catholic Church, kickstarting a couple of centuries of religious wars that took in most of Europe and made of Catholic Ireland a back door for the invasion of England as well as a seat of ever greater rebellion. It was, though, Henry's daughter, Mary, herself a Catholic, who initiated the policy of Plantation, the Latinized form of 'land grab', carried on by her sister successor Elizabeth I and by James I (already James VI of Scotland), the first of the Stuart monarchs, who came after her.

---

* The genealogical website geni.com gives his 'occupation' in full as 'King of England, Count of Anjou, Duke of Normandy, Lord of Ireland, King, English Monarch, KING OF ENGLAND, King of ENGLAND (1154–1189), duc de Normandie (1150–1189), duc d'Aquitaine (1152–1189), comte d'Anjou, de Tours et du Maine (1151–1189).'

The Plantation in the north-east differed from the Plantation in the rest of the island in that a great many of the Planters – as they came to be known – were, for reasons of simple proximity, of Scottish, and very particularly Scottish Presbyterian stock. The 1603 Union of the Two Crowns, which saw James VI of Scotland become James I of England and Wales, gave impetus to this particular Plantation. Historian Norman Davies in *The Isles*, published in 1999, writes of that moment, 'Protestant Ulster, run by the English, manned by the Scots, and planted on the Irish, was, in effect, the first British colony'.

(I like Norman Davies a lot – I like *The Isles* an awful lot – and I care not a jot for the word Protestant as it has been applied to me, but something inside me sags when I read elsewhere in the text of 'Protestant Ulster' as 'a retarded time capsule'. Really, Norman? All of it?)

The first concerted attempt to oust the Planters started in the north-east in 1641. The hope, as with so many conflicts before and since, was that it would all be over quickly. Instead, it was the beginning of a war that dragged on for eleven years, pulling in Scots Covenanters and two different English factions – Royalists and Parliamentarians (for this was the time, too, of the English Civil War) – in the course of which hundreds of thousands out of a population of one and a half million may have died.

The eventual defeat of the Irish Confederation was the excuse for further punitive confiscations of land and forced relocations of former landowners to the inhospitable west of the island. War returned in the late 1680s as the Catholic James II tried to use Ireland as a springboard to wrest back the English crown from his son-in-law, the Dutch William of Orange, who had the blessing of the pope, Innocent XI, although, in what was fast becoming a pattern, the geopolitical significance was overlaid with more local animosities. For many Protestants, especially in Ulster, the Siege of Derry across 1688 and 1689 – and more importantly the city's refusal to capitulate – and the Battle of the Boyne the year after, when William, 'King Billy', won a decisive victory, were defining events with a long reach: 'No Surrender' and 'Remember 1690' reverberate right down to today.

As happened in time with previous generations of new arrivals, the descendants of many of those Tudor and Stuart Planters came to think of themselves as Irish before all else and to see a need for a measure of self-government. Some went further. By the end of the eighteenth century, and taking their inspiration from the only-just-United States of America and revolutionary France, they had set their sights on full independence. Their Rising, in 1798, was in the name of a United Irishness embracing Catholic, Protestant (which is to say Episcopalian) and Dissenter (those mainly northern Presbyterians), though this was not enough to stop it from descending into an appalling sectarian bloodletting and an equally appallingly brutal military suppression that paved the way for a formal Act of Union, which in 1801 brought into being the United Kingdom of Great Britain and Ireland, aka the UK.

Which really quietened things down.

Agitation for repeal of the Union began almost as soon as it came into effect and grew in vociferousness and urgency following the Great Hunger of 1845–9, which laid bare the inequities of a landowning system that had left a majority of the rural population – the vast majority of the population as a whole – reliant on a single crop, the potato. When it failed, they struggled. When the Westminster government failed to respond, they starved. A million died. A million more emigrated, mostly to the United States. Ulster, which had a different tenant arrangement from the rest of the island, suffered less badly from starvation and emigration (the high-water mark for emigration from that quarter was actually a century before). And there were other divergences. Nationalism of the sort once espoused by northern, Presbyterian United Irish women and men was increasingly identified with Catholicism, bolstered, following Catholic Emancipation, by an expanding Catholic middle class, and by the church itself. In Britain in the years after the Famine a two-party political system emerged, with one party, the Liberals, increasingly committed to addressing the 'land question' in Ireland, which, under Prime Minister William Gladstone, became a commitment to the devolution of power to a government in Dublin, or, to use the shortened form, Home Rule.

The Liberals' Conservative opponents – full title the Conservative and Unionist Party – were adamant that not only was it wrong in principle, but that Home Rule would be resisted by a sizeable and geographically specific part of the population. 'Ulster will fight, and Ulster will be right' became their rallying cry, even though it was coined by a Liberal Unionist, Joseph Chamberlain, whose son Neville, as prime minister in September 1938, famously declared Britain and Germany would not fight and everything would most likely be all right.

Successive Liberal Home Rule Bills were defeated, the first in the House of Commons, the second, more controversially,

9

as the nineteenth century drew to a close, in the unelected House of Lords. The Liberals, though, came back a third time following the 1910 general election (*elections*: the first produced no clear majority), which left the Home Rule-supporting Irish Nationalist Party holding the balance of power. The Liberals had other grievances with the Lords, other socially progressive legislation they wanted to enact. One of the first things they did was remove the Upper House's ability to reject bills outright. All it could do in future was delay their implementation. The way was clear for Home Rule to pass into law, which it did in 1912. That same year, more than 400,000 people signed 'Ulster's Solemn League and Covenant' (the title comes straight out of the Scots Presbyterian tradition that was so pronounced in the north-east) pledging to use 'all means that may be found necessary to defeat the present conspiracy to set up a Home Rule parliament in Ireland'. The following year an Ulster Volunteer Force was formed. (There was a strong tradition of volunteering, too, and not just in Ulster: it was out of an eighteenth-century Volunteer movement that the United Irish rebellion emerged.) Early in 1914, this 'UVF', by now numbering almost 100,000, imported tons of arms from Germany.

And then Archduke Franz Ferdinand was assassinated, and Austria-Hungary declared war on Serbia and then Germany declared war on Russia, Belgium and France, and then Britain declared war on Germany and Home Rule, with a temporary opt-out for Ulster, was put on hold.

The UVF joined the British army en masse to fight the Germans who they had just bought guns from, as did many of the Irish Volunteer Force, which had formed in the image of, but in opposition to, the UVF and which had similarly brought in guns from Germany. Many others, though, especially those who looked on Home Rule as nothing more than a stepping stone to full independence, saw the war as 'England's difficulty', which provided Ireland with a once in a generation – once in many, many generations – opportunity.

On Easter Monday 1916, the Irish Volunteers, and the smaller Irish Citizen Army, steered by a circle of conspirators from the Irish Republican Brotherhood, rose up in Dublin, occupying key buildings and issuing their Proclamation of the Republic: 'We declare the right of the people of Ireland to the ownership of Ireland, and to the unfettered control of Irish destinies, to be sovereign and indefeasible ... We place the cause of the Irish Republic under the protection of the Most High God. Whose blessing we invoke upon our arms and we pray that no one who serves that cause will disgrace it by cowardice, inhumanity or rapine.'

The British army, vastly superior in numbers and weaponry, put down this Easter Rising within a week.

All seven signatories of the Proclamation were executed the following month, along with several more of the military commanders and a few months later the Ulster born diplomat Sir Roger Casement, who had been captured the week before the Rising after arriving in Ireland aboard yet another vessel set sail from Germany.

And all the while in northern France the British and French armies were preparing for a major offensive along the River Somme, an offensive which, when they finally launched it on the morning of 1 July 1916, saw the 36th Ulster Division – the UVF by other means – suffer dreadful losses.

Support for the Rising, muted in Easter week, grew in the wake of the executions of May (and, in Casement's case, August) 1916, as did antipathy to the British. In the general election called in the immediate aftermath of the Armistice of November 1918, Sinn Féin, the party most identified with the independence cause, won a landslide, everywhere but the north-east. Rather than take up their seats in Westminster, the party convened the first Provisional Government in Dublin. That same day in early 1919 a group of Volunteers – the germ of a new Irish Republican Army – killed two members of the locally recruited Royal Irish Constabulary in Co. Tipperary, signalling the start of, and setting the tone for, the War of Independence that carried on into 1921 and spread into most parts of the island. As ever, the north-east was an exception. There, the years 1919–21 were characterized more by intercommunal strife and in Belfast in particular attacks on the minority Catholic population. In the middle of the violence, in December 1920, the Home Rule Act that had been suspended when the world went to war six years before was enacted with two separate parliaments, one in Belfast, one in Dublin, though only the Belfast Home Rule parliament ever sat (to the despair of Edward Carson, the Dublin-born Unionist leader, who wanted neither Home Rule nor Partition), the appetite in Dublin being now for a complete break with Britain.

Or appearing to be.

After negotiations in London in the autumn of 1921, a Provisional Government delegation signed a treaty that fell well short of independence, offering Ireland, in effect, Dominion status. Civil war broke out between those who accepted and those who rejected the Treaty, the pro-Treaty side now styling themselves the National Army, the anti-Treaty side sticking with IRA.

Pro won.

Anti, eventually, regrouped and entered back into the political system in the shape of Fianna Fáil, under the leadership of Éamon de Valera, who had escaped execution in 1916 due to his American birth. There remained, though, a sizeable group of irreconcilables as opposed to the existence, or the limits, of the 'Free State', as they were – as, admittedly, all the Southern parties were – to the very fact of a Northern Ireland in any shape or form. Its exact shape and form was confirmed by a Boundary Commission intent – they made no bones about it – on the creation, to the north of the boundary, of a permanent Protestant majority, or as permanent as 1924 could envisage. One third of Ulster's nine counties – Donegal, Cavan and Monaghan – were omitted from the new northern state. Or, if you preferred, statelet. (It could have been worse, or smaller. At one stage Fermanagh and Tyrone were to be cut adrift, too, leaving only Antrim, Armagh, Down and   to give it its official Northern Ireland name – Londonderry.) Within it, Catholics (about 35 per cent of the population) faced discrimination and exclusion, with limited entitlement to voting in local council elections, and, while having equal voting rights in general elections, no hope whatever of seeing a party that reflected their views or represented their interests ever dislodging the ruling Unionist Party from their seat of power in the grandiose new Parliament Buildings at Stormont.

A Special Powers Act, brought in during the violence of the early 1920s, was never repealed. The UVF that had become the 36th Ulster Division now supplied numerous recruits to the three categories – A, B and C – of the Ulster Special Constabulary, created to support the new Royal Ulster Constabulary. A and C were soon lost to history, but the part-time 'B Specials' remained as a constant irritant to the Catholic community. Sectarian violence returned to the streets of Belfast in the mid-1930s, by which time Fianna Fáil had come to power in the South and, as well as legislating to take the Free State out of the Commonwealth, through a new constitution, had taken action against those irreconcilables still styling themselves the IRA. Four years after the end of the Second World War, known as the Emergency in the South, which largely sat it out, the 26 counties declared themselves, and by virtue of the territorial claim in Articles 2 and 3 of the constitution, the 6 counties of Northern Ireland, a republic. Seven years after that again the IRA, numbering some two hundred active members, launched a 'border campaign' that, far from driving Britain out of Ireland, had, by the time they called it off, driven their own organization to the brink of extinction. In the South in particular, the IRA took a leftward, grassroots-politics turn. When the golden anniversary of the Easter Rising rolled around, in 1966, Northern unionists had almost to invent the present-day bogey with which to scare themselves silly, although that is not to say there were not behaviours and attitudes on display that could give the gullible, or the easily led, succour. It was also, of course, the golden anniversary of the Battle of the Somme. The UVF name was dusted down and adopted by a group of extreme loyalists, some of whom were, at the very least, inspired by one Ian Paisley – a correspondence-course minister, master of his own Free Presbyterian Church and dyed-in-the-wool demagogue – and all of whom were as opposed to the mildly reformist regime of Unionist prime minister Terence O'Neill as they were to the (mostly imaginary) IRA. Seemingly unembarrassed by the connections between him and the UVF gang that carried out a series of nakedly sectarian murders in Belfast in the spring and summer of 1966, Paisley was to the fore of the opposition to the Northern Ireland Civil Rights Association formed early the following year under the banner of 'One Man One Vote'. As civil rights marches grew in size so did the counterdemonstrations and the level of violence from police and B Specials. The disorder became general, as the decade entered its final year, and more intensely sectarian.

British troops arrived.

A new IRA – the Provisionals – was born, in the way that IRAs usually were, by a split from the 'Official' IRA.

Protestant paramilitaries burgeoned.

The Troubles had begun.

Within three years – that had seen, to pick out some of the lowest lights, the introduction of internment, the commencement of a mass IRA car-bombing campaign resulting in multiple civilian casualties (though loyalists too did their bloody bombing bit), widespread sectarian murder and the massacre of fourteen people by the Parachute Regiment in Derry* – the British

* To this must be added the massacre, which it took the British government fifty years to acknowledge, and then gracelessly, of ten others of its own citizens in Ballymurphy, by the same regiment, six months before Bloody Sunday.

government had called time on Northern Ireland's parliament and introduced direct rule from Westminster. At the beginning of the following year, 1973, the United Kingdom and Ireland, along with Denmark, joined the European Economic Community – 'the Common Market'. It was the beginning of a period of gradually improving relations and closer cooperation between London and Dublin (if laced still at times with suspicion), especially over the issue of Northern Ireland. In 1985, the two governments signed an Anglo-Irish Agreement and following another near-decade's violence, ended by the IRA's ceasefire in 1994 (then started again by the IRA's bombing of London's Docklands, then ended again by another ceasefire in 1996), brokered, with American assistance, the talks that led to the April 1998 Belfast Agreement, known to the world as the Good Friday Agreement. About as many people had died in the quarter-century of the Troubles as were killed in the four earlier-twentieth-century years of the War of Independence and the Civil War that followed.

Under the Good Friday Agreement, endorsed by referendums North and South, the 26-county state renounced its territorial claim on the 6 counties and recognized that they would remain part of the United Kingdom until such times as there was a majority in both jurisdictions (accounted for separately) in favour of Irish unity. The Agreement stated that the power to trigger such a referendum resided with the British secretary of state for Northern Ireland of the day, but only where they were satisfied that a majority of those voting there would express a preference for a united Ireland. In the event that the secretary of state had called it wrong, and the result was in favour of

Northern Ireland remaining in the UK, another referendum could not take place within the next seven years.

A new Stormont power-sharing government came into being, led at first by the Ulster Unionist Party and the nationalist Social Democratic Labour Party (SDLP), but – after several suspensions and protracted squabbles over the implementation of the Agreement, including on the timing of paramilitary disarmament – eventually, and perhaps inevitably, by Sinn Féin and Ian Paisley's Democratic Unionist Party.

In the South, meanwhile, the role and authority of the Catholic Church – such a dominant force since the State's inception – was weakened by a series of revelations, each more shocking than the last, of child abuse and the ill treatment of unmarried mothers and their babies, stretching back decades. Little by little and then all in a rush, a new, more socially liberal Ireland emerged. Queen Elizabeth II visited in the spring of 2011, paying her respects to the Irish dead of the War of Independence and reflecting that 'with the benefit of historical hindsight we can all see things which we would wish had been done differently or not at all'. All seemed set fair for the next decade and beyond.

Then, in June 2016, the UK voted to leave the EU, as it now was; or, to be territorially exact, a majority who cast their ballot in England and Wales voted to leave, the majority in Scotland voting to remain a part of it, along with the majority in Northern Ireland.

The border between North and South became, as ought to have been predicted, a central sticking point in the attempts to find agreement on the precise nature of the UK withdrawal and of its future trading arrangements with its former European partners.

Hard borders, soft borders, tech borders, sea borders.

The question that had seemed for a time before Brexit to be drifting out towards the fringes of the political conversation (excluding Sinn Féin's, and even their hearts did not always seem to be in it) came right back into the centre: was it time to talk seriously about getting rid of the border altogether? Should 6 go into 26 again?

Imbolc

It is 1 February. The Feast of St Brigid, or Biddy's Day, named for the fifth-century Irish nun born just south of the Ulster–Leinster border in Faughart, close to present-day Dundalk. In Irish embassies across the globe in recent years, Biddy's Day has become a celebration of women and women in the arts in particular, with readings and talks and performances by artists and thinkers and makers from North and South, *St* Brigid having been elided with an earlier, pagan Brigid who held the Celtic gods and goddesses' poetry portfolio. A friend reminds me it is also Imbolc, one of the 'quarterly beats' of the Celtic year, the turning towards the light and traditionally in Ireland the first day of spring. I say, 'in Ireland', but when I run the notion by friends here in Belfast I am met with as many blank looks as bright lights, which may admittedly mean only that I have discovered a new test for determining which of my friends here in Belfast are Protestant and which Catholic, a thing that we are otherwise far too polite these days to ask, or even surmise.

The first of February is also this year, 2020, the first day of the Brexit transition period. The first *full* day: it actually began at 11 p.m. our time last night (the UK starting a goal down, having to go by the EU's hour-ahead clock), to the accompaniment of waving flags and fireworks and 'Rule, Britannias' – and tears, too, and fuck-fuck-fucks – and Sophie Raworth on the BBC's News Special apologizing that Graham Norton was going to be a little late tonight. There are still eleven months of transitioning to come, still many, many details to be worked out, which is a bit like saying that a lorryload of bricks and slates still have many details to be worked out before they have transitioned to house. Along with the rest of the United Kingdom, though, or, rather, along with Great Britain, for no Northern Ireland means no United Kingdom, the North will be leaving the European Union of twenty-seven nations (including the South), by the end of the calendar year. Leaving under the terms of the Northern Ireland Protocol, a late addition to the withdrawal negotiations, which means it will be simultaneously part of the UK internal market and the EU single market, which means in turn there will be some sort of regulatory checks at Northern Irish ports, which is another way of saying a border in the Irish Sea. As I am sure all concerned asked themselves when they were devising it – as I am sure many have asked themselves in the past when devising cunning solutions and exceptions for this corner of the island – what could possibly go wrong?

And it is Saturday. And although it is far from spring-like, it is bright. I have walked, this first February lunchtime, the mile or so from my house to the Parliament Buildings at Stormont in Belfast's near east suburbs for a pitch event to a delegation from One Young World – styled by CNN the 'Junior Davos' – to bring their global convention to the city in 2023.

I am fifty-eight. I am there strictly in a supporting role.

I am, as it happens, there with some of the same people, from Fighting Words Belfast, the children's writing charity, I was with in June of 2019, at St Anne's Cathedral, to receive an award from the American Ireland Funds in the name of Lyra McKee, the journalist and LGBTQ+ campaigner, murdered just two months before by the New IRA. I was writing a book then about Northern Ireland in the grip of a Brexit whose precise shape – or even likelihood of ever coming to pass – was still uncertain, but whose impact on relations within Northern Ireland, and between it and the rest of the island, was already considerable. I did not know it then, but the account of that night in St Anne's would end up being the closing pages of the book. I chose for an epigraph an off-the-cuff line from the poet Scott McKendry, at another June 2019 event, this time in the Sunflower Bar on Union Street: 'where we live is basically a piss-take of the whole world'. At that particular moment – with the Northern Ireland Assembly not having sat for two and a half years, with politicians from the former coalition parties seemingly more intent on winding each other up than looking for common ground, with no sign of progress on issues such as abortion reform or marriage equality it seemed like, and was received by the audience as, a pretty fair assessment.

Seven months on, the mood in the Long Gallery on the first floor of Parliament Buildings could not be more different. Rachel Woods of the Green Party welcomes everyone on what is her own first time in the Long Gallery. The Assembly has only been sitting again for a matter of weeks, and Woods was co-opted as a Member of the Legislative Assembly (MLA) during its suspension in place of former Green Party leader Stephen

Agnew. (Co-opting is regularly used by all Stormont parties: once the former Members of the European Parliament have returned from Brussels and are absorbed into the Assembly's ranks, a full sixteen Members – or getting on for 20 per cent – will be occupying seats to which they have not, themselves, actually been elected.) 'How lovely,' she tells us, 'to have you all here while it is functioning.' I think she means it in the sense of, 'now that it is functioning again', but history since those heady days of the Good Friday Agreement teaches us it is well to be cautious.

The (mostly young) people gathered, however, are positively buoyant. Conor Houston, a former solicitor advocate, now head of Houston Solutions Ltd, is here; indeed, Conor – in his role as director of something called Connected Citizens – might be the reason why everybody else is. I once wrote of Belfast's great nineteenth-century social reformer Mary Ann McCracken that she could not stand still for two minutes without a committee forming around her; with Conor Houston it is more like a conference, or indeed a convention. There is, quite possibly, something a little self-selecting about some of this particular group. Conor introduces a twenty-something speaker as 'one of the Top Ten Young Entrepreneurs in Europe', and she corrects him, pleasantly but firmly, '*the* Top Young Entrepreneur'. That, though, only accounts for part of the room. There are others here from community groups and organizations, like Fighting Words – here, of course, at the encouragement of Conor, but keen all the same to have their say. Brexit, which is all of fourteen hours old, is spoken of as an established fact. Whether you were for or agin, whether you were behind it in the abstract but not in the concrete shape it has assumed, whether you cried last night or waved a flag, it is here. The emphasis this afternoon is on what we – or, rather, they, the next generation – do now.

Conor, in order to impress upon the One Young World delegation that the next generation might get to air all of this and other matters of concern right here in Belfast in 2023, has clearly called in a number of favours. Elizabeth Kennedy Trudeau, the US consul general in Belfast, is here. The US Consulate General in Belfast is the second oldest in the world – 'second oldest *continuously operating*', the Embassies and Consulates website specifies, but, you know, *second* … in the whole wide world – established by George Washington himself in the last full year of his presidency.* Belfast in those 1790s days had a reputation for radicalism that was without equal on the island. As that Embassies and Consulates website goes on to say, 'Settlers from Northern Ireland [sic] participated in the signing of the Declaration of Independence and numerous American presidents could trace their family backgrounds to this region.' Both the radical reputation and the clout with the American administration have lessened more than somewhat in the intervening couple of hundred years: gone South, you might almost say.

From where I am sitting in the Long Gallery, I cannot work out whether Mary Robinson is actually here, too, or just invoked

---

* Washington did not come to Belfast himself, although Benjamin Franklin did, and had a bar named in his honour, the Dr Franklin Tavern, or more familiarly 'Peggy Barclay's', one of the principal hangouts of the United Irish movement in Belfast, which is as good a definition of hiding in plain sight as you are likely to find. Or not hiding: the tavern was raided and half the leadership arrested.

so often that she might as well be. Mary Robinson these days is one of the One Young World Counsellors, revered in those circles, as elsewhere. From her election as the seventh president of Ireland in 1990, when she was just forty-six, many people date the beginning of the transformation of Irish society. Not only was she the first woman to hold the post, she was also the first president since *the* first president, Douglas Hyde (1938–45), not to come from the Fianna Fáil list, having been a Labour senator before her elevation to the presidential residency, Áras an Uachtaráin, in the middle of Dublin's Phoenix Park. Interestingly, she split from the Labour Party in the mid-1980s over its endorsement of the Anglo-Irish Agreement, the negotiations for which, she argued, ought to have included Northern unionists, whose own opposition brought hundreds of thousands of protestors on to the streets and gave rise to the infamous 'Ulster Says No!' campaign, and Ian Paisley's 'Never, Never, Never!'.

Although, as president, Robinson held no executive power, the very fact of her being in Phoenix Park, as someone with a track record of campaigning on issues such as decriminalization of homosexuality and access to contraception, sent out a powerful signal of a wider desire for change. It was certainly picked up as such in the North, where the presidency was, for many of my generation certainly, associated still with Éamon de Valera, who in one capacity or another was at the forefront of Ireland's politics from the time of the Easter Rising to the joining of the Common Market. Her subsequent term as UN High Commissioner for Human Rights further cemented her reputation, and

Ireland's, on the world stage.* And though her successor as president – after a second term – reverted to type in having a Fianna Fáil connection, she, Mary McAleese, chalked up a couple of records of her own: first Northerner to be elected president, and first woman anywhere in the world to succeed another woman in a country's highest office.

Definitely not in the room, at least not to begin with, is the British government secretary of state for Northern Ireland, Julian Smith, who has sent his apologies along with his fervent hopes of joining us later. Though you would have to say, if anyone could plead pressure of work this first day of February/spring/Brexit transition, it is Julian Smith. Back at the start of January with talks between the Northern Ireland parties over the restoration of the Assembly still seemingly deadlocked, Smith, appointed by Boris Johnson when he took over the party leadership in August 2019, walked out one dark and rainy night, the Irish Tánaiste Simon Coveney by his side, to meet reporters gathered in front of these same Parliament Buildings. Together they announced the 'historic' New Decade, New Approach Agreement, which none of the parties in the talks had actually yet agreed to, or even had sight of (what there was to have sight of: the document being waved around looked suspiciously like a home-printed cover folded around whatever bits of paper had been lying around on someone's desk), but to which none of them could

---

* Her reputation takes a bit of a hit, when, just past Imbolc 2021, it comes to light that Princess Latifa Al Maktoum of Dubai, with whom the former president had posed for photos – at the invitation of the United Arab Emirates government – was in fact being kept a prisoner and had been subject to beatings and torture.

afterwards very well say no.* Arriving against the backdrop of an unprecedented strike by members of the Royal College of Nursing, and the worst waiting lists in the UK (350,000, or 20 per cent of the entire population), the Agreement's headline priority in restoring the Executive was transforming the health service. Legislation on the Irish language was provided for under 'a new framework both recognising and celebrating Northern Ireland's diversity of identities and culture and accommodating cultural difference'.

The announcement is a brilliant piece of theatre and no more dishonest in its deadpan delivery than others in the long line of historic announcements that have preceded it. And it helps that Smith has the slightly dishevelled air of the late comedian Tommy Cooper. And that – unlike others in the longer line of hapless-through-to-hopeless secretaries of state before him (there are honourable exceptions, but they are few) – he is at least *getting good stuff done*. He has already enacted equal marriage legislation for Northern Ireland and is working hard at abortion reform.

'I know,' he says, when he does eventually arrive in the Long Gallery, 'that there are differing views on [abortion], but, finally, it's a woman's right to choose.'

And that, as indeed it should be and should always have been, is that.

I get the feeling that, even in the face of the difficulties ahead, even as one who would rather not be leaving the EU

---

* I have adopted this as my own preferred method of making announcements, about everything from children's contribution to housework to repayment of debts. If nothing else, it gets me out of the house for a few minutes and entertains the neighbours' cats.

at all, *he* is optimistic, too. I get the feeling, moreover – again unlike the long line of the hapless and hopeless – he actually likes being here.

Conor Houston, in winding up proceedings, quotes Seamus Mallon, the Northern Ireland power-sharing Executive's inaugural deputy first minister. (It bears repeating, and often, that our deputy first minister – DFM – is in fact a *joint* first minister, so that it is common to refer to the office – O – she shares with the first minister as OFMDFM.)* 'I don't care,' said Mallon, and says Conor now, 'what we call this place, as long as we call it home.'

I have got up, by this time, to stand by a radiator under a window that looks out over the Parliament Buildings' front steps and down the dipping, mile-long driveway to the front gates and the east–west aligned Upper Newtownards Road on the other side. Which is when my mouth falls open. A group of protestors, seventy- or eighty-strong, are making their way up the drive. They are not the curiosity. Protests outside Stormont are – I would say – an at-least-weekly occurrence. I have walked up and down that driveway time without number myself, although the practice these days is to save your legs and your voice and enter the Stormont grounds by the side entrance, joining the driveway a good four-fifths of the way up, where stands the statue of Edward Carson, accidental founder of the Northern Irish state; as indeed these particular protestors may have done,

---

* My friend Emily Dedakis and I get lost looking for the toilets up on the first floor of Stormont. I think, as we try various doors, we are going to end up in an office: *in office*, possibly. I tell her I will be WTFM: What the Fuck Minister. She opts for SWTFM. The S is for Seriously.

because they are all, when I see them, on the far side of Carson and making for Parliament Buildings' steps. They are mostly young and colourfully dressed, and I automatically assume they are protesting against Brexit. They are not. As they draw closer, I see that the banners and placards they are carrying all relate to mental health.

'I can't believe we are protesting this again', reads one.

Northern Ireland has been in the throes of a mental health crisis for years now. Although the figures have recently been revised down a little, suicides among young people in particular have been running at truly terrifying levels.

Neither the sight of the protestors themselves, though, nor, alas, the reason they have turned out today is what causes my jaw to drop.

Coming up behind them, starting at the gates, rather than the statue, coming, that is, south to north, and in an undeviating straight line, is a wall of cumulonimbus, looking for all the world like the nemesis of Carson's own defiant claim:

'We will not forsake the blue skies of Ulster for the grey mists of the Irish Republic!'

The cloud trails its swift downpour over the protestors, darkens the front of the Parliament Buildings (though with the lights on in the Long Gallery it barely registers) and passes like a shiver overhead and into the Craigantlet Hills beyond.

In the rest of Ireland this Saturday lunchtime, the campaign for the general election, called in the middle of January by Taoiseach Leo Varadkar, has entered its final week.

Just this morning at breakfast I was talking through the election with my younger daughter.

'So, I know the UK has Labour and Conservatives, left and right. Where are Fine Gael and Fianna Fáil?'

(That was her to me, but it could easily have been the other way.)

'Right and ... right.'

'Which is further?'

'It's kind of neck and neck.'

I explain, as best I remember it, about the first wall-to-wall Sinn Féin Dáil, about the War of Independence, the split over the 1921 Treaty, the birth of Cumann na nGaedheal as the party of government, its merger a decade later – as the anti-Treatyites returned as Fianna Fáil – with the Blueshirt movement, and, hey presto, Fine Gael ...

'So, Fianna Fáil is what was Sinn Féin.'

'The other part of what was.'

'So, what is Sinn Féin then?'

'That is a very good question.'

As I was walking up to the One Young World pitch, I suddenly thought of an answer. If political parties were retail premises Sinn Féin would have had a sign in the window sometime around 1916, 'Under New Ownership'.

Sinn Féin in its original manifestation, in the early years of the last century, was, in the words of the historian F. S. L. Lyons, 'not a party but a demand', though what exactly that demand – for independence – would mean in practice or how it would be achieved was less clear. The framer and namer of the 'Sinn Féin Policy', Arthur Griffith, led the Irish delegation sent to London in 1921 to negotiate the Treaty with the British. And, whether from a sense of honour – I negotiated it so must own it – or from genuine preference, Griffith was the biggest single advocate of the 'Dominion' terms agreed.

Sinn Féin, you could say, helped split everybody else from it, including the party that now bears its name.

As for the other two ... viewed from Up Here, Fianna Fáil and Fine Gael these days are like the children of rebellious parents who in their turn rebel by becoming bankers or oil industry executives. My Dublin-born brother-in-law, Jonathan Shankey, of whom more later, tells me that Fianna Fáil was traditionally the party of the working classes, as opposed to Fine Gael, who represented prosperous farmers and merchants, and their lawyers, though there was always something anarchic and corrupt in its (Fianna Fáil's) make-up. Not for nothing did Seán Lemass, a founding member and future Taoiseach, describe it as 'a slightly constitutional party'. Jonathan tells me, too, that in a previous election (he thinks the 1990 presidential campaign when they were trying to portray Mary Robinson as a raving Trotskyite), Fianna Fáil had proudly campaigned under the banner 'The Party with no Philosophy'. That distinction, though, from Fine Gael has become increasingly blurred and it is not uncommon to see their initials elided – FFG – reminding me of the short-lived art-rock hook-up between Glasgow's Franz Ferdinand and LA's Sparks – FFS – who in 2015 scored a minor hit (it ought to have been major) with the jaunty 'Piss Off': 'Tell everybody to piss off, tonight. They should piss off and leave you alone in your world tonight.'*

I mean if ever you wanted something to play at a victory rally, when it was too late for the suckers to change their minds …

Northern Ireland has featured in the election campaign barely at all, even though Northern Ireland in a sense dictated its timing: Leo Varadkar, and his Tánaiste Simon Coveney, were coming off the back of two major diplomatic successes, in ensuring in the first instance the removal of the threat of a hard border on the island of Ireland as a consequence of Brexit, and, in the second, getting the Stormont Assembly back up and running. Why not cash in while you are ahead? Oh, Sinn Féin have in their manifesto a commitment to a referendum on reunification though they do not, there at least, put a timeframe on it and have concentrated for most of the campaign, as might be expected, on the outgoing Fine Gael government's record, and the failure of Fianna Fáil when in power to do much better. 'Time for Change' the election posters tell the Southern electorate, 'Time for Sinn Féin'.

Then in the final televised leaders' debate before the election, host Miriam O'Callaghan asks the Sinn Féin president Mary Lou McDonald about Paul Quinn. In the autumn of 2007, the nineteen-year-old from South Armagh was lured to a barn just over the border with Co. Monaghan where a gang of men beat him, brutally, methodically, and – though he clung to life for

---

* The Sparks keyboard player and songwriter, Ron Mael, famed for his wide-eyed stare and toothbrush moustache ('Have you seen Sparks?' John Lennon asked an interviewer in the early Seventies. 'They have Hitler on piano!'), in his granddad suits and slicked-back hair, actually always put me in mind of Éamon de Valera.

several days – finally, fatally. A great many people, including Paul Quinn's parents, laid the blame at the door of the South Armagh IRA, with whom they said their son had had run-ins. Sinn Féin's Conor Murphy, at the time MP for Newry and Armagh, and therefore the Quinn family's own elected representative, denied any IRA involvement, suggesting instead that the murder was connected to a fall-out among fuel launderers: 'Paul Quinn was involved in smuggling and criminality. I think everyone accepts that.'

Following the restoration of the Northern Ireland Assembly in January, as a result of that historic New Decade, New Approach agreement, just before the Dáil was dissolved, Sinn Féin handed Conor Murphy the job of finance minister. Breege Quinn, Paul Quinn's mother, asked, as she had asked many times in the years since the murder, if Minister Murphy would retract the accusations against her son. The minister said nothing. His party said nothing.

And now with five days of the campaign left to run, the party leader has been put on the spot. She stumbles over what Conor Murphy said he said and what she had previously said she thought he had said and whether even the thing she thought he had said as opposed to what he had said should ever have been said.

The leaders of her election rivals light on her obvious discomfort. Micheál Martin, leader of Fianna Fáil, says he cannot believe it took Conor Murphy thirteen years to apologize for his scandalous comments and questions his fitness for office. If he is basing his judgement of fitness on that one incident, I cannot believe it has taken him and his party, and Leo Varadkar and his, thirteen years to get around to noticing. But, then, for all of those thirteen years Sinn Féin were not breathing down their necks, beginning even, if the latest opinion polls are to be believed, to show them a clean pair of heels.

Eventually Mary Lou McDonald lets it be known that she will be ringing Breege Quinn herself 'at 5.30' on Thursday, 6 February, a little over thirty-six hours before the polls open. After so many years of inaction and evasion and out-and-out misrepresentation (I only opted for that to keep up the end rhyme, I would have preferred 'lying'), it is an almost comically precise promise. She does phone, and Breege Quinn, with great dignity, acknowledges the gesture, even though she never gets what she most wants, a retraction by Conor Murphy on television – the same medium on which the original comments were made – of the allegation that her murdered son was a criminal.

It is clear, though, throughout, that there are other voices asking what any of this has to do with the current general election. Even if the IRA was involved, it is all 'history', and Northern history at that, never mind that the murder was committed nine years after the Good Friday Agreement, endorsed by the Irish electorate, which was supposed to have brought an end to all that 'history', or that the barn where it occurred was in the South. The North – and what went on, and is still going on, there – is different. The *Irish Times* editorial the morning before the election says as much:

The notion that Sinn Féin has a right to be involved in government in the Republic because it is part of the

power-sharing Executive in the North does not stand up to
scrutiny.

Northern Ireland is not a sovereign state, but a part of
the United Kingdom whose misgovernance for so long
necessitated a political experiment in local administration
designed to force all sides to work together.

The governance of this Republic, a basically well-run and
wealthy sovereign* State is an entirely different matter. The
political parties in the Dáil are perfectly entitled to say no to
coalition with those they regard as a threat to its values and
its future prosperity.[1]

It is as though the *Irish Times* leader writer has forgotten or
is just not bothered that these words are going to be read above
as well as below the borderline.

Not that the below-the-borderline electorate appears to take
a blind bit of notice. A week and a day after St Brexit's Day a
smidge under two-thirds of them turn out to cast their votes and
return Sinn Féin as the largest single party, with 24.5 per cent of
first preferences, a gain of almost 11 per cent on the previous
election in 2016, and the party's best result since 1923. Fianna
Fáil's vote is down more than 2 per cent, Fine Gael's nearly 5
per cent. It may have taken a century, but it looks, at first glance,
as though the country has come full circle: SF – FG – FF – SF.

So much for cashing in on Brexit success and restoring the

---

* Pause there just for a moment at 'wealthy', ask yourself what exactly that
signifies, then double back to 'basically well-run' ... Wow. I mean, like, just
wow!

Stormont institutions. Simon Coveney, who will now be clearing his desk in the Tánaiste's office, is not the only one wondering what you have to do to keep a job these days: a month after standing shoulder to shoulder with him announcing New Decade, New Approach, Julian Smith is on his way, too, victim of a Boris Johnson reshuffle. He did the job that was required of him, but he still has to be punished for being too soft on Brexit.

If anything, the fact that Stormont was functioning again may have played into Sinn Féin's hands, countering the impression, voiced by one Southern voter early in the campaign, that 'when they're above in the North, it's no, no, no to everything'.

That something seismic has happened is everywhere recognized. Commentators at home and abroad rush to put a name to what it is exactly. Even commentators who would not normally be well disposed to Sinn Féin can find some positives in the vote. In the *Irish Times*, Fintan O'Toole castigates as lazy those who would see it as an Irish form of populism: it is, rather, 'entirely sensible', a responsible demand for an expansion of public services.[2] That word 'change', which featured so prominently in the Sinn Féin campaign, features just as prominently in the analysis: root and branch change to how Southern society is organized, from access to affordable housing, to healthcare.

Certainly, it is the word Mary Lou McDonald wants to focus on. As one commentator notes, when it came to the leaders' debates – presumably even the one in which it seemed as though she was on the ropes over Paul Quinn's murder – it helped her party's cause that 'the only female leader on the debate stage was also the only one who had never been Minister for Health'.

She dismisses as an unhelpful distraction the election-night speech of David Cullinane, elected on her party's ticket on the first count in Waterford, where Kevin Lynch, a republican prisoner in the Maze Prison outside Belfast, on Hunger Strike for political status, stood in June 1981. 'What a fantastic moment it must be,' Cullinane says, 'if [Kevin Lynch's] family is watching on, and people in the North are watching on, to see Sinn Féin get over 20,000 first-preference votes in this constituency. They did not break the Hunger Strikers. They did not break Bobby Sands and Kevin Lynch. They will never break us. They will never break Sinn Féin. Up the Republic, Up the Ra and Tiocfaidh ár Lá!'*

Never mind for the moment that Kevin Lynch was a member of the Irish National Liberation Army (INLA), with which, the Hunger Strikes aside, the IRA had a fraught relationship. Cullinane's 'they' who could not crush Sinn Féin, like the choruses of 'Come Out Ye Black and Tans' that break out at other counts, appears to conflate Britain with the twenty-six-county Ireland of Fine Gael and Fianna Fáil, making an enemy, rather than simply a political opponent, of the very State in which he has stood for election.

All the same, almost before negotiations have begun to see whether Sinn Féin can put together a coalition government with smaller parties and independents, both Mary Lou McDonald and her predecessor as party president Gerry Adams are calling for an accelerated track to a United Ireland referendum and for

---

* For the benefit of anyone who earlier baulked at Poblacht na hÉireann, it means 'Our Day Will Come' and is pronounced Chucky, from which comes the disparaging 'Chucks' for republicans.

the EU to come out as a promoter of unity, as it did with East and West Germany after the collapse of the Berlin Wall in 1989.

They are, of course, right to argue that a greater percentage of the electorate has just voted for the party that had a border poll in its manifesto than has voted for any other *individual* party, although, despite an exit poll suggesting that 59 per cent favoured reunification, more than three-quarters still cast their vote for parties that did not.

A few days after the election (on the day, in fact, that Julian Smith gets the heave-ho) I am at the launch of a British Council book, *Britain and Ireland Lives Entwined: Shifting Borders, Shifting Identities*. The event takes place in the Duncairn Centre in north inner-city Belfast, a few hundred yards up the Antrim Road from Carlisle Circus, one of the Northern Ireland Troubles' most complicated interfaces. Although the population of this part of the Antrim Road is overwhelmingly Catholic, the Duncairn Centre is in a former Presbyterian church, a reminder of a time when the city was not so divided along religious lines. Among those with essays in the British Council book is Ian Marshall, who in April 2018 became the first self-designating unionist to be elected to Ireland's Upper House Seanad Éireann since the 1930s. In January 2020 he became the first unionist to lose his seat in Ireland's Upper House ... but, still, for a year and a half he was there. *

---

* First self-designating unionist, but not quite first Northern Protestant. Writer and former Northern Ireland Labour Party member Sam McCaughtry was there for a while in the mid-1990s, as, a little before him, was Gordon Wilson, whose daughter Marie died by his side under the rubble of the IRA bomb at the cenotaph in Enniskillen in November 1987.

I am conscious several times in the panel discussion, by contributors from both sides of the border, of what you might call dropouts or glitches, moments when the differences of experience, the terms of reference of our everyday lives, become apparent. We are all, I would say, more than averagely interested in the politics of one another's jurisdictions, but no matter how frequently we travel between one and the other there are now and then things we just do not get. Lives not so much entwined as broadly overlapping.

Afterwards I get into conversation with a retired senior Northern Ireland civil servant who pours cold water on the 'vote for change' reading of the Republic's election result. Those half-million people who gave Sinn Féin their first preference – and all of those whose transfers got the party to the thirty-seven-seat mark – may have voted for change, he says, but what they have got is a lot of people in Sinn Féin who are unreconstructed republicans.

Or maybe, knowing that a lot of people in Sinn Féin are unreconstructed republicans, half a million people voted for them anyway. Because that, too, is a change from the softly-softly, nicely-nicely approach to Irish unity.

Ten days later, in the last full week of February, at the London launch of the book in the Irish Consulate on Grosvenor Place, the talk, on the panel as in the standing around and chatting before and after, is of a protracted period of negotiations before any new government is formed. There has already been one session of the Dáil at which four different people were nominated as Taoiseach, and four different people failed to secure enough votes. I hear all the different permutations of coalition partners talked through and tested. Nothing at this moment can be entirely ruled out.

The only thing, in fact, that looks certain tonight is that the coronavirus epidemic that has shut down the Chinese city of Wuhan, in China's Hubei province, since the turn of the year (only in China, we agree, could you shut down an entire city), and that has now been reported in alarmingly high numbers in Lombardy, northern Italy, is heading our way.

The Dublin launch of the book, mooted for March, does not take place in the end until the middle of July, via the – largely unheard of in February – medium of Zoom. A lot has happened betweentimes, and a lot that might have been expected to happen has not.

I am not sure any more where on the scale of unexpectedness to place the announcement in the third week of June   more than four months after the election – that Fianna Fáil and Fine Gael, arch- and occasionally deadly rivals since the Civil War of the 1920s, have, with the support of the Greens, agreed a programme of government for the next four years of the 2020s, with the Taoiseach-ship passing from Micheál Martin back to Leo Varadkar halfway through.

FFG (with a brackets &G) has come to be.

All together:

'Tell everybody to piss off tonight ...'

I cross the border just once in the days between the end of February and St Patrick's Day. I have been working for the past couple of years on a film about Johnny Logan, the only person ever to win the Eurovision Song Contest twice – one of those films, alas, that despite everyone's best efforts, and much goodwill, seems unlikely now to happen – and together with my co-writer and our producer have a couple of meetings lined up, in Meath and then in Dublin. We talk while we drive, reminding ourselves why we are doing this. It is a great story, of course, of triumph in the face of adversity. (Our strapline is 'Winning should have made him, instead it nearly killed him, the only way to save him is to try to win again.') It is also, though, a celebration, of Eurovision, first, foremost, but of Europe more generally. For all of us, as Northerners, from, as we say, various backgrounds, the film is a journey into a very different Southern Ireland from the Ireland of today. That is, in part, what these meetings, and previous meetings, are about: imagining our way back. Shay Healy, whose house is our final port of call, wrote the first of Johnny Logan's winning songs, 'What's Another Year'. He is well up in years now, Shay, and ravaged by Parkinson's. He welcomes us into a room filled with the paraphernalia of illness and the memorabilia of an extraordinary career, all sort of tossed together. He is courteous, he is helpful, he is occasionally scandalous, as he has every right to be.

He had a long relationship with RTÉ, starting there as a cameraman when he was just twenty in 1963. He would later present a satirical chat show, *Nighthawks*, produced by Anne Enright before she devoted herself full-time to writing. He could claim to have helped bring down a government: in an interview in January 1992, Sean Doherty, a former Fianna Fáil cabinet minister, revealed that the Taoiseach, Charles Haughey, had been fully aware that journalists' phones were

40

being tapped a decade before. Within a fortnight, Haughey was gone.

Truly, I can say I knew nothing of this, or, if I had ever known, I had forgotten it. Haughey was the apotheosis of that Fianna Fáil anarchy and corruption my brother-in-law spoke of. There was, from the very start of his career, so much scandal and rumour swirling around him that the phone-tapping tipping point would not have surprised me, but the fact that it had come to light on *Nighthawks* had somehow passed me by. I was living in England at that stage, although that is no excuse. Even when I was in Belfast the news from a hundred miles south generally reached me via Broadcasting House 450-plus miles away in London. And even if I *had* been able to pick it up on my mum and dad's TV, I do not think it would ever have occurred to me to switch on RTÉ. I do have it now. Once a month I remember and watch the main evening news.

RTÉ did not recommission *Nighthawks* after that fourth series ended in the spring of 1992. The broadcaster terminated Healy's contract at the beginning of 1995, a few months, as it happens, before I arrived to present an arts review series called *Black Box*. I was told before I went there that RTÉ was a hotbed of Civil War-era politics and even had it put to me that the decision to employ me – Northern and Protestant – as presenter was a way of one of the sides getting at the other. (What can I say? I was a pretty feeble sort of weapon: the station dropped me after only one season.)

The programmes were recorded as live about an hour before they were broadcast, at nine o'clock on a Monday night. The last train from Dublin to Belfast in those days left at 8.15 p.m., far too early for me to make it from the studio to Connolly Station. The first few weeks, RTÉ booked me into a guesthouse a few minutes' walk from their compound in the south Dublin suburb of Donnybrook. I happened, one Tuesday morning when I was checking out, to see the bill. Something, I recall, in the region of IR£80, which at the time was not much different in £ without the IR. Back in Belfast I got in touch with a friend who drove for one of the city's main taxi companies. I asked him what the fare would be from Dublin. It would depend, he said, but if it was a regular fare – it would be regular, I told him – then maybe seventy, seventy-five pound. He let me know pretty quickly he would not be interested himself, but he put me in touch with a friend who worked on the switchboard. Maybe she would be able to sort me out. She was able to, all right: she offered to drive me home herself.

The only slight problem was that Edie (I'll call her), who came from the bottom of the Shankill Road, did not know Dublin at all. Her mate Dee did, though, and so the arrangement was that he would come with her the first week. Donnybrook even so was a couple of steps too far. We rendezvoused in the Burger King on O'Connell Street across the road from the GPO, where on Easter Monday 1916 Padraig Pearse read the Proclamation of the Republic.

Even after that first week, or first couple of weeks, when she was getting her bearings, Edie kept bringing Dee, or Dee kept volunteering to come, for company. (The ceasefires were less than a year old, we were still living, and driving, with some of the old anxieties.) Dee and Marc Bolan both. Edie had T. Rex's *Electric Warrior* on cassette. T. Rex's *Electric Warrior* might have been all that Edie had on cassette. It is certainly pretty much all the three of us listened to. 'Beneath a bebop moon, I wanna croon with you-a-oo, a-oo-oo, with you ...'

My memory is that the journey in those days took us about three to three and a half hours. (Four full plays of *Electric Warrior* and time to spare.) I was smoking then. We counted off in cigarettes the towns and villages out of Dublin into Meath: Balbriggan, Stamullen, Julianstown, Monasterboice, Castlebellingham ... If I have been through them once in the quarter of a century since RTÉ politely (but very firmly) dropped me, that is as much as I have. Stretch by stretch, village by village, town by town, that entire route has been bypassed. I could tell you more about Applegreen service stations these days than I could about any one of them.

(There is, admittedly, plenty to tell you about Applegreen, which has, in less than thirty years and under the ownership of the same two men, gone from a single filling station in Ballyfermot, west Dublin, to over five hundred stations across the UK and Ireland and now the USA with an annual revenue in excess of £3 billion. Even a global pandemic could not put a dent in its performance: share prices in December 2020 jumped 40 per cent in a single day after rumours of a takeover, which in turn followed the news in the autumn that the company had been successful in its bid to build, and operate, twenty-seven new service stations on the 570-mile-long New York State Thruway.*)

---

* Nowhere can I find a snapshot of its share performance for the September day in 2019 when a rat was filmed emerging from an open bag of Brennans – 'Today's Bread Today!' – sliced wholemeal pan, in the food prep area of its station in Cherry Orchard, Dublin.

Even if I did smoke, I doubt I would now have the opportunity to spark up. There are no traffic lights, no obvious breaks of any kind, from the moment you leave Dublin until you arrive in Belfast. If you hit the Drogheda Toll Plaza right, you barely have to slow down there. The same is true on the other side of Dublin, on the road I most often travel, the M7 to my wife's home city of Cork. The traffic jams at Kildare used to be so bad you could have got out and picnicked at the side of the road and not added to the delays. You could have grown, picked and toasted the tobacco in your Marlboro Light.

Now, I have no real sense of where Kildare is, or, rather, I have no real sense of when I am proximate to where Kildare is. More than that, I have no real sense of how Kildare is, or thinks, as in votes. (The answer it turns out is 'variously': one Sinn Féin candidate, one Fianna Fáil, one Fine Gael returned in both Kildare South and Kildare North, with an Independent in the former and a Social Democrat in the latter completing the constituency sets of four.) I have put thousands and thousands of Southern Irish miles on the clocks of my various cars in the years since Ali and I met, eighteen months before the *Black Box* stint. And I have never been more acutely aware, driving through is not the same as travelling in.

I never finished the Shay Healy story. On the way to his house, we stopped for coffee and a sandwich at a roadside place where Meath shades into north Co. Dublin. 'Tainted Love' was playing on the radio and the teenage girl at the sandwich counter was throwing dramatic shapes for the teenage boy across the shop floor at the till when we went in – then and every time after that we turned our backs on her. (It was written all over the boy's face.) Ours was the only car in the car park, and as we pulled away I could still see her dancing, and never mind that it was late afternoon and the tubs of sandwich fillings were barely touched.

It was like something from *The Last Picture Show*, but overlaid with something altogether more disturbing, something whose outlines were only beginning to be glimpsed.

Shay Healy died while I was completing this book, on Friday, 9 April 2021. The same day as Prince Philip. Such was the blanket coverage of the latter's death across all the UK channels that it was not until Saturday, 10 April that the news about Shay got through to me. I wish I had chosen that as one of my nights to watch RTÉ.

Beltane

I had planned back in February to spend this first day of May
– and, by Imbolc-extension, of summer – in Dublin. I would
leave Belfast at first light and drive down the old road again,
by myself this time, stopping for breakfast somewhere on the
far side of Dundalk.

For lunch I had in mind somewhere around Talbot
Street in Dublin city centre. I still remember the shock of
unrecognition, reading Sean O'Reilly's 2004 novel, *The Swing
of Things*, with its depiction of Talbot Street as one long line
of internet cafés and shops offering international phone cards.
If there is one street in Dublin every Northerner who ever
took a train south knows it is Talbot Street, running from
the side entrance of Connolly Station all the way down to
O'Connell Street. (We have other, more shameful reasons
for not forgetting Talbot Street: the bomb that the UVF left
there in May 1974, killing fourteen people.) 'He's got this all
wrong,' I remember thinking, only to find, next time I got
off the train myself – and when, after all, had the time before
that been? – that he had got it exactly right, and that with
every new stretch of the M50 that opened, making still more
seamless the connection between the M1 and M7 – between

Belfast, ultimately, and Cork – Dublin itself had become, for me, all too easily bypassed.

O'Reilly's central character, Noel Boyle, is having to make his own adjustments. A former IRA prisoner, from Derry, he has arrived in Dublin to study philosophy. Boyle, O'Reilly said in an interview around the time the book came out, is forced to confront the failure of his own mythology about the place. 'The Free State. Dublin has moved on.'

It has changed again, or changed more, in the years since *The Swing of Things*. Still, Talbot Street felt like just the place to strike up a conversation about what a United Ireland might mean for anyone who had only recently made the Republic their home.

On the way back I would drive out on the Drumcondra Road and on then to the Swords Road as far as Dublin Airport for dinner and idle chit-chat.

For a great many people here in the North, Dublin Airport has become the destination point of choice for international travel. We have our own Belfast International Airport – actually in Antrim, fifteen or twenty miles from the city – but its mainstay these days is package holidays.

For travel to the USA in particular, Dublin is probably the best airport anywhere on these islands, that is if you do not want to wait for another seven hours at the end of your six-hour flight in the immigration hall of an American airport being barked at by Customs and Border Protection officers. There is, down an escalator in Dublin's Terminal 2, a little bit of Ireland that is already the property of the government of the United States – the line is clearly marked on the floor. Pre-clearance, is the official name. Unofficially it is 'The 51st State'.

You still might get barked at, and you will definitely have to queue, but not for anything like as long as you would on the other side, and, besides, you are at the very start of your journey; you are still up for it. Although it has crossed my mind, more than once, to ask whether in the event that my papers or my explanations did not satisfy – worse, set some computer's alarm bells ringing – I would be handed back over to the Irish side of the 51st State line, or taken further in – all the way across? – to the actual USA.

The journey by car from Belfast is not much more than eighty minutes on a good day, M1-A1(   )N1-M1;[*] by bus it is still well under two hours. There are at least four competing bus operators: Translink, whose Goldline service leaves from the Europa Bus Centre on the hour and takes you eventually, if you were to stay on beyond the airport, into the main Busaras station on Store Street, Aircoach, which leaves on the half hour from Glengall Street, literally on the other side of the fence (well, railing) from the Europa Bus Centre, and which, unlike the Goldline, runs right through the night; the Belfast–Dublin Express, which runs, again from out on Glengall Street, less regularly than Aircoach and Goldline both, but unlike Aircoach and Goldline has a toilet onboard; and a fourth one that nobody in my extensive research (emails and texts from my desk) has actually taken or can even remember the name of, although everybody is agreed is the really cheap one, 'seven or eight pound one way', compared to, say, the Goldline's standard fifteen.

We have very good connections, is what I am saying, and

---

[*] Principal routes with invisible border in between.

are increasingly inclined to use them. There are probably more people from the North in Dublin Airport at any given moment than there are in all of the greater Dublin area, a sizeable number of them people who would not dream of travelling the extra ten miles into the city proper. A neutral space. Where better to try to find out, three months in, whether the transition period had changed in any way views on how close the two parts of the island should in the further future be?

As I say, that, back in February, was my intention. Instead, where I am as May begins is where I have been for most of the past six weeks: confined to quarters, like everyone else, everywhere else on the island. *The Day of the Triffids* overtook *The Last Picture Show*. Coronavirus is the only story in town. Never mind all night, I am not even sure that the Belfast to Dublin buses are still running during the day.

The first documented case of Covid-19 in Northern Ireland is believed to have entered *by* bus, from Dublin Airport on 26 February, having found its way into the system of a passenger returning from a skiing holiday in northern Italy.

(I just looked again at the photograph of the Department of Health officials making the announcement. They are all sitting at the same table, their elbows practically touching … *I don't even do that with my own family now*.)

The Republic of Ireland recorded its first case three days later, that one-year-in-four day, 29 February (officials again sharing a table), and was rating the chances of further cases as 'moderate to high'.

You could not accuse them of scaremongering.

Nothing at all is as it was on that Saturday afternoon that I stood at Stormont listening to Julian Smith and watching the raincloud roll up the driveway.

And yet the seasons change regardless, and whether we are in lockdown or out, sick or well, fearful or resigned, this is still Beltane, 'bright yellow day' (the weather, here in Belfast, is doing its level best to oblige), the flora and the fauna must do their this-particular-tilt-of-the-axis thing. The current pandemic will, given a few hundred, or even score more of these planetary tilts, be fully absorbed into the aeons-long sentence of human life on earth – Black Death reset or Spanish Flu blip. In the first few weeks of the outbreak, the European Union, a recent subclause in that human-life-on-earth sentence, behaved like the twenty-seven self-interested entities that the Union's whole existence was meant to dissuade them from being. It creaked and at moments seemed almost to teeter, but as the first phase, or wave, at last shows signs of receding and governments begin to ease, or to talk about how they will eventually ease, lockdown restrictions, the impression grows that the Union, again, will – notwithstanding a few borderline cracks – come through intact.

Two of these islands' main party leaders – had negotiations back in February in the South worked out differently that would read the islands' two premiers – Mary Lou McDonald and Boris Johnson, have fallen victim to the virus. Johnson might have died, although already I wonder whether in the aftermath there will be some who doubt or dispute this, who see Boris's spell in intensive care as a ruse to get him out of the firing line for a while, or to garner much-needed public sympathy: his government's initial response to the unfolding emergency came across as, at best, complacent, at worst completely cavalier. Sometimes, though, people whose politics we do not agree with just get sick, too. The key word there being 'people'.

Mary Lou McDonald, in her first major interview following her own bout of Covid-19, has declared that coronavirus could be an even greater catalyst for unity than Brexit, which it 'dwarfs' in highlighting the dangers of Partition.[3] An intervention that Northern Ireland's First Minister, the DUP's Arlene Foster, at the next day's socially distanced news briefing – this, not elbows touching, being the new way – describes as 'constitutional navel-gazing' in the midst of a crisis. Michelle O'Neill, deputy first minister, and therefore Foster's colleague, and vice-president of Sinn Féin, and therefore McDonald's second-in-command, comes down somewhere in the middle. This is not a political matter at all, she says, but a matter of basic common sense.

(I remember once, in my teens, a football team turning up with only ten men – well, boys – for a match against the team I played for. I was down as substitute that day, so our manager and theirs agreed that I could be loaned to the opposition for the afternoon. Just occasionally I look at Michelle O'Neill standing at her lectern, two metres from Arlene Foster's, and remember that game, that feeling that the best I could hope for was a draw.)

In general, the South seems to think that it has 'done better' so far than the North in handling the pandemic. True, many in the North think that the South has done better than the North, where according to one narrative, summed up by Sinn Féin again in the voice this time of Declan Kearney, junior Stormont minister, 'some Unionists' have sided with right-wing elements in the Tory cabinet in putting the economy ahead of health by not being consistent, or wholehearted enough in their enforcement of the lockdown. And though comments like this often feel, and read, like an exercising of the muscle or a way simply of allowing Sinn Féin to maintain that balance of being a party of government in one part of the island and an opposition party in the other, and indeed in the island next door, Michelle O'Neill herself does on occasion join in, taking a hatchet, as it were, to a leg of the Executive stool on which she is standing.* Speaking at the start of April, on BBC Northern Ireland's *The View*, she had a go at a fellow Executive member, Health Minister Robin Swann of the Ulster Unionist Party (smaller these days than the DUP), accusing him of 'slavishly following the Boris Johnson model when it came to testing', despite the fact that Northern Ireland at that point was, by some distance, out testing the rest of the United Kingdom, and despite the fact, too, that Swann was beginning to emerge as one of Stormont's most trusted ministers.†

'I have made these arguments privately,' she said then, 'and I feel it is my moral duty, given the severity of the situation we are dealing with, that I have to say those things when they are not right.'

'In the space of one interview,' said BBC Northern Ireland political correspondent Jayne McCormack, 'the concept of collective responsibility practically vanished.'

---

* Or, if you prefer the analogy of me-as-loanee, turning and heading a corner into the goal she is supposed to be defending.

† A Lucid Talk poll on 1 June gives Swann a 71 per cent approval rating. Among the six leaders – and joint leaders – of the islands' parliaments and assemblies, Michelle O'Neill comes in fourth, with 53 per cent, behind Nicola Sturgeon, Leo Varadkar and Arlene Foster, and ahead only of Mark Drakeford and Boris Johnson.

The health minister received threatening, sectarian messages that very same day, messages that the deputy first minister was quick to condemn, but a week later she was on his case again, accusing him of going on a 'solo run' in requesting from London the assistance of British troops in the building of a Nightingale Hospital on the site of the former Maze Prison, which, whatever your views on the subject (and, God knows, there are few combination of words more emotive here than 'Maze Prison' and 'British troops'), coming just eight days after her own interview and Jayne McCormack's comments on it, was possibly just a tiny touch rich.

That said, there is plenty of evidence that people here have chosen to look both ways or chosen which of two ways to look – south of the border or across the water – according to their pre-existing views on Irish unity, or, more awkwardly for how we all rub along here, trying to put labels behind us, according simply to their religious background. When Leo Varadkar, still Taoiseach despite having come third in the election six weeks before, and in Washington, mid-March, for the annual 'shamrock ceremony', announced from the steps of the White House that schools in the Republic were to close 'until the end of the month', some Catholic Maintained Schools (as they are known) north of the border decided to follow suit and closed their doors, or just did not reopen them after the St Patrick's Day holiday: a full week before the Northern Ireland Executive made its own schools closure announcement. Arlene Foster, justifying the delay, said that once schools did close it would not be 'to the end of the month' but for at least sixteen weeks, which would carry us beyond the end of the Northern Irish school year. In certain predominantly nationalist areas, shops, too, were apparently suspending trade in advance of Boris Johnson's speech to 'the British People' on 23 March introducing the lockdown. Not for the first time, I found myself, in search of a comparison, reaching for China Miéville's 'weird fiction' novel *The City & the City*, in which two cities, governed by different laws and speaking different languages, occupy the same geographical space, only instead of cities here it is countries: within the one border both a United Ireland and a United Kingdom of the hand (that locks the school gate, or pulls down the shutter) as well as heart.

One (hu)man's weird fiction, I suppose, is another bunch of humans' right here right now.

The tug of war between Dublin and London, and whose lead Stormont should be following, carries on into the early stages of the emergence from lockdown. Leo Varadkar chooses the later afternoon of 1 May to announce a five-stage '101 Days to Normality' plan with precise dates, running into June, July and early August, for the reopening of non-essential retail and hospitality and the gradual enlargement of gatherings outdoors and in. As with the announcement from the White House steps, this seems to have taken our own first and deputy first ministers by surprise. Boris Johnson's 'plan', which is set out in a televised address on 10 May, is built around the advice (instantly lampooned) for people to 'stay alert'. At least he says he consulted across 'all four nations of the UK', which means Arlene Foster and Michelle O'Neill had a bit longer than the rest of us to get their heads around lines like 'work from home if you can, but you should go to work if you *can't* work from home'.

The Northern Ireland Executive waits another two days

before publishing its exit strategy. It has five stages, which presumably satisfies those calling for North–South alignment, although – give with one hand, take with the other – the actual stages are not all the same as the rest of Ireland's and, here in the North, there are no dates attaching to any of them, creating a rare unanimity in the public at large by satisfying practically none of it.

All of this in a week when it becomes clear that in accordance with the terms of the Northern Ireland Protocol, due to kick in on 1 January 2021, the Westminster government is indeed going to have to introduce physical checks at the three main ports – Belfast, Larne, Warrenpoint – on goods coming into Northern Ireland from Great Britain. Becomes clear, even more gallingly for unionists who have, since the announcement of the Protocol, been dead set against any such thing, in a question asked in a Stormont committee meeting by Sinn Féin's Martina Anderson of her colleague Declan Kearney, who adds that the Executive Office has been informed by Westminster itself that 'delivery on that infrastructure needs to start as soon as possible'.

And all of *that* despite Boris Johnson's 2019 'Tayto Castle Declaration' – made after a visit to Northern Ireland's most famous potato-crisp factory, in Tandragee, Co. Armagh – that the Protocol would entail no physical checks and that if any Northern Irish businesspeople were asked to fill in a Customs form, they could get straight on the phone to the prime minister who would instruct them to throw the form in the bin.*

---

* And the award for the best Tayto Declaration photo caption goes to … The *Irish News*, for 'Cheese and Union'!

Listen carefully to that speech, though, and it is clear he is talking about goods – he singles out those Tayto crisps – *leaving* Northern Ireland.

When, a couple of days later, the government docs publish its four-point plan it is a little less alarming for unionists, fearful that the Protocol marks the beginning of an economic United Ireland by stealth, than what was trailed by Declan Kearney – there is no mention, for instance, of the complicated tariff levy and refund scheme for goods *not* carrying on through Northern Ireland into the Republic – even if many still see the acceptance of *any* additional controls as a major U-turn. This particular turn, filtered through Michael Gove, a past master in obfuscation and belittling, amounts to 'some limited additional process on goods arriving in Northern Ireland, conducted taking account of all flexibilities and discretion [and with] the minimum possible bureaucratic consequences'.[4]

To quote the son of a friend of mine when, the Christmas after he turned eleven, she sat him down and delivered the Santa Claus U-turn, 'Yeah, right.'

The chances of any of this actually being ready in time look, seven months out, with something like sixty-four different agencies and statutory bodies to coordinate, and the small matter of a global pandemic to deal with, slight at best.

Amid all the gloom and uncertainty and outright fear, the BBC's adaptation of Sally Rooney's second novel *Normal People*, set principally in Sligo and Dublin, is being screened, to rapturous reviews and to yards of column inches and features in newspapers across the islands.

There is an exchange in the novel that does not make it into the adaptation (written by Alice Birch and Sally Rooney herself), following the 2011 Irish general election in which Marianne and Connell, the main characters, vote for the first time.

'Fine Gael in government. Fuck sake.' [Connell says.]

'The party of Franco.'

I loved, when I first read it, the author's decision not to gloss this for the non-Irish reader. Actually, for the non-Southern reader. For all the reasons previously stated, I do not know how many people reading Up Here would get it straightaway, though there is, of course, a difference between getting 'it' and getting the gist, which nearly always is enough.

It will be a while again before I can hear 'Fine Gael' myself without fuck saking under my breath in a vaguely Sligo-y accent.

Normal People looks like being one of those things that makes the English in particular love the Irish even more. Because the English, in some part of their psyche that they would prefer not to contemplate, have always, always loved the Irish. Or maybe it's just a London–Dublin thing that occasionally leaks out into the rest of the islands.

(These *are* big, broad brushstrokes, I know, especially when it is difficult in these streaming days to put an exact figure on the numbers viewing in any one country. It is a strong indicator of the series' appeal in the UK, though, that it broke all records on both BBC3 and BBC iPlayer.)*

---

* The iPlayer record was previously held by *Killing Eve*, which by my logic means that the English love affectless Russian contract killers only slightly less than they love the Irish.

I mull over the director's – or was it the scriptwriters'? – decision to change the code in the school football match shown in Episode 1 from Association, i.e. soccer (as it is in the novel), to *Gaelic Athletic* Association, aka GAA, aka footandhandball. It could be a simple recognition that soccer nearly always looks shit when staged – and it has to be staged: you need your star to do something, or suffer something; you cannot rely on the bounce of the ball. I cannot help wondering, though, if it is, at least in part, a signal: this is *us*, this is *here* ... and maybe even (a little fond jibe to all those others looking in and longing), *this is something else you cannot do as well as we can.*

Connell and Marianne are completely without any of what might be considered by outsiders to be traditional Irish baggage. Marianne is 'not much for mass'. Connell has only ever set foot in a church once: for a funeral. The novel, on the other hand, does contain one piece of recent baggage that is, almost certainly for reasons of budget, absent from or greatly reduced in the series: the abandoned house where Connell and Marianne meet in one episode is all that is left on screen of an entire 'ghost estate', of the kind first introduced to the wider world in Donal Ryan's *The Spinning Heart*, and of which, at the time the novel was set, in aftermath of the 2008 global financial crash, there were reckoned to be over six hundred spread across just about every one of the twenty-six counties. That there were so many is testimony to the rapid and finally unsustainable growth of the preceding couple of decades. That there were so few in the North is testimony to the divergence between the two economies in those decades, a divergence that had effectively flipped the chart, leaving Northern Ireland on almost every indicator trailing in the Republic's wake. It is hard to find figures from the same source for the two jurisdictions, but it looks as though the average salary in the South for the 2019–20 financial year was €50,789, or just over £43,050, compared with £35,545 in *Belfast*, which is usually considered the highest-earning part of Northern Ireland. (Another survey puts the average across the six counties at £32,895.) This would be consistent with a 2014 report in the *Belfast Telegraph* that put the earnings gap at £8,000 in the Republic's favour and found a gap, too, of almost £5,000 between Northern Ireland and the rest of the United Kingdom.[5]

Northern Irish people are paying a premium for being Northern Irish people, or, rather, are not being paid it. Although I suppose looked at another way we are, on the face of it, a cheap date. On the face of it.

The North, by the way, barely features in *Normal People*, beyond Connell's Trinity College pal and all-round good guy Niall, for which, perhaps, we should all be glad. It is tempting though to think that – again, at the time it is set – within the world of the novel, the island, constitutionally speaking, is a more settled and agreed place than it is now.[*]

A little bit of something like harmony, meanwhile, has broken out in the Stormont Executive, at the very top of it, in fact. In an interview from a room in Stormont on Sky News on the penultimate Sunday in May there is the first inkling that Arlene Foster and Michelle O'Neill have developed something

---

[*] Belinda McKeon's equally fine – and Trinity-based – *Tender* was published only three years before *Normal People*, but set in 1998, the year of the Good Friday Agreement and, more importantly for the novel, the Omagh bomb.

more cordial than a mere working relationship. Seated, the regulation two metres apart, on straight-backed chairs, but looking comfortable in one another's company, they are both keen to stress that, whatever their long-term aspirations, their focus is on serving the people of – oh, precious and versatile and unloaded word – *here*.

'We're elected *here*,' Michelle O'Neill says, and then again for good measure: 'We're elected to represent the people that send us *here* ... So, you can look to London and you can look to Dublin and you can pick good and bad in all approaches, but for me this is about our own approach to Covid-19.'

I watch each of their faces in turn when the other is speaking. They have almost certainly been wired off in advance about the interviewer's questions, but even when he steers the conversation round to Brexit neither looks in the least concerned that the answer coming from their left, or their right, will in any way discomfit her.

So, of course – applying the *Normal People* story arc and a basic knowledge of Northern Ireland politics – that is the moment when you would expect it all to go awry. Only the how is ever in doubt. Though the cause of the rupture, when it comes, is completely unforeseen.

It begins, on 21 June, with news of the death of Bobby Storey while undergoing lung surgery in England.

In the years following the first IRA ceasefire in August 1994, Storey had emerged as one of the most important and recognizable figures in the republican movement. Unlike most of the other well-known names, and faces, he did not hold any elected position, and although he was sometimes referred to as head of Sinn Féin in Belfast most people not in the party loop saw him first and foremost as Gerry Adams's right-hand man and fixer. One of the first occasions, indeed, when he broke cover and spoke publicly was the Police Service of Northern Ireland's arrest of Gerry Adams in 2014 over the abduction and murder forty-two years before of Jean McConville. 'That they would dare touch our party leader! The leader of Irish republicanism on this island!' Storey thundered at a rally in west Belfast, while beside him then deputy first minister of Northern Ireland Martin McGuinness gave a little chuckle.

Unofficially Storey was the Provisional IRA's director of intelligence and in that role the person principally responsible for a series of post-ceasefire 'spectaculars', such as the break-in at – and removal of hundreds of files from – the PSNI's Special Branch headquarters at Castlereagh in east Belfast, and the 2004 Northern Bank Robbery.

Storey's funeral, nine days on from his death, is huge.

Hundreds line the streets; scores upon scores walk them, in formation, behind the forty to fifty mourners who flank and bring up the rear of the coffin.

Mary Lou McDonald and Sinn Féin colleague Martin Ferris have travelled from Dublin. Pearse Doherty has come from Donegal. Michelle O'Neill has not had to travel so far, but in terms of Northern Ireland hers is perhaps an even more problematic journey.

The guideline on attendance at funerals since the start of lockdown has been a maximum of six family members.

It seems Sinn Féin is taking advantage of some eleventh-hour changes by the Executive to the rules on numbers allowed – so eleventh hour in fact that the public has not even had a chance to be properly informed of them, so eleventh hour that they have not even been signed off by ministers. Michelle O'Neill suggests that church leaders who express concern at the conduct of the funeral – its sheer size – at a time when so many have been denied the opportunity of paying their last respects to their own loved owns may have been 'confused' ... They could be forgiven if they were, since it takes another two days for the revised guidelines to appear on the Department of Health website.

Looked at from the outside, it might seem as though one party of government had asked another for a favour – 'I know you never saw eye to eye with him, but it's Bobby ...' – and then, having got it, whistled through their fingers for all their mates to come and join them.

There is no denying Bobby Storey's iconic status, or the genuine affection in which he is held by republicans (although there were many, too, who feared him): Sinn Féin claims 250,000 watched its live stream of the funeral. The size and nature of the crowd that turns out rather than tunes in, however, is not entirely down to a spontaneous outpouring of grief. Sinn Féin has sent out emails with muster points and transport arrangements, along with precise details for mourning wear: black trousers, white shirts, black ties, or, as the call-out terms it, 'black and whites'. You could say it ensures that all those walking behind the coffin will be ... uniform.

And then there is what amounts to a rally afterwards at the republican plot of Belfast's Milltown Cemetery, where more than seventy-five IRA volunteers are buried, though not, at least there and then, Bobby Storey himself, his remains having been taken for cremation to Roselawn Crematorium on the other side of the city: Roselawn, where a whole other set of new arrangements have fortuitously come into effect that very morning, enabling the attendance of as many as thirty mourners, unknown, alas, to the eight other families whose loved ones were due to be cremated that day; families left literally standing at the front gates watching as hearses went on up the long, curving driveway to the crematorium building alone.*

A journalist friend who was at Milltown tells me that the whole thing looked and felt to him calculated in more ways than one. Instability in the North, he maintains, suits the republican movement's longer term aims. The Stormont Executive has been cooperating too well on the coronavirus. Here was a golden opportunity, while simultaneously honouring a hero of their cause, to do something about that.

Whether intentional or not, it has the effect of driving a wedge between the parties and the leaders in particular, putting paid, for the moment at least, to interviews with indulgently smiling two-shots … Putting paid, in fact, to any public appearances together, including at briefings on the progress of the pandemic and the efforts to deal with it.

This is one of those moments, I tell myself, looking at those men in their black and whites, to store away, to call to mind when you think it is you who is crazy or paranoid, that, you

---

* A report eight months later concludes that, in respect of Roselawn, Sinn Féin did not seek to influence Belfast City Council. Again, last-minute changes to regulations were made that were not communicated until much later to the rest of the public.

know, maybe the IRA Army Council does not really exist and therefore can't possibly have influence over Sinn Féin both south and north of the border, or indeed when you are next asked to put your X or your 1, 2, 3 on the ballot paper. If you are comfortable with the idea of political parties and uniforms, go right ahead. If you are not … well, you cannot say you did not know.

In the meeting next day of the Stormont Executive Office Committee, at which the conduct of the funeral is interrogated, Sinn Féin's Martina Anderson addresses the deputy first minister. It is like the scene in the movie where the audience realizes that the human vessel that is the co-opted MLA for Foyle has been inhabited by members of the cult which has based its entire worldview and diction on the character of Aunt Sarah in Lisa McGee's *Derry Girls*. 'Michelle, you had to be there yesterday. The republican family needed you there yesterday. Because you gave us comfort and guidance, to the family of Bobby Storey and to the wider republican family … I want to thank you on behalf of all of us because we couldn't have got through yesterday without the support that you have given us.' A performance that SDLP leader and fellow Foyleside elected representative Colum Eastwood (he defeated the Sinn Féin candidate at the 2019 general election) sums up in two words: 'sycophantic drivel'.

She knows a lot about giving comfort, does Martina Anderson. See her tweet off the back of the announcement by Justice Minister Naomi Long that the so-called Troubles Pension, which Sinn Féin had to be compelled by a court ruling to enact, despite its having been passed into law seven months before, was going to cost in the region of £800 million: '£8000M 4 Pensions mainly for those who fought Britain's dirty war in Ireland ... £800M mainly 4 those involved in Collusion.'

The court ruling followed an action by Jennifer McNern whose role in Britain's dirty war was to go for coffee in the Abercorn Restaurant with her sister Rosaleen on Saturday, 4 March 1972. In the no-warning IRA bomb that exploded twenty minutes after they sat down, at the table next to the one the bombers had just vacated, the sisters between them lost five limbs and one eye. Martina Anderson did remove the tweet soon after and later issued an unreserved apology, to which Jennifer McNern said, 'I personally don't need apologies, I just need the payments made.'

South of the border, meanwhile, only three days before the funeral, even the new Taoiseach's wife was absent from the traditional swearing in at the president's residence in Phoenix Park due to Covid restrictions.

Included in the new coalition's programme for government is a 'Shared Island Unit' within the Office of An Taoiseach. The rhetoric is specifically designed not to scare any unionist horses, long on working towards a consensus, short on (actually, completely devoid of) border polls: '[t]his unit will examine the political, social, economic and cultural considerations underpinning a future in which all traditions are mutually respected ...' I am no engineer, but I think I might tread very warily indeed on anything underpinned by a mere consideration, no matter how well examined. The Unit and its brief were actually trailed early on in the negotiations between Fianna Fáil and Fine Gael. Blogging for the London School of

Economics, Etain Tannam, lecturer in Peace Studies at Trinity College, points to several key changes between the draft and the final version, some subtle – like the desire to 'enhance' the role of the British Irish Intergovernmental Conference, a unionist bête-noire, rather than, as previously, to 'expand it'; some that could fairly be described as headline-grabbing. Gone from the text published in the Programme for Government is the earlier draft's use of the term 'united island', which now looks to have been the middle rung on a word ladder on the climbdown from 'United Ireland'. Unless, of course, you are inclined to see 'Shared Island' as the first rung on the way up ... as An Taoiseach himself seems to suggest, just a few weeks into his premiership.

Speaking to the *Irish Independent*, only a day after repeating that a border poll at this stage would be far too divisive, he says that the Unit has to be preparing for the day when England (he was very specific) gets 'turned off' Northern Ireland. 'They may just say "we're not as committed to it as we were in the past". That may not happen for quite some time, but we have to be prepared for all sorts of eventualities.'

Comments in which Arlene Foster says she is 'disappointed'.

Not so her prime minister, or not noticeably so. On a flying visit to Belfast a short time later he tells unionists that they should engage with the Unit 'in a confident way'.* (Apparently

* Dear Prime Minister, I know nothing about the inner workings of political unionism, but I have a feeling that one sure way to undermine any person's confidence is to say one thing to their face and then quite another the moment their back is turned or the moment you find yourself in negotiations with someone else. Yours, etc. Glenn

not having so much as glanced at any recent issues of the paper in which he is writing, he uses an article in the *Belfast Telegraph* to marvel at Northern Ireland's response to coronavirus, 'the way dividing lines that have existed in the past simply ceased to matter in the face of a foe that cares nothing for politics or faith'. Tell that to Robin Swann.) Anyway, he has really, really, exciting news of his own to deliver. Looking ahead to 2021, a hundred years on from the formation of Northern Ireland, there is going to be a new Centenary Forum! And a Historical Advisory Panel!

Now it is the deputy first minister's turn to be less than wowed. There is nothing to celebrate in the centenary, she says, and the anniversary period would be better spent in honest conversation about Partition and its failures.

Cue the party horns extending halfway,

drooping,

hitting their flattest note.

Still in his first days as Taoiseach, Micheál Martin nominates Eileen Flynn as the first woman from the Irish Travelling community to sit in the Seanad. In the wake of the murder in Minneapolis of George Floyd and the Black Lives Matter protests it provoked, the racism directed at Ireland's indigenous ethnic minority has come more and more to the fore, a reminder that prejudice and discrimination on the island is not just a Catholic–Protestant conversation.

(Precise figures are again a little hard to come by, but there would appear to be something like twelve times as many Irish Travellers living in the South as the North.)

On 13 July, Rethink Ireland* adopts Imelda May's poem 'You Don't Get to be Racist and Irish' – first broadcast on RTÉ at the start of June – for a (twenty-six-county-) nationwide billboard campaign to promote its €3 million Philanthropic Equality initiative.

The poem, in essence, tells listeners – Irish listeners very particularly – that they cannot cling to memories of past wrongs done to their country, their ancestors, or resent the persistence of prejudice and demeaning stereotypes, while at the same time ignoring, or worse still adding to, the wrongs done in the present day to people living in their midst.

It is powerful stuff.

Latest population figures show that the North is now one and a half times smaller than the South, or the South is two and a half bigger than it. The North is also getting older faster. It is also considerably whiter: 98 per cent compared to the South's 88 per cent, which is not far off England's 85 per cent. Northern Ireland in this regard more resembles Scotland, 96 per cent of whose population identify as white.

For an idea of how radically things have changed in the past several decades, my brother-in-law suggests I have a look at a photograph of Pope John Paul II's visit to Ireland in the autumn of 1979. 'There were maybe three million people in Ireland then,' Jonathan says, 'over a million and a quarter of them are at the mass in Phoenix Park on the Saturday, and they are all white.' Not only that, he says: 'Look at the men. *They all have the same haircut.*'

---

* That is, 'Social Innovation Growth Fund Ireland Limited trading as Rethink Ireland'. The title, you might think, was a sensible place to start.

The question arises, has the South grown more diverse because of its policies, or have the policies followed the diversity? And what has prevented that diversity from crossing the – let us face it – not particularly noticeable border?

One obvious reason might be the Republic of Ireland's enhanced international profile. In almost their last act as Taoiseach and Tánaiste before entering into coalition with Fianna Fáil, Leo Varadkar and Simon Coveney successfully oversee the country's election onto the United Nations Security Council, getting the nod over Canada after a campaign costing €800,000.* Money well spent, according to Coveney, ensuring that 'Irish values and Irish foreign policy is shaping decision-making for the next two years ... For a small country, we have a lot of influence.' (Northern Ireland, of course, could claim to be on the Security Council already as part of the United Kingdom – a permanent member – but in matters of international diplomacy such as this it is a well-disguised part. The British voice rarely comes with a Northern accent.) And if that sounds a little like preening, he is only echoing what others, beyond these shores, are saying. *The Economist* runs a feature – 'How Ireland gets its way'[7] – in which it refers to the country as 'an unlikely superpower', citing not just that Security Council success at the expense of Canada ('another country often flattered by comparison with a bigger, sometimes boorish neighbour'), but also Finance Minister Paschal Donohoe's election to the

---

* The *Irish Times* runs a story headlined, 'How pub sing-songs and Bono brought Ireland to a seat at the highest table'.[6] It is possible some of the €800,000 was left behind in the till of a pub in Crosshaven, Co. Cork.

presidency of the Eurogroup, 'the influential club of euro-zone finance ministers', beating the French and German governments' preferred candidates, as well as commissioner Phil Hogan's being handed the European Commission's trade portfolio. (Again, the laws of TV drama dictate that the higher a character rises the further they will fall.) And, of course, the fact that the EU's position on Brexit was, in *The Economist*'s eyes, 'shaped by Irish diplomats'.

'On a per-head basis,' the article concludes, 'Ireland has a good claim to be the world's most diplomatically powerful country.'

In the accompanying graphic the Irish gold harp symbol is replaced by a flexed, and impressively muscular, arm.

Speaking at an *Irish Times* Summer Nights Festival earlier the same week, economist David McWilliams reckons that Ireland is only three decisions away from being a perfect country – 'Scandinavia, but more fun'.[8] He is good on pithy sayings, David McWilliams. 'Ghost estates' was one of his, back in the mid-Noughties. One of those three decisions relates to land – landlords hoarding it should be penalized, through taxation, to help solve the housing crisis; one relates to multinationals – simply put, 'they are our friends, not our enemies'.* The first, however, is to sort out Northern Ireland and to enter into dialogue with unionists, whom he styles 'the most petrified people on the island'.

---

* Ireland's tax arrangements for multinationals – and very particularly Apple – have come under near-constant scrutiny from the European Commission since the early 2010s, and from many within Ireland itself.

It is almost sixty years old now, but one of the best summations of the Northern unionist dilemma I know comes in a series of interviews conducted on the streets of Belfast on the eve of the first visit to Northern Ireland by a serving Taoiseach – Seán Lemass, of 'slightly constitutional party fame' – in the opening weeks of 1965.[9] (A visit met by a one-man protest at the gates of Stormont by Ian Paisley, forty-three years before he returned there as first minister of a power-sharing government with Sinn Féin.) Following on from an Orangeman who thinks the South is a foreign country, and a man who has many good Catholic friends 'in Éire' and finds them to be very decent people, following on, too, from a couple of Falls Road Catholics who are happy enough with the way things are, either side of one who thinks all Ireland should be united 'politically and religiously', is a man in his late thirties or early forties with the most pained and perplexed expression I think I have ever seen.

'Up until I was eighteen,' he tells the interviewer, 'I would have considered myself more British than Irish. It was only when I went to England in fact that I realized I was Irish … but then going down [South] I find I'm not Irish either … I feel rather forlorn and adrift. I'm primarily an Ulsterman. I think Ulstermen have been a separate entity since ever there was an Ireland.'

First and foremost, it is the visible presence and palpable influence of the Catholic Church in the South that he notices, but he expresses the opinion, too, that the only way he is likely to belong Down There is if he changes in relation to it, rather than hope that it will change in relation to him.

Half a century on, the presence and the influence of the church has diminished greatly. Only 78 per cent of people in the

2016 Census gave their religion as Catholic, down from 84 per cent in the Census before that, and 91 per cent in Census before that. (The Census does not record the number of actual churchgoers among those nominally Catholic, although all other evidence suggests that it, like the number of new recruits to the priesthood, has dropped precipitately.) The second largest grouping was no religion at all, which now accounted for a shade over 10 per cent. The various Protestant denominations between them made up just 4.2 per cent of the total population. This is actually a rise on the historic low in the 1940s and 1950s (as recently as 1998 and the referendum on the Good Friday Agreement it was 3 per cent), but still well down on where it stood a hundred years ago. Numbers – which had already dropped to around 10 per cent by the opening decades of the twentieth century – declined even more noticeably in the years immediately following Partition.

I remember the hand   but not, embarrassingly, the face or the name – of the person who once counted off for me on his fingers the several reasons for this decline: Ne Temere, inter-marriage, flight, loss of heart, a class of civil servant that left when the British administration got the boot.

Some now dispute the importance of the first of these, the Catholic Church's decree of 1907, whether it introduced the idea that children of mixed marriages had to be brought up Catholic, or simply restated it, or whether its greatest impact was its insistence that all marriages involving Catholics, including marriages between a Catholic and a non-Catholic, were invalid unless witnessed by a Catholic priest.

Co. Clare has the smallest population of Protestants in the State. Along with its neighbouring 'Midwest' counties of Limerick and Tipperary, it also accounted for the second smallest number of visitors from Northern Ireland, in the last available Tourism Ireland figures for overnight stays (when any of us were still able to go anywhere): 41,000 annually, though it far outstrips the four midland counties – Longford, Westmeath, Offaly and Laois – which between them can only muster 15,000. My maths is not the strongest, but I think that means that on any given night in 2019 there were ten people from the North lying in bed in each of those counties … More people from Northern Ireland, on the other hand, visited the Border Counties – Cavan, Monaghan, Donegal, Leitrim, Louth and (a stretch in every sense, this, of 'border') Sligo (the closest to the North it gets is Leitrim) – than came from the from the entire twenty-six counties to *any* part of Northern Ireland. In fairness to the people of twenty-two of those twenty-six counties, not too many of them could be bothered to stay the night in the midlands either.[*]

I am reading, quite by chance, the day I spend poring over all those Census figures, Elizabeth Bowen's *The House in Paris*, published in 1935. The aunt of one of the central characters lives in the Co. Cork village of Rushbrook (do not go looking for it on the map), having married, after years of widowhood, a certain Colonel Bent. Rushbrook is 'full of Protestant gentry, living down the misfortunes they once had'. Outside the bathroom door are 'black, staring photographs' of the ruins

---

[*] The ever-improving road network might again play an unwitting part: there are a fair few places in that least-visited counties list that you would really have to want to get to, places which these days you have every incentive to by-pass.

of the Colonel's previous home, Montebello, burned by the IRA in the troubles – note the small t – of 1919–21.

Literary critic Kelly Sullivan has a great line in an essay about Bowen, which picks up on the recurrence of ruins in her novels. 'It is,' she says, 'the suspense of the non-catastrophe – the anticipated event that never happens that most urgently permeates Bowen's writing.'[10] Though for Colonel Bent the catastrophe most definitely has. He is, in Bowen's words, 'an unfledged bird who has already been blown out of his tree once'. (Talking of great lines.)

Relatives in England are perplexed by the Bents' insistence on remaining in Ireland, as opposed to settling in, say, Devon, which is pretty much Cork folded along the axis of the Irish Sea.

It would be like 'Aunt Violet', they think, to set a premium on her company by living across the water, but acknowledge, too, that 'Uncle Bill' might, very simply, want to cling 'to the edges of his own soil'. In fact, though he and she do talk about the 'old times' it is only to reinforce the conviction that 'one had to make the best of things now', a formulation that recalls a sentence of Colm Tóibín's (in a review of Roy Foster's *Paddy and Mr Punch*, which deals with Bowen): 'No one wants territory' – this some four and a half years before the Good Friday Agreement – 'merely a formula of words ambiguous enough to make them feel at home.'[11]

One scene in particular strikes a chord with me. As the boat bringing the Bents' niece Karen to visit for the weekend makes its way up the River Lee to Cork Harbour it passes – among the gothic villas and terraces of tall, pink houses and, eventually, boxy warehouses – a house with a white plaster horse visible in the fanlight.

I remember having one such house pointed out to me, sixty years later, when I moved to Cork in the early 1990s. This, the person doing the pointing out told me, was a Protestant house, or had been when the horse was put there. I deduced from this that the horse was a Williamite symbol – William-III-ite, that is to say – the horse from the murals so familiar to me growing up in Northern Ireland, albeit without King Billy himself sitting astride it, sword pointing, 'Onwards to the Boyne!'. It seems likelier, though, that it dates from a century later, a three-dimensional representation of the white horse that appears – on a red shield, surmounted by a crown, against a very papal-looking background of yellow and white horizontals – on the flag of the House of Hanover: a sign of loyalty, is one theory, in the violent aftermath of the 1798 United Irish rebellion, when militias supporting the crown were hunting down rebels, which some were inclined to interpret simply as Catholics. A Georgian version of the lamb's blood struck on the doorposts of the Israelites when I-*am*-the-Lord passed through the land of Egypt smiting the firstborn.

An item in the Dublin *Evening Herald*, from February 1937, suggests that the white horse caught on as a piece of domestic ornament, devoid of any political connotation, but still with the lingering notion that it somehow conferred safety on the household.[12]

Even without the white horses, though, Protestant houses continued to be conspicuous.

My brother-in-law, Jonathan Shankey, is Protestant, or as he would more often say, it being the Protestant way to denominate,

Church of Ireland. His was a relatively affluent, south Dublin, suburban upbringing. And in the early 1970s, his early childhood, someone shoved shit through the letterbox of the house his family had just moved into.

'They thought we were Brits,' he tells me. 'Brits', that is, by simple virtue of not being Catholic.

A short time after that, someone else, labouring under the same misapprehension presumably, took a shot at the front window with a pistol – a .22 calibre, which, Jonathan says, made only the smallest dent in the glass. He remembers that dent all the same. Remembers running his finger over it. His awareness of being different – and of being singled out as different – was *sensory*. And then there were the flags: theirs was the only house on that south Dublin street not to have a yellow and white flag out for the pope's visit in 1979 and again – or such at least was his impression – the only one, two years later, at the height of the Hunger Strikes in the North, not to hang out a black flag on the death of the first prisoner to die, Bobby Sands.

Which is not to say that the family were without sympathy, or Jonathan himself: 'Even people who didn't support the IRA could see [that the British government's stance on the prisons] was an injustice.' Politically, in fact, his father was a republican – 'Fianna Fáil through and through'. *His* father was headmaster at the school Jonathan himself went to for a time, Kilkenny College. He would have been, in those pre-Partition times, a unionist, but he was, crucially, a temperance man, too: a temperance man above all things. During the War of Independence, which did not know yet to call itself by that name, a detachment of

Black and Tans were billeted in the school gymnasium.* He was appalled by their indiscipline, their drunkenness in particular. If this was the best that Britain could do in defence of the Union, he wanted no part of it.

Jonathan's father was a mariner, who, after a decade as an apprentice officer on 'deep sea' routes, spent the rest of his career with the shipping division of the Guinness Brewery in St James's Gate. He was, you could say, the person who kept fuelled the argument of whether porter travelled well or not. And then Jonathan tells me something I have never heard before: almost all the employees of Guinness when his father started there in the late 1950s, maybe four thousand of them in total, were, like him, Protestant.

Guinness loans put Jonathan, his brothers and his sister through university. Guinness doctors still, more than five years after his father's death, look after his mother. (He tells me another story, about his mother, with three children already, making discreet inquiries about contraception – this at a time of Catholic Church, and by extension Irish state, prohibition – and being introduced through 'the Protestant network' to a doctor who gave her a Dutch cap, already lubricated, with instructions for how to fit it. She got herself ready only for it to shoot from her hand and land in a corner of the side room the doctor had shown her into. She picked it up, covered in dust and hair, and

* For any latecomers to early twentieth-century Irish politics, the Black and Tans – along with the Auxiliaries – were mostly British, frequently ex-military reinforcements drafted in to the otherwise locally recruited Royal Irish Constabulary. The War-of-Independence-that-did-not-yet-know-that-it-was was known colloquially as 'The Tan War'.

put it into her handbag, which was as close to her person as it ever came again. Less than a year later, Jonathan was born.)

I say the fact that the Guinness workforce was largely Protestant was news to me, but it is not in the least news to the various friends from the South to whom I talk in the days and weeks after my conversation with Jonathan. How could I *not* have known? they ask me.[*]

All the same, I am intrigued to know still – given that the vast majority were likely to have been neither mariners nor managers, given that there had to be far more blue collars worn than white, and by women as well as men – where all those workers went when the workforce contracted; about the Protestant working class more generally. Martin Maguire at Trinity College, who has written a lot on this subject, puts forward the novel explanation that, actually, across the past century and more, working class Protestants, in Dublin especially, were far less sectarian than their Northern neighbours. Intermarriage was as a result much less of an issue. In fact, with so many young Protestant women marrying soldiers – as many as a third – intermarriage for young Protestant men was practically a necessity if they were going to stay in Ireland; even without Ne Temere to enforce it, many Protestants, Maguire says, were happy to convert even if only in name.

Jonathan and my sister-in-law sent their elder daughter to a 'C of I' school in Dublin. I use inverted commas because there

---

[*] I tell them (badly) the joke someone else told me about a resident of south Dublin who has been having an affair for twenty years. 'How did you get away with it for so long?' a friend asks. 'Simple, we did it northside.'

are, my niece tells me, only five Protestants in her year, 'and,' she says, laughing at the low level of her own observance, 'I'm one of them – oh, and I'm going out with one of the others.'

Whatever way you cut it, or account for it, though, you would have to say that when it comes to sharing the island, or at least sharing twenty-six counties of it, the current Republic has not a great deal of recent practical experience. There is a more than mathematical difference between 4.2 per cent and the something closer to 20 per cent that a United Ireland would bring.

It is one of the key differences between the South and the North that the minority – Protestant – in the former was negligible. In the latter, the minority – Catholic – was, despite all the creative border-making at the time of Partition, never less than a third. There may not have been in the South anything quite on a par with the first prime minister of Northern Ireland Lord Craigavon's (the former Sir James Craig's) infamous 1934 speech – popularly rendered 'a Protestant Parliament for a Protestant people' – but the evidence for how the State viewed its relationship with the Catholic Church is pretty inescapable. The 1932 Eucharistic Congress in Dublin – think a liturgical Olympics – coincided with the election of the first Fianna Fáil minority government under Éamon de Valera, who clearly, given the long lead-in time, could not claim any credit for having brought it there, which naturally did not stop him trying. He called another election early the following year and this time won an outright majority.

Looked at from the outside, and I am going to say not just from a Northerly island aspect, with Dublin in particular swagged and garlanded, and a High Altar erected in Phoenix

Park, the Congress had something of the look of an act of betrothal. Ireland, said de Valera at the height of it, had always been a Catholic nation.

Vast public outpourings such as the Congress, or the visit of Pope John Paul II half a century later, did not spring from nowhere, but were fed by a near-constant round of religious devotion at parochial and diocesan level. A friend tells me that in his north Dublin neighbourhood in the 1960s speakers were strung up on lamp posts and the Our Father intoned in Irish for the annual parade of the Host through every street in the parish, while parishioners knelt by the roadside reciting the rosary. Lambeg drums being battered on the Twelfth it was not, but still his memory is that his Methodist neighbours got offside for the day. My wife, growing up in the Seventies and Eighties, remembers Cork city centre practically grinding to a halt and a huge cross being erected at the foot of the main shopping drag, Patrick Street. The church's declaration of 1954 as an international 'Marian' year, meanwhile, triggered an unparalleled craze for grottoes dedicated to the Blessed Virgin in public places and private gardens alike.

Many people before me have pointed out that not only is that 'a Protestant Parliament for a Protestant People' line a misquotation, but that it was also contained in a speech that referenced comments emanating from south of the border. As Patricia Craig, who, despite her surname*, could never, in a

---

* Her great friend Ciaran Carson, poet, novelist, translator, flautist, brought up in an Irish-speaking household off the Falls Road, literally rejoiced in the dissonance of his own surname.

lifetime of perceptive literary and cultural criticism, be accused of having a unionist axe to grind, writes: 'everyone remembers Sir James Craig's comment ... but not that it was a riposte to De Valera's boasts about Southern Ireland.'

What Craig said in fact, in response to a question from George Leeke, Nationalist MP (one of only nine in the fifty-two-seat chamber) for Mid Londonderry was: 'The Honourable Member must remember that in the South they boasted of a Catholic state. They still boast of Southern Ireland being a Catholic state. All I boast of is that we are a Protestant parliament and Protestant state ... I am doing my best always to top the bill and be ahead of the South.'

That last line, I have a sneaking suspicion, is the sound of a unionist lord trying to be down with the 1930s kids. He catches something all the same of the escalation in rhetoric across that decade. De Valera's Tánaiste, and future president, Sean T. O'Kelly was no slouch at the 'this country and that church up a tree' sort of talk. True, the revised Irish constitution of 1937 annoyed the Catholic Church by not explicitly establishing it as *the* church in Ireland, opting instead (Article 44) for a recognition of its special place in the State – which the constitution took to mean all thirty-two counties – while also recognizing the Episcopalian Church of Ireland, the Presbyterian Church, the Methodists, the Quakers and Jewish congregations; and true, even this 'special place' was amended out of existence by public referendum in the winter of 1972 (one of the lesser celebrated, but surely most significant referendums of the last half-century that could be said to be the precursor of the transformative referendums on divorce, same-sex marriage and abortion);

religion, though, is not all about practice or moral guidance, it is oftentimes simply a set of shared cultural experiences and assumptions.

Mary Burke, now at the University of Connecticut, but with degrees from both Trinity College Dublin and Queen's University Belfast, has written of a 'perception of Irish Protestants as colonial hangovers who were less than full citizens of a de facto "Catholic Republic"'. This in an article about abuse in Protestant institutions, abuse which was, she says, not hidden, but ignored, not forgotten, but 'disremembered', a dialect term she uses to mean a failure to recall something of which one has been repeatedly reminded.[13]

A good word that, 'disremembered'.

The ellipsis in that speech of Craigavon's, by the way: the words it stands in for are, 'It would be rather interesting for historians of the future to compare a Catholic state launched in the South with a Protestant state launched in the North and to see which gets on the better and prospers the more. It is more interesting for me at the moment to watch how they are progressing.'

I can only think that 'at the moment' he was speaking he thought the comparison showed in Northern Ireland's favour. Looking now, though, from his future … well, he was not wrong, it is rather interesting. Maybe just not in the way he would have imagined.

*

I am reading online an article on the 1932 Eucharistic Congress, which touches on the importance of advertising, and includes images of some of the souvenirs on offer. E. C. Handcock of Burgh Quay, Dublin, is selling a series of what it styles 'Paskelite' Lamps for windows, the bulbs set within glass in the shape of flames – single, 'duoform', and 'triform', at five shillings, ten shillings and thirteen shillings respectively – and, at thirty-five shillings, a 'Paskelite' Altar, a three-tiered affair with a cross lamp in ruby natural glass on top. 'The Altar,' the listing concludes, 'is of Dublin manufacture', there being besides adverts in the papers of the time warnings about foreign-made goods coming in, English goods in particular, including 'wrongly designed' Eucharistic Flags. The official flags sold at a shilling each and were flown alongside yellow and white halved papal flags and the Irish tricolour.

I end up on eBay looking for more souvenirs (I have been working all day; this is my way of bringing the plane gently in to land) and find a postcard showing these last two flags, staffs crossing in the stem of a chalice. And if there is a shade of a difference in the yellow half of the papal flag and the third band of the Irish flag, for the life of me I cannot see it.

Which gets me thinking.

It is in the Irish constitution, Article 7, pages 8 and 9. (The constitution runs to 260 pages, or 130 pages twice: once in Irish, the official language of the State – see Article 8 – and once in the second language, English, though, curiously, the Articles are published in the second language first and the first second.) 'The national flag is the tricolour of green, white and orange': 'an bhratach trí dhath .i. uaine, bán, agus flannbhuí, an suaitheantas náisiúnta.'

The constitution does not expand on the choice of colours or apply to them a symbolic gloss, though it is generally understood to represent nationalists (green) and unionists (orange) united in peace (white). There is a similar tradition about the Newfoundland tricolour, possibly my favourite flag in the world: green, white, and – startlingly – pink, this last supposedly a representation of the English rose.

The story goes that the green, white and orange flag was first presented to Thomas Meagher Jr in France in the revolutionary year of 1848, modelled on that country's own flag, by a group of women who would themselves have to have invented the 'white for peace' bit, since that is not what it has traditionally represented in the French tricolour. There are several theories about what it does stand for there – the clergy being one – the closest to 'peace' being 'égalité' to the 'liberté' of blue and red's 'fraternité'. (Newfoundland's white is for Scotland – from the colour of the St Andrew's cross.)

So, why, I am wondering, did I grow up referring to the flag as the 'green, white and gold'? Because, you might say, I am a Northern Protestant by birth and the people I did my growing up among had a red white and blue interest in selling the Irish tricolour short. So why then, I am wondering, too, did my wife, Southern Catholic by birth, starting her growing up eleven years behind me all the way down in Cork, home of then Taoiseach Jack Lynch, know it as the green, white and gold, too?

When I am not searching eBay for Eucharistic Congress souvenirs on those late-evening descents, I can lose myself for half an hour in a Wiki-hunt for the kits of teams competing in some international football league or other, trying to see if any colour theme emerges and, if it does, how that theme relates to the national colours.*

Jack Lynch was the first Taoiseach to have been born in Cork and the last until Micheál Martin was sworn in, in June 2020. An All-Ireland Hurling Champion with his county, Lynch played his club hurling with Glen Rovers, formed the year of the Easter Rising. Its original colours of green and gold hoops with white shorts were augmented by a third alternating black hoop in honour of the Rising's executed leaders. Elsewhere in the county Bride Rovers also wear a strip of green, white and gold, with a blue away kit, because they were, as their website says, 'clashing with [so] many teams in various grades e.g. Newtownshandrum, Blackrock & Ballymartle'.

I hold my saffron-bound notebook up to a photograph of the flag flown above the GPO in Easter 1916. The rightmost stripe of the flag is a shade lighter than the notebook's cover, though I am bound to say the green is more jade than emerald. It could just be faded, as it has been suggested to me other flags are that I have drawn to people's attention down the years. Or it could just be a really, really, really light orange. As to the recurrence of the *word* gold, that should be read, or heard, as poetic licence: what, after all, rhymes with orange? See 'The Dying Rebel' by the ever-reliable Wolfe Tones: 'My only son was shot in Dublin /

---

* Two things in my defence. In my pre-teens when our parents were out and he was having card schools with his friends downstairs, my brother would let me read his otherwise off-limits *Book of Football* magazines, which always featured team kits in an almost identical graphic style to Wikipedia's. Also, I count to a hundred before I get out of bed in the morning. Every morning.

Fighting for his country bold / He fought for Ireland and Ireland only / The Harp, the Shamrock, Green, White and Gold ...'

Here's a tip: if you cannot find a rhyme, do as the Newfoundlanders do and start from the fly side and work back: 'The pink the rose of England shows / The green St Patrick's emblem bright / While in between the spotless sheen / Of St Andrew's cross displays the white / So hail the pink, white and green ...' ('Flag of Newfoundland').

At various moments Irish nationalists have been as keen as unionists to tone down the orange and, rather than unite the traditions, the flag has been used to deepen the divide. And I do not mean just in the dim and distant either. Even in the South there has been a perception that it has been misappropriated or enlisted for sectional ends.

Jonathan Shankey again tells me that the 1990 World Cup, 'Italia '90', when Ireland under the management of Jack Charlton made it all the way to the quarter-finals, helped him and others of his generation at last to embrace the tricolour. It was not just 'theirs' any more, the thirty-two-county republicans. 'It was ours,' he says.

If there is a referendum any time soon, if there is a vote in favour of reunification, then the flag is going to have to form part of the conversation. I am not saying it could not ever be 'all of ours', but there would be a monumental amount of work required before that day was arrived at, with no room along the way for further gold-rhyming or other liberties with the colour wheel.

Maybe we could invite Newfoundland into the equation. Think about it: between us we could have the whole North Atlantic sewn up. And we could throw that pink into the mix.*

But, here I am getting hung up on flags and, look! The sun is out! Restrictions are lifting! It is time – at last! – to load up the car and hit the road south …

… -westish.

---

* A little flaggy footnote. In early September, the BBC apologizes following an item on its *Breakfast* show in which an Irish tricolour was used to represent Northern Ireland in a graphic showing the different quarantine arrangements in place in the four constituent parts of the United Kingdom. It may have been an act of kindness, enabling DUP members to exercise their 'this is disgraceful' and 'I demand an apology' muscles while Stormont is in recess (they seize the opportunity, loudly). Or it may have been that whoever was tasked with creating the graphic just did not, you know, in keeping with a great many people on the big island, have the first fucking clue.

Lughnasa
(Less or More)

'Bundoran is getting ready and the shutters are being opened, doors unlocked, the kitchens are being prepped and now we are ready to welcome you all back to Bundoran's famous hospitality and wonderful scenery and back to our fabulous activities and back to support local businesses. Bundoran is ready, we can't wait to see you soon.'

Message from Bundoran business owners,
Fermanagh Herald, 2 July 2020

Back at the start of May, when he announced his place holding government's five-stage plan to lift lockdown restrictions, Leo Varadkar talked of '101 Days to Normality'.

Stage 4, beginning on Day 81, 20 July 2020, allows for inter-county travel and the reopening of hotels and restaurants under strict social distancing guidelines. Sometime around Day 22 or 23 I made a pre-emptive booking for the Great Northern Hotel in Bundoran, right down in the south-west corner of Donegal, almost on the county border with Leitrim. I confess I may have thought when I was making it that I was booking a hotel in Buncrana, seventy miles further north, on the other side of the six/twenty-six border (and up the road a way) from Derry, which is the end of Donegal I know better. I confess, too, that I might not have been anywhere near either this particular week if flights had been taking off as they always had, as I had every reason to think they always would, when I sat down to book a holiday in Day 2 or 3 of January in what seemed set then to be a year like any other.

Bundoran, though, I realize very quickly, nearly always comes with some sort of explanation tagged on, an unspoken – and occasionally right out loud – 'actually'. No one you run into – and over the course of four days I run into a surprising number of people I know – appears to be there by choice.

'Actually, I have family in Leitrim, we just stopped off here on the way ...'

'Actually, a friend has a house – outside the town – and let us have the use of it for a couple of days.'

'Actually, we had to cancel the holiday in France because of the pandemic.' (OK, that was me.)

'It can get a bit wild at weekends,' says a friend, who lives in Fermanagh, the closest Northern Irish county. The quickest route from Belfast takes you through the Fermanagh village of Belleek and into the South via a bridge across the River Erne, which unlike much of the rest of the border does at least feel as though it is a line between one thing and another, even if that is one friendly thing and another. Rossnowlagh, this friend tells me, just a little further up the Donegal coast, is a better spot by far.

Last time I was over Bundoran direction was six or seven years ago, doing the Donegal leg of the island-long Wild Atlantic Way, which had only just opened, or at least had only just been joined up in Irish government thinking, as a way of boosting tourism all down the west coast: a 'unifying theme' as one hotelier in Co. Clare put it at the time. There were hopes that the BBC's *Top Gear* programme could be attracted over – hopes which, I understand (I would drive to Donegal and beyond to avoid ever seeing it), did come to pass a couple of years later: Chris Evans and Matt LeBlanc driving a couple of Rollers around the Kerry to Cork leg.

That last time I passed through the town it was a Sunday morning, out of season and raining. My wife and I drove along a strip of road, the Atlantic Way itself, below the Main Street, between blocks of blank-faced holiday apartments and the amusement park – the Merries, as we call it in our house, using the term imported from Tramore, where my other brother-in-law and his family live. The whole strip looked out-of-season, rainy-Sunday bleak and un-Merrie.

The strip does not look a great deal cheerier as we pass it this Monday morning on the road (the Sea Road) that dips then rises off Main Street to where the Great Northern Hotel perches, a few dozen yards on the offside from the cliff edge. The holiday apartments have not yet reopened, or if reopened have not yet been let, the few amusement park rides that do seem to be working look as though they are simply going through the motions, passenger-less. But the sun *is* shining in the breaks in the fast-moving clouds, and I am, not just because of the wind that whips my breath away, too, when I step out of the car in the hotel car park, almost speechless with excitement. Because we are anywhere. Because we are very particularly here, looking across the broad bottom of Donegal Bay, and the narrow slice of Leitrim coastline, to the headland at Mullaghmore, Co. Sligo, ten miles away.

There are golfers all around – the Great Northern stands in the middle of one of the oldest links in Ireland – but even their presence cannot dim the delight.

'Who owns the sea? Who owns the green sandy field by the sea?' I find myself thinking in quotation marks, and for a while cannot remember where the words come from. They have the ring of Flann O'Brien – I have been re-reading *The Third Policeman* during lockdown – and, when I finally get a proper hold of them, something of the surrealness of O'Brien, too. In the days after I made the booking, reorienting myself from -crana to -doran, I came across a court case, from nearby Ballyshannon District Court.[14] The summer before last a traffic warden on duty at Bundoran's seafront car park noticed a 'big lad with a longish beard' sitting on the grass with his shoes off, playing the harp. When the warden stopped to speak to a woman about paying for parking, the big lad got up and told him not to be taking money from her. 'You're only a fucking cleg,' the big lad said and 'dunted' the warden, who reeled back 'four or five feet'.

Defending himself in court, the big lad said that it was the feast of Lughnasa and that he had been playing the harp for a family – from the North, he was keen to stress (one of the girls was dancing) – when the warden appeared. 'That got up my nose,' he said, 'we were there for a cultural gathering.'

Which was when he asked the question about the ownership of the sea and the green, sandy field beside it. The judge told him that court time was precious and that the question must be relevant. This is the moment at which, no matter where you stood to begin with, you start siding with the big lad. He apologized to the warden, then squeezed in another line about how 'we' used to run free on those fields next to where the car park was, and how no man or council owned the sea.

When confronted with his previous convictions for traffic violations and burglary, he said simply, 'A man is more than his past.'

'We are going away from our culture,' he said in conclusion, 'and my conscience is clear.'

He might have called me as a witness on the going away from our culture point.

I thought right up until the moment I sat down to read it for the first time – early 1990s, I am thinking (it would be years before I saw a production of it) – that the Lughnasa at which the characters in Brian Friel's great play were dancing was somewhere else in Donegal.

Dancing at *Lammas*, on the other hand, I would have got right away.

Lammas (from Loaf Mass) falls, in most of those places where it is observed, like Lughnasa, on 1 August, although like Lughnasa (the Lugh there is an ancient Irish god), it can extend well into the month of August. In Northern Ireland, in fact, the Auld Lammas Fair takes place, as it has for more than four centuries, in the final days of the month, in the north Antrim town of Ballycastle, to the end of whose name every Northerner will automatically tack on an 'o', helpless slaves to the song in celebration of the fair by John Henry McAuley:

At the Aul' Lammas Fair
Were you ever there?
Were you ever at the fair in Ballycastle-o?

It was always, in my childhood, the last act of the school holiday and for that reason, well, that and the fact that it was in Ballycastle(-o), which never conformed to my idea of a seaside town (my grandfather *loved* it), I never wanted to go.

I pause work to watch a YouTube clip of the fair in 1964, complete with school-age Irish dancers, the boys in saffron kilts, the girls with matching sashes draped over one shoulder.

The big lad from Bundoran would be in his element.

With a version of 'She Moves Through the Fair' playing over the footage, it looks closer to the Forties than any 2020 person's idea of the Sixties; it looks, if I am honest, with the knowledge of the atrocities that the next few years would usher in, like a massacre waiting to happen – those carelessly, or, rather, carefreely crowded streets – and indeed loyalist paramilitaries did try to bomb the town at fair time, several years after the signing of the Good Friday Agreement, which we had fondly hoped when we voted on it had put an end to all that sort of thing.

A second, shorter clip from 1976 includes a cutaway to a poster torn down the middle but still clearly declaring Sectarianism Kills Workers. There is another flyer further up the wall: Roger Casement Anniversary. I am guessing of his death, by hanging, sixty Augusts before, for his part in the events of 1916, although his birthday (he was approaching his fifty-second at the time of his execution) falls on the first day of September. He had family connections in Ballycastle, even asked that his body be taken back and buried nearby.

It never was.

O.

I got it wrong earlier. The Great Northern does not perch, it sprawls. (Southfork springs to mind. Southfork with Work Done.) Opened twenty years before the outbreak of the Great War, it is a relic of that pre-Partition, historical nine-county Ulster, when the province had the whole top end of the island uncomplicatedly sewn up, and when the railway would carry you via Enniskillen from the Great Northern Railway Station in the centre of Belfast. The railway is long gone, along with the original four-gabled frontage of the hotel. Or if the gables remain, they are submerged beneath more recent additions and reorientations.

There are, of course, everywhere evident, more recent additions: Perspex screens and strict one-way systems and at every door hand-sanitizing posts.

I make a note on the first night in the hotel to the effect that you know you have crossed the border when the member of waiting staff taking your dinner order asks you if you would like any 'dilute' in your water. 'Although,' I write, 'I did not know you knew until I did and they – she: her name is Shannah – did. She means what I would have called squash growing up, though when I was growing up the squash, the concentrated fruit drink we thought *was* juice, went into the glass, or I suppose jug first, the thing to be diluted. Here you water first, dilute second.

Ali, to my right at our round dinner table, is wide-eyed in the presence of a flashback to her Cork childhood. 'I think we used to call it *dilutie*.'

Later, in the hotel bar, populated mid-evening (or as the continuing restrictions demand semi-populated: every other table free) by families like ours, she points out that the most common order is 'a pint of X [for him], a glass of Y [for her], and a jug of dilute [for them]'. Purple seems to be the younger children's dilute of choice, as Ribena on the rare occasions it was offered – and when it was offered it was always offered by name – would have been mine, although on looking again at the bottles being tipped into the water jugs on the Grand Hotel's bar counter, these to me are more cordials than concentrates. And, yes, it is a small thing, and of course every country has its regional variations, but I am struck by the fact that something as familiar this far north in the island, as it is a couple of hundred miles to the south, at the other end of the Wild Atlantic Way, draws a complete blank if you travel a couple of dozen miles to the east. (I pause to canvas the opinion of a friend from Castlederg, on the eastern, which is to say Northern, side of the Donegal/Tyrone border. It was 'diluting juice' there. But always the juice first.) And that word, dilute, six parts of one to twenty-six parts of the other ... Or, there again, twenty-six parts of one with six parts of the other thrown in. Now mix.

Bundoran plays a heartbreaking cameo role in *Big Girl, Small Town*, the debut novel by Michelle Gallen, who (like my friend) grew up on the Tyrone side of the border with Donegal. Majella, the central character, spends a couple of days in a caravan a friend has given her family the use of in return for her father's having fixed his car. 'Hardly Tenerife, is it?' his wife says sourly, and the holiday is all downhill from there.[*]

The town has 'come up a bit'. That is the 'actually' of another woman we know from Enniskillen who we bump into on our first morning, at the end of the West End Cliff Walk, which has taken us out through a little wicket gate at the side of the hotel, down on to the promenade, past the blue-flag beach on one side and Water World on the other – still shut against the day when the government triggers Stage 5 of its lockdown easing – and up into the town at the foot of Main Street just short of the bridge where it hands on the baton to the Sligo Road.

(Another morning we will turn right instead of left as we come out through the hotel gate and follow the wilder route, taking in Fairy Bridges and Wishing Chairs to the surfing mecca that is Tullan Strand: as untouched – beach and cliffs all around it – as any stretch of coastline I have ever trodden on this island or the next.)

A plaque on a gatepost on the promenade close to Water

---

[*] Michelle Gallen's book should be required reading for anyone harbouring the slightest doubt about the effects on border communities of British army road closures during the Troubles, as it should be for anyone overly dewy-eyed about the attitudes and actions of Northern republicans: the biggest event in the town of Aghybogey in the course of the Troubles was the IRA's April Fool's Day bomb, which flattened houses and destroyed the Catholic church, but left its intended target, the town's RUC station, intact. Blackly funny, but not without precedent in what it daily feels harder to think of as the real world.

World says the enhancements were made possible by the second phase of the European Union's Programme for Peace and Reconciliation – aka PEACE II – which, like PEACE I before it and PEACES III and IV after it, encompassed the Southern Border Counties in its purview. Back in January 2020, the EU committed to a further seven years of funding – Peace Plus – that would carry on, either side of the border, despite Brexit.

A report by the Northern Ireland Council for Voluntary Action in 2005, looking particularly at the impact of funding in east Belfast, Strabane, in Co. Tyrone, and Cavan, south of the border, points out that 'PEACE II is not a conventional regional development initiative. Its overall strategic aim is to "reinforce progress towards a more peaceful and stable society and to promote reconciliation".'

The focus in the main is on inter- and intra-community relations, but there is, too, a recognition that economic regeneration across the board has a significant role to play.

'At the very least,' the report concludes, 'this research has shown us that PEACE II has contributed to putting in place an environment where individuals and organisations have to consider the needs of others. Whether or not this has fully translated into addressing divisions and engendering greater inclusivity within our society is debatable.'

'Don't be too cynical,' my wife says when I go back a couple of days later to take a photograph of the plaque on the promenade. She has already seen me that morning take photographs of the 1916 Societies stickers on a number of the lamp posts up the town – 'One Ireland One Vote' – and of the A4 bills posted here and there by the Irish Republican Prisoners Welfare Group: a green raised fist behind three strands of barbed wire. The thumb and two of the clenched fingers are green, too, but the middle finger is white and the ring finger very definitely yellow. No question of fading here: these posters have only recently gone up.[*]

There is one back up at the top of Main Street, a hundred yards or so from where it joins the Sea Road again, in front of the Irish Gift Shop, which forms part of a white-painted-stone-faced row of houses. The windowsills, doorsills and lintels are all the green of the post box set in the wall between the shop and the house next door with a sign in the window saying Rooms to Let. Just below the first-floor windows a string of bunting runs, green, white and orange. The Gift Shop itself has two windows, reflecting its two faces. It is, in the one, a shamrock mug and tea-towel fest, and, in the other, a shrine to a particular version of Irish republicanism. A note, in biro, in the window beside the right-hand door jamb, advertises flags for sale: Ireland, Starry Plough,[†] Palestine. (A bar a little way down the street appears to have bought the first and third.) Another newer sign – sign indeed of these Covid-times – says Only 4 People In Shop at One Time, which at least means if the INLA were here on an away day they would not need to split again to go in.

---

[*] If the juxtaposition of the PEACE II plaque and the A4 bills is intended to reflect badly on anyone it is certainly not PEACE II.

[†] The original Starry Plough had a yellow plough and white stars in celestial Plough formation on a green background, although the version more usually seen now dispenses with the plough and places the stars on a sky-blue background. The flag of the Irish Citizen Army at the time of the Easter Rising, since the mid-1970s it has been most readily associated with the Irish Republican Socialist Party and the ever-smaller paramilitary organizations it gave rise to: INLA, IPLO, IPLOBB …

I pass the shop for the first time on the afternoon of our second day in town, about an hour – as it happens – after my editor Neil Belton phoned me to say that Head of Zeus were definitely acquiring this book. And there, right in front of me as I enter, stuck to the glass next to the bumper sticker that reads Keep Ireland Tidy, Throw Your Rubbish in England, is another sticker: $26 + 6 = 1$. Actually, there are two versions, one with all the numbers in black, another with an orange 6 and a green 26 and 1. (Note, in dilute terms, the addition of the six does not change the colour of the 26.) So, of course I tell myself I will have to get one for Neil, but then...

'Excuse me ...'

I look up.

The woman behind the counter points to the other customers standing to her left, my right: one, two, three ... ah ...

'Sorry, I'll call back in a while,' I say.

Any time I do call back, though, there are already a couple of people standing outside waiting for one of the four inside to leave.

And then, before I know it, it is our last morning, Saturday. I head up straight after breakfast and – wouldn't you just know it – the green shutters are still down. They are still down at just past eleven o'clock when Ali and I go back up together, a last walk before checking out. I take a few photos of the front of the shop, of the Irish Republican Prisoners Welfare Group flyer, kicking myself. We walk back to the hotel along the PEACE II-funded promenade.

'We can swing back that way when we're leaving,' Ali says. Which is what, twenty minutes later, with Ali at the wheel, we do.

'You're in luck!' she says and, almost before the car has stopped moving, I am out and feeling in my pocket for my mask.

The elderly man behind the counter this (late) morning is already completing his first sale of the day, to a customer who seems anxious to get away.

'There you are now' – setting down a well-wrapped package next to the till – 'Would you like a bag?'

'I'm all right. I'm parked out the front.'

'Right, that's €25.' The customer is ahead of him and has a twenty and a ten in his hand. 'Thirty. Wait now I'll get you your change.'

'Just give me five sticks of rock.'

The sticks of rock are on the counter next to where I am standing, waiting my turn: €1.20 each, or 5 for €5.

'Five sticks of rock,' the elderly man says, as he must, it is now clear, say everything that has already been said or that he has totted up in his head. He moves in their direction using the counter and the shelves behind for support and balance. 'What kind?'

'Any kind at all.'

Picking five of any kind presents more of a challenge than five of one kind. It looks to me as though he is going for *all kinds*, rather than, say, four of this one and one of that.

'Five sticks of rock,' he says eventually and brings them back to the till. 'Will I wrap them?'

'The car's right outside the door.'

'Right, right.' He sets his hand flat on the sticks of rock on top of the package. 'And you're sure you don't want a bag?'

'I'm OK. Really.'

It does not occur to me until later that that first customer, whose car was parked right outside the door, who might, like me, have been expecting the shop to be open earlier, might have seen me taking photographs of the shuttered front, of the lamp post and the A4 flyer. Maybe he had only started to be anxious the moment I walked back in the door.

Finally, finally, he gets his package.

'There, they'll never know what's in it,' the elderly assistant says, by way of a parting joke. I think.

I have all the while been having a better look around than I managed the first day I was (half) in. The Irish republican stock falls into two main categories: the Easter Rising, and aftermath, and the Hunger Strikes. There are posters there are plaques there are plates there are clocks with the faces and the names of the executed leaders of the former and the ten men who starved themselves rather than wear prison uniform in the course of the latter,* although despite solo appearances by one or two of the others – a large poster showing the arrest, or capture, of Francis Hughes in the south Derry countryside, in 1978, following a gun battle with British soldiers – there is from each era, one undoubted star: Michael Collins and Bobby Sands.

Very slowly it dawns on me that, whatever the actual time they are showing, the clocks here stopped in 1981: no Sinn Féin candidates standing for election on the back of the Hunger Strikers' electoral success, no Armalite and Ballot Box strategy,

---

* This is not to ignore the other four of the 'Five Demands' (the right not to do prison work; the right to free association; the right to a weekly parcel, letter and visit; the restoration of lost remission), but the Maze protests began with the refusal to wear the uniform and escalated from there.

no Back Channel to the British government, no Hume—Adams
initiative, no ceasefire (marks 1 or 2), no Good Friday Agreement
(no bomb either at the cenotaph in Enniskillen, thirty miles
down the road and across the bridge at Belleek), no revoking
of Articles 2 and 3, no recognition of the principle of consent,
no entry into government with the DUP, no largest single party
in the Dáil, no official opposition to the Fianna Fáil / Fine Gael
pact ... although, hang on a minute: Michael Collins? Did he not
negotiate – and die defending – the Treaty that led to Partition,
the Treaty that the IRA of Bobby Sands and the other nine
Hunger Strikers rejected, hence to this day the difficulty that
some elected representatives north and south of the border
have accepting, much less saying, the name of the country in
whose legislature they sit?

Is he not one of the 'they' that could not break Sinn Féin?

Any journalist worth their salt would pursue this.

The only salt on me, though, is what blew in off the sea just
now as I walked along the promenade to the car.

'What can I do for you?'

The man with the they'll-never-suspect package has left the
building. The elderly assistant has taken up position in front
of me.

'I was looking for one of those 26 + 6 bumper stickers.'

'One of what?'

'The 26 + 6 bumper stickers?' I hear my voice go up at the
end. Maybe you do not call them bumper stickers here. He
inclines his head. The cavity of his right ear is completely taken
up by a transparent moulded hearing aid. (I think of the jellyfish
I have seen in the pools below the hotel, taking on the shape

of the rock where the tide has left them.) 'Round here, on the front of the counter, they're like a long narrow strip: 26 + 6 = 1.'

He shakes his head. He is still not getting me. I realize it is my mask. (These are early mask days: we are all struggling.) I pull the fabric out a fraction from my mouth and nose, repeat my request. He comes out, not quickly, from behind the counter, in order, I think, to see what I am pointing at, but instead he crosses to the wall just inside the door where he puts his hand on an unfurled Donegal flag.

'No!' I say, and he turns, but does not stop what he is doing, which has nothing to do with the flag and everything to do with the bank of light switches that the flag has been obscuring. The bulbs in a row above the front windows all come on. That first customer really must have been out of his car and into the shop before the door was even half opened.

'Now,' he says.

I point at the bumper (or alternatively designated) stickers. 'The one with the green and orange numbers.'

In behind the counter, he goes again. He pulls out a couple of cardboard boxes from the back shelves at seeming random, pushes them back in again.

'Have you had a bit of a run on them maybe?' I ask.

'What's that?'

He offers me his left ear this time. The same species of hearing aid as the right. I pull down the mask I had only just pulled back up. 'I was wondering if maybe you'd had a run ...'

He does not even wait for the end but returns to pulling out boxes. 'There's a lot of stuff hasn't come up from Dublin. We're only open again two weeks. We weren't so bad here, but it was raging down there, you see.'

The virus he means.

There are several notices about the shop warning customers off taking photographs, but if I am not to have my sticker, I at least want a picture. I pull out my phone and snap quickly, though in truth I would have had time to set up a tripod and proper lighting. Finally, he turns to face me again with a sorry shake of the head. 'Not to worry,' I say, and then for want of anything better, 'I was looking at your wooden plaques.'

'Plaques?' He got that. 'Those aren't wood, those are stone. Look …' He moves round to a shorter counter at right angles to the first and reaches in for one of the Hunger Strike commemoration plaques, saying, as he does, 'There's the two boys that started the whole Hunger Strikes going.'

'Bobby Sands and Francis Hughes?' I say.

'Gaughan and Stagg,' comes a voice from behind me, which is the first I realize that another customer – another two customers, a woman, and the man who just spoke – have come in while all this plaque chat has been going on.

The elderly man is pointing to roughly where Michael Gaughan and Frank Stagg are on the plaque *next* to the one he has lifted, which shows only the names and the faces of the Maze Hunger Strikers. 'They died in British jails, and if you think they had it bad in Belfast you can imagine what it was like over there.'

(He is not wrong, of course. Prison doctors in Parkhurst Prison force-fed Michael Gaughan, who was twenty-four, on seventeen separate occasions, the last the night before he died, contributing to or directly causing his death.)

The man and the woman nod firmly. I may have failed the interview. Although there may be something here too of local or regional pride: Gaughan and Stagg were Mayo men, South – and not just politically South, but geographically west – to the Maze-10's North.

'Do you make those here?' I ask.

'No, those are up from Dublin, too. Twenty-five euro.'

I point out that the price tag says forty. The man does a double take then puts out a hand and takes my wrist, laughing. 'So it does!'

I am trying hard to be not best disposed to this man, but it is not really working. It occurs to me now the real reason his first customer was so keen to get away as I was coming in the door was that he had just received an unexpected €15 discount, or €10 cash and five free sticks of Bundoran rock.

I tell him I will weigh up the €40 and maybe drop in again, even though I know my wife and daughters are in the car round the corner somewhere, ready for the road home.

'Do that,' he tells me. 'It's dead here. We had our summer in May. You don't get two summers in the one year. If it's from over in the North you are, you'd be better in Rossnowlagh. The cars were lined up there on the beach all last Sunday.'

None of these sentences fall into the category of obvious sequiturs, though as best I can tell from the tone of the last of them, he does not altogether approve, and would rather there was a little less 6 lined up in this neck of the 26, thanks very much. Nothing against me.

As I am leaving, the man and woman who had come in behind are themselves leaning over the counter with the plaques.

It does not look like being a busy morning for the shamrock side of the house.

Ali is parked up on the other side of the wall from the Peace II promenade.

'No stickers?'

'They're waiting for them coming up from Dublin.'

'They get them from Dublin?'

I think the wrong one of us went in there.

We follow the Wild Atlantic Way out of town (me writing on a sheet of A4, folded small, while the conversation in the shop is still fresh in my mind) in the opposite direction to the one we travelled those several years ago, through Ballyshannon, birthplace of Rory Gallagher, who for a few mid-Seventies years, when no one else would come, was pretty much the whole of the Belfast touring music scene, and on round the headland that overlooks and gives a name to Rossnowlagh – and, indeed, though it is only a shade after midday, there are already lots of cars right down on the beach, even if we are a bit too far away to see whether they are sporting Northern or Southern plates.

As we turn inland from the strand we chance upon a Presbyterian church – a little corrugated iron affair, with red painted window frames set into its brown walls and a weathered red pitched roof complete with campanile. And only *then* do I remember that, since the late 1970s, Rossnowlagh has been the location of an annual July Orange Order parade, often referred to as the Donegal Twelfth, though like many another 'Twelfth', everywhere but Northern Ireland (except when it falls on a Sunday), it does not actually take place on the twelfth itself, but on the nearest Saturday preceding. And hard on the heels of that comes the thought that that might have been what the elderly shop assistant intended when he mentioned the Northern cars parked there. And that maybe – just maybe – he had me pegged from the start, or at least from the moment I got the Hunger Striker question wrong.

Rosita Boland, author of the brilliant *Elsewhere* ('One woman, one rucksack, one lifetime of travel'), visits Bundoran for the *Irish Times* a few days after we leave.[15] The town's Tourism Officer tells her the place has been 'mental' since the lockdown restrictions were eased, though that is not quite how Boland herself would describe it. Much of the excess for which Bundoran was notorious after dark, or on those summer nights when darkness was late in coming, has been reined in, and the town, one resident confides in her, is all the better for it. Someone else tells her that instead of the working-class Northern Irish families who make up the bulk of their clientele in normal years they are seeing more middle-class southerners. That 'southerners' jumps out at me. He means southern as in Tipperary, Cork, Longford, Kildare, Wicklow, 'even Galway', although again when you are in Donegal everything is south, but I wonder is there, too, a lingering sense of apartness, the awkward remainder of that early twentieth-century equation that looked at the map and saw Ulster not as a province but a population that would quickly preclude a unionist majority unless three of its nine counties were cut adrift from the new Northern Ireland state.

I put down the paper after reading Rosita Boland's article (I am not sure whether I am relieved or disappointed that she makes no specific mention in among the 'many souvenir shops' of the one at the top of the town) and realize not just that I miss Bundoran, but that I always miss Donegal keenly when I return from any bit of it.

I realize, too, it is 1 August. Lughnasa good and proper.

I am heading off again in a couple of days.

The festival of Lugh, the three-faced god, this year coincides with a call-back to February and that pagan/Christian Brigid mashup that is the modern Imbolc, or Biddy's Day, a celebration of women in and of Ireland.

In the final days of July, the Advertising Standards Authority for Ireland withdraws from Irish television screens an ad for Tampax – it is set up to look like a chat show – that includes the line 'you gotta get them up there, girls'. This decision on the basis of eighty-four complaints, from which the Advertising Standards Authority has extrapolated that while the ad may not have caused *grave* offence, the offence it did cause was likely to have been *widespread*.

If that is so, it is as nothing to the offence that *that* judgement – and the subsequent decision not to review it – causes.

To a great many of those who take to print to vent their anger, it appears as though, for all the changes that it has undergone in recent times, Ireland's celebration of women does not go all that deep. 'Everyone outside this nation,' Anna Nolan writes in the *Irish Independent*, 'is aware that only in Ireland could this happen.'[16] (I agree wholeheartedly with the sentiment, but know that there are nations where such an ad would never have got near a screen to begin with.) A letter to the same paper reminds readers that in 1944 Archbishop John Charles McQuaid – who enjoyed an enormous amount of influence over successive Taoisigh and their juniors – had let a minister in the department of health know that he had been briefing 'the Bishops', as he said, 'very fully' on 'the evidence concerning the use of internal sanitary tampons, in particular, that called Tampax'.[17]

At that stage it seems Tampax had been unavailable in Ireland for a year and a half, but the Archbishop had been tipped off, by a chemist who was also a Knight of Columbanus, that new stock was soon expected.

'On the medical evidence made available,' McQuaid concluded, 'the Bishops very strongly disapproved of the use of these appliances, more particularly in the case of unmarried persons.'*

The projected shame, the confusion, the simple lack of information, all of which the Tampax television ad are intended to redress, are, of course, not unique to the Republic of Ireland: one of the best films of 2020, Sarah Gavron's *Rocks*, set in present-day London, features a scene in the school toilets that is almost a carbon copy of one from her own school days thirty-something years before that Anna Nolan writes about in her *Irish Independent* article.

And God help us – or maybe on second thoughts, God, stay out of it, please – there are probably plenty of people up here in the North and not just on the Unionist right who will be inwardly celebrating the ASAI intervention, who in fact would be delighted if the advances made in recent years in the South

---

* The letter in fact echoes another letter to the *Independent* back in January 2013. I have started by quoting the first and segued into the second, which in turn alludes to an article in *Irish History*. It seems the 'Knight Chemists' conspired to ensure that Tampax remained off the shelves for another while at least.

were not only halted at the border, but rolled back below it. In the summer of 2018, following the repeal of the Eighth Amendment, overturning the ban on abortion in the South, a campaign in which Sinn Féin had latterly at least been very active, Arlene Foster was met with scorn when she claimed that some nationalists and republicans in the North were thinking of voting DUP because of the party's trenchant anti-abortion stance. Her DUP colleague Ian Paisley Jr went further in claiming a priest in his constituency had written to him saying he would be urging his parishioners to back the party. The letter that he finally produced proved that the priest had done no such thing, although he did thank the DUP for its pro-life policies and did appear to suggest, too, that the South had become 'a cold house' for 'traditional Catholics', who might as a consequence feel more at home now in the North.

I have kept an eye on the population figures in the three years since. I am here to tell you there has been no detectable upswing from that quarter.

Lughnasa
(Good and Proper)

Another month, another seaside town, south-east this time instead of north-west: Tramore, Co. Waterford, the despair I am reliably informed (if you consider second-hand pub chat reliable) of urban planners: 'This place? They'll never make it work. Down the bottom for tourists, up the top for locals, Main Street at a forty-five-degree angle ... No chance.'

It is true that Tramore does not so much run down to the sea and all its ancillary attractions as gallop like a three-year-old on a promise of a bucket and spade.

(I have learned for the sake of the brake pads to approach from the side.)

There is an alternative history of modern Ireland that revolves around surfing. Tramore hosted the first Irish National Surf Championship in the summer of 1967, although the sport had been gaining a foothold for a couple of decades before that. One of the pioneers was a teenage boy in Dundalk who accidentally caught a wave while out on his homemade paddleboard (he had copied the design from *Reader's Digest*) in 1949, the same year that the Republic of Ireland Act came into force. Nowhere is completely watertight, not even (least of all?) an island. Other influences will always leak in.

The house in Tramore where my brother-in-law now lives was for a time in the late 1960s Surf Central, the home, and surgery, of a doctor whose sons were all keen surfers. Delightfully – to me, anyway – the Irish Surf Association (ISA) split not long after its formation, giving rise to the Surf Club of Ireland (SCI), leaving the ISA representing only the Dublin area. Would that that had been the deadliest split on the island in those years.

Never mind alternative history, there is a *movie* to be made about the spring 1966 'Surfari' that started in Strandhill, Co. Sligo, then curved up through Bundoran, Rossnowlagh (home to another couple of surf pioneers), Cruit Island, Marble Hill Strand in Dunfanaghy, and finally into Northern Irish waters at Portrush. And all the while the rest of the Republic, and a fair whack of the North, celebrated the fiftieth anniversary of the Easter Rising and old initials were given a dusting down and repurposed for a new murderous era: fifty-five years, some of them, and counting.

A few days after writing those lines I follow the story of two cousins from Co. Galway who were swept out to sea on their paddleboards one early August evening and who drifted for some thirty kilometres before managing to couple their boards to the buoy of a lobster pot off one of the Aran Islands, from where, seventeen hours after they had entered the sea, they were eventually rescued. The *Irish Times* map accompanying the rescue story ('created with Datawrapper') has a red rectangle around Galway Bay, and a gaping hole where Northern Ireland should be. According to this map, those 1966 Surfarians would have rounded Malin Head beyond Marble Hill Strand and tumbled straight down into Monaghan. This actually looks like (former) Tory adviser Dominic Cummings'* dream come true: Northern Ireland – as he is on record as having wished it – swallowed by the sea, although it is perhaps unfair, for once, on Cummings to single him out in this way. The 'tow it out and sink it' brigade has never lacked for recruits, or at least armchair brigadiers.

The *Guardian*, meanwhile, runs a feature on the Top 20 pit stops off main UK holiday routes and illustrates it with a map of Great Britain only.

Talk about being neither here nor there?

The Waterford constituency, which includes Tramore, returned deputies from three separate parties, along with a fourth independent, in the February 2020 general election, though none for the first time in the history of the State (if you allow a straight line from Cumann na nGaedheal) from Fine Gael. By far and away the biggest winner was Sinn Féin, whose candidate David Cullinane was elected on the first count with 20,597 votes, getting on for double the quota and more than double what he had got at the last election. Which is what emboldened him to make his 'unhelpful distraction' of a speech about 'them' never breaking the Hunger Strikers and never breaking Sinn Féin, Up the Ra and Tiocfaidh ár Lá.

I go for a mid-afternoon stroll alone, with a vague hope of seeing Rocky Mills, Tramore's celebrated Elvis impersonator,

---

* I fondly hoped, following his departure from Downing Street, that I would have to use this footnote to explain who Cummings was, but the stake has not yet been devised that is sharp enough to keep him from returning.

who according to the satirical *Waterford Whispers News* website has been on the scene since at least 1911. Within minutes, however, I am in sea fog so thick I could be surrounded by Elvis impersonators and not know it. In fact, I could – for all that I am able to pick out of the present century – have stumbled right back into 1911, somewhere between that June day of *Ulysses* and Partition. I find myself, I could not begin to tell you how, at the outer limits of the promenade, beside a section of sea wall with a sign before it saying, 'Woman's Slip', cliffs rising up on one side, and, on the other side, a forty-five-degree slope down to the beach. 'Cliffs' and 'beach' in this instance are both suppositional. They are for the moment simply higher fog and lower. There are, incredibly, still people out there in the lower fog, children as well as adults to go by the sound of the voices, paddling and swimming and … are they …? I have to go down the slope a little way, straining my eyes, to make sure… they are, yes: building sandcastles. Sandcastles in the sea fog. I think I may have stumbled as well into the mother and father and giddy toddler of all metaphors.

Back up on the street again I encounter the glowing end of a cigarette being inhaled, from which I infer a smoker in the three-foot-six to four-foot-two height range, or a taller one, seated.

Whatever they breathe out makes no dent in the fog.

'I've never seen fog to beat this,' I say.

'You haven't been in Tramore much.' A male smoker. Middle years. Then, 'Is it from above in the North you are?'

'It is. Just down for a quick visit. I'm writing a book.'

'Don't tell me.'

For a moment I don't.

'Wondering whether there will be a referendum ...'

He does not even ask me on what. The cigarette end glows again. 'There will be.'

'What way do you think it will go?'

'Only one way it can go.'

'You sound very sure.'

'I am.'

The cigarette rises a couple of feet – so the man on the end of it was seated – and is flicked to the ground. Full stop.

Later when the fog lifts, my brother-in-law, my wife and I take the dog for a walk, way down at the other end of the promenade, beyond the Merries and the Men's Slip, and the Lifeboat Station, where *Trá Mór* really grows – if a little stonily (another image: two teenage girls sharing a pair of flipflops to hop down to the sea) – into its Big Strand name, all five unbroken kilometres of it.

It is perhaps in the nature of beaches on an early August Friday evening, but the strollers and bathers and dashers from the waves crashing against the sea wall are more young than old. In ways I cannot quite put my finger on, there is an air of confidence about them, or maybe it is just that the fog too of uncertainty, and anxiety, that has hung over past few months, has (for now at least) lifted.

What there are not, that I can hear at any rate, are any other Northern accents, although as they would tell you in Bundoran July is the Northerner's month – or, more specifically, the middle two weeks of it, *half* month – of choice. And in the past, there was not a great deal of choice about it. The 'Twelfth Fortnight' was the holidays whether you celebrated King William III's victory at the Boyne or not.

My brother-in-law and his wife used to have a pair of Dalmatians, Nollaig and Samhain, Christmas and Halloween, the former one of the few Irish words I instantly recognized, the latter a word I would have known to see, but not to hear, or not known when I heard it (*sow*-en) that it was how you gave tongue to that combination of letters.

This latest dog is called Leia, a nod, I think, to my brother-in-law's early-teen *Star Wars* obsession. Sometime late in the evening I comment on the fact that they have departed from their tradition with dog names – that Leia is clearly not in the same idiom as Nollaig and Samhain. Actually, my sister-in-law says with infinite patience, it is not just in the same 'idiom', it is in the same language: it means grey. Leia – or Liath, as I now know her to be called (just as I now know, or am newly reminded, that Princess Leia is pronounced *Lay*, and not *Lee*) – stands there incontrovertibly greyly before me, head cocked: 'Seriously ... *Star Wars*?'*

I lie in bed that night wondering about the Irish language in any reunited or even reconfigured Ireland. Article 8 of the constitution (I sleep with it under my pillow), which

---

* Fast-forward to Christmas/Nollaig. My wife and I are searching online for gifts for our Tramore niece and nephews. 'The younger lads still love anything to do with *Star Wars*,' my brother-in-law has said, so we have found our way onto a site with Stormtrooper costumes – and look, there is Luke, too. 'We should see if we could find a Princess Leia costume for the dog,' I say. 'You mean like this?' my wife says and turns the screen to face me. There is even a little 'hair' attachment with side buns. 'Yeah,' I say, 'but do they do it in grey?'

states in English before Irish that Irish not English is the national language, though both have the status of official language, also contains the following clause: 'Provision may, however, be made by law for the exclusive use of either of the said languages for any one or more official purposes, either throughout the state or in any part thereof.' Those last five words might almost have been written with anxious unionists in mind.

It is a point frequently made, though well worth making again, that in the North as well as the South during the post-Famine decades Protestants were prominent in efforts to revive – in some parts save – the Irish language. There have in recent times, too, been well-publicized and enthusiastically adopted Irish-language classes in working-class Protestant parts of Belfast. Even better publicized, though, is the if not outright hostility towards Irish – suspicion at the very least that the language has been enlisted in a broader cultural war against unionism in general. The DUP has almost single-handedly and by pretty much every means at its disposal, including Looking-glass logic ('The Irish-speaking community appears to be growing in Northern Ireland, where we do not have an Irish Language Act, and declining in the Republic of Ireland, where there is legislation ... An Irish Language Act would not necessarily help the language,' Edwin Poots MLA, 2007) blocked the implementation of a language act that would give Irish official status in Northern Ireland as well, although FactCheckNI, the independent fact-checking service, supports the party's claim never to have given a commitment to an act, only a strategy.'[18] The act's supporters, Irish speaking and non-, say that this is not a question of forcing the language on anyone. It is about dignity and equality. Presumably, under a new dispensation, its guarantees would be subsumed into Article 8 of the constitution, though with what implications for that article's 'any part thereof' exclusion zone is moot.

Presumably, too, any future thirty-two-county Ireland would have oversight of, or an opinion on, the running of the current Northern Irish 'state' – for which read Protestant – schools, and might well exempt them, if requested, from the otherwise compulsory teaching of Irish. Proficiency in Irish is no longer a requirement for entrance to the Republic's Civil Service, or for post-primary teaching jobs, though all new primary school teachers are still required to have taken the language to Leaving Cert (A Level stage in the North), or to have taken a diploma. Aside, though, from whether pupils in schools that did not offer Irish (and again assuming that were an option) were materially disadvantaged in the jobs market, there is the question of the disadvantages that might accrue from voluntarily closing them off to what might by then be a pretty pervasive part of the culture.

Irish, I see, is not at present required for university entrance for *non-Irish* students. The framing of that, too, would clearly

---

* The FactCheckNI verdict parses it thus: 'Although they signed up to the [2006] St Andrews Agreement, this includes a commitment by the UK government, and not the DUP. After devolution, responsibility for a language policy was transferred to the Northern Ireland Executive, but this did not include a commitment to establish an Irish Language Act.' Even New Decade, New Approach falls short of *act*. And still the DUP baulks.

need to be looked at again in any future where north and south were purely geographical terms.

My Tramore nephews go, as their younger sister, my niece, will eventually go, to an Educate Together national school, a movement that grew out of a single multidenominational school – the so-called Dalkey School Project – set up in Co. Dublin in the late 1970s, with the support of the ruling Fianna Fáil party under Charles Haughey. Now, as then, though, there is opposition, or lack of cooperation, from within the Catholic Church. The Dalkey School was initially labelled 'atheistic'. The Knights of Columbanus too rattled their sabres, or lances or whatever the latest Knight fashion is, in its direction. As recently as 2016, Fr Paul Connell, President of the Association of Management of Catholic Secondary Schools, was warning that dismantling the Catholic ethos of schools risked creating a vacuum that could express itself in nihilism and self-harm, although I am bound to say that his comments were given pretty short shrift in many quarters. Michael Clifford, writing in the *Irish* (formerly *Cork*) *Examiner*, recognized that they could be seen as offensive by bodies like Educate Together and 'entirely alien' to 'anybody interested in values such as equality of treatment for all'.[19] More than anything, though, he suspected that to most people in the South, Fr Connell's views were simply irrelevant. The church had lost whatever claim it might once have made to be the arbiter of morality in Ireland.

Which does not mean it has lost entirely its ability to harry or dismay.

Tramore Educate Together, which my brother-in-law helped establish in 2014, has outgrown its original building. There is a school building sitting empty, not too far away, which they would move into in a heartbeat. Except it belongs to an order of nuns, who object. 'Or some senior nuns do,' my brother-in-law says. 'Hashtag Not All Nuns.'

I am reminded of the integrated school movement in Northern Ireland, which despite repeated assertions that integration from an early age is one of the surest ways of addressing the problem of sectarianism in our society, still only accounts for about 7 per cent of the school population, not least because of the rearguard action of the Catholic Church. And I am reminded, too, that the entire make-up of the school system is another of those areas of Southern life on which I am a little vague, as though the border were not a wayward and mostly invisible line, but a gauzy curtain for ever in the mid-distance.

A little later in the year, the *Irish Times* reports on an 'unpublished document' – I think the technical term is 'kite' – being discussed/flown by the Department of Education to consider the phasing out of Catholic symbols from the majority of state, or Education and Training Board (ETB) schools in the South, or alternatively the incorporation into them of symbols that reflect the diversity of the school's enrolment.

(As the department's website explains, 'the post-primary education sector comprises secondary, ETB schools and community colleges. Secondary schools are privately owned and managed. ETB schools are state-established and administered by Education and Training Boards … while community colleges are managed by Boards of Management of differing compositions.' In case you were, as I was, wondering.)

Around seventy ETB schools will be exempt from the proposed changes, due, the report says, to explicit and 'binding agreements with the Catholic Church that guarantee certain provisions for Catholic children'. That article of Michael Clifford's at the time of Fr Paul Connell's 'nihilism and self-harm' address makes mention of the church's 'excellent political skills' in keeping control of the vast majority of schools in the Irish state. You would have to think, or hope, that even those skills would not be enough to maintain its dominance in an all-island Ireland.

Further evidence of the potential for future disputes comes in November, when the Republic's Workplace Relations Commission (WRC) determines that a so-called 'Designated' Community College discriminated against a child by rejecting her application of the grounds of her religion. 'Designated' here is understood to mean 'representative of a particular religious denomination', almost always Catholic. In this instance, though, the college is designated Church of Ireland. (There was no fee-paying Church of Ireland School in the part of north-west Dublin where the school was established.) It is the pupil that, the WRC has found, was discriminated against who is Catholic. The case against the college was brought under the Equal Status Act of 2000, an act that clearly has in its sights marginalized or under-represented sections of society, and I think in that instant of the DUP and its use in the Stormont Assembly of mechanisms intended to protect minorities.

Mick Fealty, founder of the news and opinion portal *Slugger O'Toole*, in an article headlined 'WRC asserts right of student from majority population to take the place of one from a tiny minority', maintains that never, even in the worst days of post-Partition, Unionist-dominated Northern Ireland, was there any state interference in the selection of pupils for Catholic Maintained Schools.[20] He sees the case as part of a wider question of how well minority rights in education could be protected in the event of reunification. 'Whether we like it or not,' he writes, 'other people will pick up and interpret the signals you send, even the ones you don't intend for them to pick up … nationalism is giving off signals that even the standards of pre-power-sharing Northern Ireland don't need to be adhered to.'

That might be coming on a bit strong – certainly quite a number of the *Slugger O'Toole* below-the-line commentators think so – and you would have to say it is a bit of a jump from the Workplace Relations Commission to 'nationalism', but it is perhaps one more example of a thing that is more or less serviceable in the current dispensation being far from adequate in the event of constitutional change. Reunification, like Brexit, is going to mean change in every area of life in the South as well as the North. Or if not change then at the very least taking a good long, hard look.

We arrived down in Tramore by car, but for reasons of other work I am travelling back up, ahead of everyone else, by train. I get a lift into Waterford city centre, crossing over the River Suir to the railway station, wedged between the river and a pretty impressive cliff face. I could not have told you before I fetched up here this morning that the station is named Plunkett, for Joseph Mary Plunkett, one of the seven signatories of the Easter 1916 Proclamation of the Republic. Just inside the station doors is a frieze-style monument to his life and Easter Rising involvement: 'Joseph Mary Plunkett changed Ireland and Here's How …'

A little over half an hour after leaving Plunkett Station, Dublin-bound, the train makes its first stop at Kilkenny – or as I now see it is called, MacDonagh Station, after Thomas MacDonagh, another of the seven Easter '16 signatories.

Connolly Station – the station on the north side of Dublin that I have been using for more than four decades, the station from which I will be leaving for Belfast again later today – is, although the connection has been worn down in my mind with too frequent use, named for James Connolly, leader of the Irish Citizen Army and, like MacDonagh and Plunkett, a signatory of the Proclamation.

I sit up in my seat and start running through the stations of the Iarnród Éireann network in my head and then – when that is exhausted – on DuckDuckGo: Cork Kent Station, after Thomas Kent (executed in Cork itself after the Rising), a near homophone in Galway named for Éamonn Ceanntt, another of those Proclamation signatories. Dublin has, besides Connolly, Heuston, where the Waterford train terminates, and which takes its name from Seán Heuston (Officer Commanding in the Mendicity Institution), who used to work there when it was still Kingsbridge Station; a Pearse, after both Padraig and Willie, only the first of them a signatory, though both were executed; and, at Dun Laoghaire, a Mallin (Michael of that ilk, commander of the Irish Citizen Army at the Royal College of Surgeons in Easter week and executed in the yard adjacent to the one in which Seán Heuston had been shot just a few minutes before). A little beyond that again, in Bray, Co. Wicklow, is (Edward)

Daly Station, for the commandant of the battalion that seized Dublin's Four Courts.

That is already a fair number of the names off the Bundoran souvenir shop Easter 1916 clock face. And there are more.

Between Connolly and Newry, the first stop north of the border, the Enterprise (as the Dublin–Belfast service is known) stops at Drogheda – MacBride (John), number two to MacDonagh at Jacob's Biscuit Factory – and Dundalk – Clarke (Thomas), Proclamation signatory. Add to this Michael *O'Hanrahan* (another of the Jacob's Biscuit Factory battalion) in Wexford, Con *Colbert* (assumed command of a battalion at the moment of surrender to save a married superior officer) in Limerick, Sean *MacDiarmada* (Proclamation signatory) in Sligo, and in Tralee Sir Roger *Casement* (hanged, of course, rather than shot, three months after all the others), and you have the network pretty much covered. Or you have had since 1966 and the fiftieth anniversary of the Rising when all these station names were conferred. The anniversary stoked the already febrile imaginations of some of the madder elements of Northern unionism. In the weeks following, a group of men from Belfast's Shankill Road operating under the name of the UVF threw petrol bombs at houses belonging – as it turned out – to people other than the ones they thought lived there, killing one elderly woman; shot and killed a man walking home alone off the Falls Road; and shot, as members of the IRA, a group of off-duty barmen who were simply Catholic, killing one of them, too.

If reunification is the fulfilment – as many republicans believe – of the Easter 1916 Proclamation, a victory beyond the grave for all those who gave their lives that week in the Post Office, the Four Courts, the Biscuit Factory, Flour Mill, Mendicity Institution, the College of Surgeons, or gave them, the following month, in prison yards, then – forget, if you can, the petrol bombers and ambushers – where are the broad mass of Northern unionists in the narrative?

To go back for a moment to Kilkenny and MacDonagh Station, where this – I give you fair warning – train of thought really began … To one side of the Up platform is a memorial, unveiled in 2018, to the dead of the First World War, sibling to a larger memorial in the Peace Park, off the town's Michael Street. In the spring of 2019, some of the madder elements of Southern nationalism set about the Michael Street memorial with a lump hammer.

By a coincidence that goes beyond the curious and into the utterly bizarre, the day I spend on the train from Waterford up to Belfast is the day before my birthday. A short time after I return home, a friend calls with a gift, including, among other things, a postcard in a clear plastic envelope. Her father was a collector. This one has, on the picture side, a portrait of Hans von Bülow inset on a tinted drawing of a concert hall whose identity eludes me,* and, on the other, in black ink over a green halfpenny stamp (only-just-King George V, surrounded by laurel wreath), the postmark 'Athlone, 14 June 1910'. It is addressed to the Reverend T. G. Sharpe of Boyle in Co. Roscommon ('Rev T. G. Sharpe, Boyle' indeed is the

---

* I say this as though concert halls of nineteenth-century Europe was my chosen specialist subject.

whole of the address). 'The knife is mine,' the message reads, 'don't trouble about it.' Which, even 110 years later, troubles me greatly. It is signed 'Robt Baile', who, my friend tells me, might have died subsequently in the Great War: the reason perhaps for her father's interest in it. I check. She is right. He – Robert Carlyle Baile – did die, aged twenty-five, on 16 October 1915; and so did his younger brother, George Frederick Cecil Baile, aged twenty-six, on 9 November 1917; and so, two and a half months after that, while attached to the 64th Casualty Clearing Station, did their father, Revd George William Baile, Chaplain 4th Class, at the age of fifty-two: of natural causes, according to the *They Gave Their Today* website. Revd Baile's one surviving son, Capt. J. Baile, was present at the funeral. The names of the fallen Bailes, father and sons, are all on that vandalized memorial in the Kilkenny Peace Park.

The Kilkenny War Memorial Group remains undaunted. Later, in October 2020, it unveils a sculpture to Thomas Joseph Woodgate, one of the youngest military casualties of the First World War, who was killed aged fourteen (he had lied to enlist, claiming to be eighteen), along with five hundred others, on board HMS *Leinster*, torpedoed between Dublin and Holyhead in the final weeks of the war. Interviewed at the ceremony, the Group's chairman Dónal Croghan says, 'I think, as a country, we have matured. First of all, these were Kilkenny men, or boys in this case. They were Irishmen and they happened to put on a different uniform. They were written out of history so that's why it's important to remember them.'[21]

The walk from Heuston Station to Connolly takes me past the Four Courts, past the front of the GPO, and up Talbot

Street, where I had a notion, at the start of February, I was going to spend 1 May.

The patterns we weave, and then unpick.

Even these several weeks after restrictions began to be eased, the street, like the rest of the city it has to be said, seems to be operating at something below half-power. And there is that extra layer of wariness that has carried over from the height of the pandemic, the *angling away from* as we walk, the averting of the face, the dip of the head. People just do not want to stop and talk, least of all answer questions. A line comes to me from a *New Yorker* article I read a while back about losing 'the habit of living in the world', though to use it in this context feels like an appropriation.[22] It is an article in fact about Ireland's system for persons in need of international protection (that, not asylum seeker, the author argues, is the term to use: a right to be claimed rather than a gift to be begged), a system, says the article, 'that is perhaps unique in its daily cruelty'. A bold statement, you might think, coming from an American journalist at a time of detention camps on the Mexican border, of migrant children separated from their parents, but she acknowledges and roundly condemns those, too, and still stands by her judgement on Ireland's forty 'Direct Provision Centres', ranging from hotels to prefab caravans, and including a former holiday camp, many miles from anywhere, whose conditions, as far back as 2015, the United Nations Committee on Economic, Social and Cultural Rights condemned as a 'severe violation of human rights'.

Talbot Street is fully pedestrianised now. At the far end of the street, just beyond the arch carrying southbound trains out of Connolly, and set out a little from the pavement, is a simple granite memorial to the victims of the 17 May 1974 UVF bomb outrage, bearing the names of the fourteen people who died here – a fifteenth, a full-term unborn baby, did not live to receive a name – and the nineteen others killed that Friday evening in attacks elsewhere in Dublin and in Monaghan town. There were other murderous loyalist paramilitary attacks south of the border, but nothing again on the scale of 17 May '74 – nothing anywhere, north or south on that scale – and equally nothing as concerted as the IRA's campaign across the water, where some three dozen shootings and bombings were carried out in 1974 alone, taking the lives of thirty-nine people.

I am passing a second-hand shop by the memorial when my eye is caught by a pile of old magazines on a stool just inside the glass-fronted shop door. I still have a few minutes before my train. I step inside. Top of the magazine pile is a copy of the *Irish Statesman* ('with which is incorporated the *Irish Homestead*'), dated Saturday 3 October 1925[23] and edited by George Russell, aka AE. The same AE who designed the Starry Plough flag for Connolly's Irish Citizen Army and who understudied Horace Plunkett (Joseph Mary Plunkett's second cousin) in the Irish Dominion League, a short-lived movement opposed to Partition, but in favour of a continued relationship with Great Britain. The IRA showed what it thought about that by burning Plunkett's house during the Civil War.

I turn to the magazine's third page – the first two being ads and the table of contents – and read under 'Notes and Comments', 'The general impression in Europe after the Sixth Assembly of the League of Nations is that Great Britain is trying to diminish the prestige of the League by obstruction to proposals emanating from the idealism in Europe.' I check the cover again: yes, ninety-five years ago, not days. The next note, or comment, is on the divisions within the British Labour Party (I am sorely tempted to check the cover again), while over the page another begins, 'Japhet in search of a father had a light task as compared with Republicans in search of a policy', at which point I pay the €10 and determine to read the rest on the train.

'At last the royal road to salvation has been found' (imagine me now in the carriage, left-sided window seat, forward-facing, pointed towards Belfast) 'and the Standing Committee of Sinn Féin has decided that the short-cut to salvation lies in a general boycott of English goods … Sinn Féin is apparently not concerned about economic reasons except in so far as they can be exploited to make political capital.'

This was a year before Éamon de Valera, president of Sinn Féin, resigned over the party's policy of abstention from the Dáil and formed Fianna Fáil, as leader of which in 1932 he entered government for the first time and promptly abolished the Oath of Allegiance and commenced an economic war with the United Kingdom, that is to say Great Britain and – more importantly for relations on the island – the six counties of Northern Ireland. The policy of protectionism was not fully dismantled until the late 1950s, helping to pave the way for Ireland's entry into the European Economic Community along with the UK in 1973, after which the whole cycle of *Irish Statesman*-like articles about Britain and Europe and splits in the British labour movement could begin again.

Japhet in Search of a Father is the title of an 1836 novel by Captain Frederick Marryat, invoked by Buck Mulligan in the opening pages of *Ulysses*. AE himself turns up in the novel, helping Stephen Dedalus out with the loan of a couple of bob. (The *Irish Homestead* had published Joyce's first stories.) Fast-forward again, from June 1904 to October 1925, and, just below Japhet in his *Irish Statesman*, AE has a note on the compulsory teaching of Irish in state schools – 'It is not the language people speak which is the real problem of education, but how they think in that language ... Knowledge of a language by itself will provide employment for none except those who are paid to teach it' – as well as one on the recent election to the Second House, the Seanad, of a Free State government whose existence was scarcely conceivable at the time of *Ulysses*'s setting, but an established fact by the time of its publication. Only around one in five voters turned out for the 1925 Seanad election, prompting the *Irish Statesman* to lament, 'No doubt the system is awkward and intricate, and, so far, the complicated mechanism gives little promise of securing the results which it was claimed would justify its adoption in practice,' *however* '[not] only our political skill, but the level of general intelligence amongst us must be even lower than our worst enemies believed if the ability to mark the Senate ballot paper is limited to one-fifth of the electorate.'

The Seanad, like many another Second House, has proved to be an ongoing headache for the Irish political system. The first premier, William Cosgrave, had promised to use his nominations to ensure representation for the Protestant minority – the 'results', presumably, to which the *Irish Statesman* refers – but this seems never to have been carried through to any significant degree. Within a few years of that 1925 election future Taoiseach Seán Lemass was expressing a preference for the Seanad's abolition. 'If there is to be a Second House let it be a Second House under our thumb. Let it be a group of individuals who dare not let a squeak out of them except when we lift our fingers to give them breath to do it.' The kind of rhetoric, you could imagine, that would have drawn hearty hear-hears from north of the border: the twenty-six-strong Senate in the Northern Ireland parliament at Stormont never, in the fifty years between Partition and the imposition of Direct Rule from Westminster in March 1972, featured more than seven non-unionists at any one time.

The first Fianna Fáil government did succeed in abolishing the Seanad completely on its way to introducing the revised constitution of 1937. The Seanad as subsequently re-established – to satisfy those, de Valera more or less said, who like that sort of thing – was, according to F. S. L. Lyons, 'but a shadow of its predecessor'.[21]

It narrowly survived a referendum on its continued existence in 2013. Unless you are a Brexiteer, in which case it won by a thumping great majority of 51.7 to 48.3 per cent. It might please AE to know that voter turnout was just short of two in five.

Since at least the 1990s, however, there has been an attempt to bring in Northerners, including some prominent figures from a Protestant background. As previously noted, though, the real challenge might be keeping them there.

By the time I have finished with the *Irish Statesman*, the train is pulling out of Dundalk's Clarke Station and is skirting the enormous, levelled area – 1.3 million square feet – that is shaping up to be – or from the looks of it *shaping up to* shaping up to be (Covid has put all sorts of projects on hold) – Dundalk North

Business Park, motto, 'It's easy getting from A to B via D.' (I think if I had shelled out big on that campaign I might be checking my terms and conditions.) The prospectus declares it is ideal for warehousing, manufacturing, pharmaceuticals, logistics and network data ... what? Storage? Amassing? Anyway, there are a lot of square feet to store/amass your data and other stuff in, with Paypal already signed up as well as Xerox and WuXi Biologics and all just forty-eight minutes by road from both Dublin and Belfast. It is a vision of a future in which the border is a complete irrelevance, and possibly national governments, too.

The early evening before we drove down to Tramore, police closed off the road that runs past the top of my street in east Belfast, stopping access to one of the main roads out of town, the Holywood Road. They closed the Holywood Road itself, at its junction with the Belmont Road, where the Strand Cinema – the *great* Strand Cinema, the last of the city's art deco picture palaces – faces Strandtown Hall, home of the East Belfast Unionist Party. I saw a camera crew at this junction when I nipped out to the shops. It was more attention than would usually be afforded a mere bomb *scare*, which is what the woman at the till in Tesco Metro told me she thought it probably was. There were simultaneous police operations at the Henry Jones Playing Fields off Church Road, about two miles away, and, across the city, at a housing development on the edge of west Belfast. Suspect devices had been planted on cars parked at each of the three locations. The fact that they had been planted *on* and not *under*, as is the norm with devices and cars, suggests either a lack of expertise or a degree of haste. The fact that they were planted simultaneously suggests the involvement of more than a small handful of people. The cars all belonged to people with connections to the East Belfast Gaelic Athletic Association Club, formed back in the late spring. To understand the significance of this club, you have to understand both the demographics of east Belfast – predominantly Protestant – and the history of Gaelic games, which, though 'established by a group of non-religious idealists', as the *Irish News* sports correspondent Danny Hughes has written, 'became a cold place for Protestants throughout Ireland from the 1960s on'.[25] The East Belfast club's formation was unusual enough that it merited a mention on the RTÉ News.

The taxi driver who picks me up off the Dublin train at Lanyon Place – formerly, laughably, *Central* – Station, driving me home past the site of one of the bomb alerts, asks me, unusually, if I was around for it. He is shaking his head. 'In this day and age,' he says. This is another thing you have to understand: taxi driving in Northern Ireland was during the years of the Troubles an almost uniquely dangerous occupation. Drivers were with good reason guarded in how they responded to questions, and in the opinions they volunteered. This is not a driver taking a calculated risk, or mistaking my religion. This is a driver who is working on the assumption that he and I are the same religion, the same religion as the people who left those 'devices'. And he is disgusted. 'Why wouldn't they support anything that brought people together?'

'Together' is, in fact, the motto of East Belfast GAA, in English, in Irish (le cheile), and in Ulster-Scots (thegither). It is incorporated, in a typeface (Farset Feirste) modelled on traditional Belfast tiled street signage, into a crest that also includes the Harland and Wolff shipyard cranes, a sunset, a shamrock, a thistle and what I instinctively want to call a Red Hand of Ulster, even though the hand, like the thistle and the shamrock, is here black. O'Neill's, the GAA kit specialist on Belfast's main shopping drag, Royal Avenue, already has a full range of East Belfast GAA kits and of accessories in black with shipyard-crane-yellow facings.

'They want to catch themselves on,' is my taxi driver's final word on the previous week's bomb hoaxers. And he is so not wrong.

In February, posters went up in parts of Derry city, showing Constable Peadar Heffron. Constable Heffron captained the PSNI's GAA team – as big a story when it was formed back in the early 2000s, after the GAA lifted its ban on members of security forces taking part in its sports, as the East Belfast GAA club was in 2020. In January 2010 dissident republicans detonated a bomb that had been attached to the underside of Constable Heffron's car. The explosion resulted in the amputation of his right leg and the removal of his bowel, leaving him with a lifelong reliance on urostomy and colostomy bags. The reason for his appearance on the posters in Derry was exactly the same reason for which he was targeted in the first place. He is Catholic and he joined the police. As well as punishing him for his choice, the bomb and the posters are intended as disincentives to other young Catholics thinking of following his example.

Peadar Heffron is on record as saying that he felt shunned by the GAA in the aftermath of the bomb that maimed him.

Never mind into 26: 6 still has trouble dividing into itself equitably and without rancour.

The reaction of loyalist paramilitaries seems not to have featured much in the discussions, in October 2019, between Leo Varadkar and Boris Johnson that broke the deadlock in the Brexit negotiations and paved the way for the swapping of the 'Backstop' arrangement for a 'Frontstop' – that customs border in the Irish Sea – in the event that no comprehensive Free Trade Agreement can be arrived at between the UK and the EU.

And nor should it have. Any more than the reaction of republican paramilitaries ought to have featured in the debate around other alternatives to the Backstop, although in that case too often it did. Michel Barnier, welcoming the October 2019 deal, sums up the EU position: 'Since day one, what really matters is the people of Ireland and Northern Ireland. What really matters is peace.'

Walking around some parts of Belfast these days, reading the stuff that is being stuck up and painted on lamp posts and walls, you could be forgiven for thinking that M. Barnier and his EU colleagues have taken their eye off one rather large ball.

Phil Hogan, whose election to the post of EU trade commissioner was cited by *The Economist* as evidence of Ireland's clout, has been back home for the summer, or, as previously suggested (see p. 71), for the fulfilment of the laws of drama. On 18 August he travels the hundred or so miles from Kilkenny, where he has been staying with a family member, to Ballyconneely, Co. Galway, for the Oireachtas Golf Society's fiftieth anniversary tournament and celebration. Him and eighty others, including several prominent Fianna Fáil and Fine Gael politicians, who together attend a dinner, at the Station House Hotel in nearby Clifden, the evening after the government reduces the numbers allowed at indoor gatherings from *fifty* to just six. Even if the new measures were not in place, or had not had time to bed in, the attendees were still contravening the old ones. Fianna Fáil minister for agriculture, Dara Calleary, who was there, resigns almost as soon as details of the dinner leak out. Phil Hogan toughs it out, as RTÉ reports: 'In a statement on Twitter, Mr Hogan said he attended the event "on the clear understanding that the organisers and the hotel concerned had been assured [by the Irish Hotels Federation] that the arrangements put in place would be in compliance with the government's guidelines."' The EU trade commissioner, and he needs someone else to help him count past fifty.

I would suggest he does not go to Sinn Féin finance spokesperson Pearse Doherty, who, appearing on Claire Byrne's RTÉ One radio show, and calling for Hogan's resignation, makes a distinction between the 'shindig' at Clifden and the funeral of 'a friend', that is Bobby Storey, in Belfast, which he himself attended, a part, as he says, of the permitted cortège of fifty.

'I think,' Claire Byrne interjects, 'the maximum allowed was thirty.'

'No, it was fifty.'

'I'm pretty sure it was thirty.'

'Yes, well, whatever the numbers were, they were the numbers that were adhered to.'

The Sinn Féin finance spokesperson and *he* thinks what previously looked to him like fifty was probably only thirty after all.

It takes another week, a whole raft of other revelations about how Phil Hogan has been spending his time while back home (including being stopped on his way to Galway by Gardaí for using his mobile phone while driving), and finally the intervention of European Commissioner Ursula von der Leyen before her trade commissioner bows to the inevitable and resigns.

The trade commissioner post goes to former Latvian finance minister Valdis Dombrovskis. Ireland, though, does not lose out altogether. In the mini reshuffle triggered by Hogan's departure Mairead McGuinness is made commissioner for financial stability, financial services and the capital markets union, which is, if not the biggest commissionership, certainly the one with the longest title. So, there, a commissioner for a commissioner. that will teach them to break the rules.

The second weekend in September, I am on the train again, via Connolly and Heuston, en route to another of the twelve stations of Easter 1916, Ceantt, for the reduced, but still, in the Covid climate, close to miraculous, version of the Galway International Festival.

Earlier in the week, the Republic's Central Applications Office (CAO) released the results of the school Leaving Cert exam – each grade having a points equivalent. At two o'clock this afternoon, about the time I am leaving Heuston for Ceantt, it publishes the minimum points required for entry to university at Level 8 and Level 7/6 Institutions. (That is how it lists them, and how they are everywhere referred to, in descending rather than ascending order.) There are thirty-two of the former and twenty-five of the latter, although some institutions are simultaneously Level 8 *and* Level 7/6. The CAO also publishes a separate points table for graduate medicine and mature nursing courses.

The train from Heuston to Ceantt this afternoon fills with young people on their way to Galway to celebrate the end of their school careers. A woman across the aisle, ten or so years younger than me, travelling with her late-teenage son, spends a large part of the journey on her phone, catching up on what points this relative or that child of a friend got. 'She *did*? Ach, that's *great* …' 'Isn't that fantastic? Good for him!' I am pretty sure in every case it is substantially less than her son got.

At any given moment in the remainder of the day and well, well into the night I will find myself wandering through a conversation of this kind or sitting somewhere as the conversation briefly surrounds me then passes on. (Everyone in Galway seems to be perpetually on their way to another, better party.) The young woman who thought she was 'going to have to go to UCC' for medicine, but finds she has the points for Trinity. The young man in the off-licence clutching the mighty carry-out he was heading to the till with when a friend of the family or former teacher puts himself in his way. 'I needed another forty for law …'

On the RTÉ main evening news, the education correspondent gives a sort of points stock market report: those subjects and institutions where the minimum points required has dropped (if the young man with the mighty carry-out is still sensate he might be pleased to know that both commerce and podiatric medicine remain open to him at the upper end of his points total) and those where the minimum has risen, or, in the case of drama and theatre studies – 'for all you budding Connells and Mariannes out there' – leapt, to just two behind law, at 564.

The much-anticipated *Normal People* bounce.

It is one of the things I liked about the novel and the TV adaptation that they got such drama out of the awarding of exam grades, without, again, ever once pausing to explain to the uninitiated how the whole points business worked (the maximum points, by the way, which only 1 per cent of pupils achieve, is 625, so do not ask me where the '732 for medicine at Trinity' I heard earlier came from), although it does, too, reinforce for me how locked in we are, North and South, to our separate systems. Which gets me thinking about Scotland, not just its distinctive Highers exams, unknown in the rest of the UK, but also its legal system, its conveyancing arrangements, the whole manner in which, even at the height of its embrace of Britishness, it retained a very clear Scottish identity, simultaneously a part of and apart from.

Lurking in the background of these thoughts is that other great Scotland conundrum: how Northern nationalists who see the island of Ireland as an indivisible unit can insist on the divisibility of the island next door, and how Northern unionists can argue for the integrity of that island and not of the one they happen to live on.

The event I have come to Galway to take part in is entitled 'Brexit and the North' and involves SDLP MP for Belfast South Claire Hanna and me in a discussion chaired by Dave O'Connell, editor-in-chief of the Connaught Tribune newspaper group.

The event has been given new impetus by the leak, earlier in the week, of details of the Tory government's proposed Internal Market Bill, aimed – the government claims – at preserving frictionless trade between Great Britain and Northern Ireland, in the full knowledge that, by seeking to circumvent provisions in the Northern Ireland Protocol of the Withdrawal Agreement, it will breach international law, although only, according to Secretary of State for Northern Ireland Brandon Lewis, 'in a very specific and limited way'.

Greater party love hath no man than this, that he will lay down his reputation and his self-respect by standing up in the Houses of Parliament and uttering such crap.

And many indeed in the days since have been the gags about specific and limited parking infringements, removals of money from banks etc., etc.

My own view – shared I suspect by a great many – is that the Internal Market Bill too will be modified or dropped in a last-gasp 'compromise' that possibly involves even more concessions by way of reparation for the bad feeling caused, with even more potential complications for Northern Ireland. To adapt Gary Lineker's 'football is a simple game, twenty-two players chase a ball around for ninety minutes and then the Germans win', Brexit often looks like a simple process in which London and Brussels negotiate for months on end and then Northern Ireland is told it has won even when a sizeable chunk of it feels it hasn't.*

* Lineker's Law true at the time of writing, 16:59 Tuesday 29 June 2021.

Claire is joining the event on screen from Belfast, having just arrived back from Westminster the day before. Dave and I are in an actual theatre together, on a stage, with an audience of forty seated in carefully spaced ranks and masked. (An observation. Sitting with a mask on, on a chair, two metres from your nearest neighbour, seems to predispose you to placing your hands on your thighs.) It has, despite the efforts of the Black Box Theatre team, despite everyone's evident delight at being out, my own delight at being there, the feel of a scene from the next novel but one by Kazuo Ishiguro.

The discussion inevitably moves from Brexit – which, to say again, the majority of people in Northern Ireland voted against – to border polls. At one point Dave O'Connell throws out the question of whether the South can even afford the North. The figure most often given for how much Northern Ireland 'costs', including jobs in the inflated public sector, is £11 billion. There is actually a Twitter account – 'End Britain's Annual £11 Billion Irish [sic] Subvention' – whose every tweet is a variation on 'cuts to school meals wouldn't be necessary if we weren't spending £11bn a year to foot Northern Ireland's bill' / 'there wouldn't be a housing crisis here in Britain if the £11bn of taxpayers' money that is forked out to subsidize N. Ireland each year…'

Sinn Féin disputes this £11 billion figure, arguing that it includes elements like pensions, which would continue to be paid for an extended period by the British Exchequer. The party puts the real cost at closer to £.4.5 billion and even this, it says, would be offset by economies of scale and by the boost to productivity and positivity that reunification would (in its eyes) inevitably bring.*

A 2018 study by economists from Trinity College and Dublin City University found that living standards in the South would drop by something in the region of 15 per cent annually in the event of reunification. Just the day before our talk, Claire's party leader, Colum Eastwood, interviewed in the *Irish Times* about the prospects of success for a referendum, points to another of the recurring questions, and issues: health, and the price of it.[26]

'A lot of people [in the North] will say to me, "I'm not paying fifty quid to see the doctor". If we don't answer that, we won't win anything.'

His solution?

'You make sure people don't have to pay fifty quid to see the doctor ... It's absolutely key to this conversation.'

Roughly a third of the population in the South, to be clear, people on benefits or lower working incomes, do not pay anything at all for healthcare. These 'Medical Card' holders also qualify for free Outpatient and Emergency Department care, where there is otherwise a charge of €100 for an unreferred visit. There are other means-tested exceptions and reductions, too, in dental care and prescription charges. For the majority, though, Eastwood's 'fifty quid' holds true.

Not only are taxpayers in the South going to have to absorb the costs of the health provision for nearly two million

---

* In news nearly too good to be true, in 2014 a seam of gold, discovered in Clontibret, Co. Monaghan, about three miles over the border from Co. Armagh, was valued at £11 billion. I imagine the ghosts of the unionist delegation to the Boundary Commission that omitted Monaghan from Northern Ireland, looking on glumly.

Northerners, in other words, they are going to have to find new ways to pay for their own. And maybe that is the way it should, and ultimately will, be sold, as an opportunity for a complete *reset* (the big autumn 2020, Covid-boosted word), overhauling all existing ways of thinking, and doing so to the benefit of the entire population, north, south, east and west.

Elsewhere in the same day's paper, meanwhile, Frank McNally is writing that 'the practicalities of reunification would still … have to unravel a century of estrangement and distrust in which the Free State/Republic was too Irish for one half of Northern Ireland and not Irish enough for the other, while in the process both halves earned a parity of disesteem in the South'.

The SDLP has set up its own New Ireland Commission, launched a month after the FFG(&G) Shared Island Unit. At the start of 2019, the party entered into a formal partnership with Fianna Fáil, agreeing (as the BBC put it in what reads like a lift from a press release), a 'shared policy platform dealing with high level themes', whatever exactly that might mean. Claire Hanna, then a Stormont MLA, temporarily resigned the party whip over it. 'I'm not a box of cereal,' she said. 'I can't suddenly become a different brand.'

The 2019 UK general election was the first electoral test since the partnership was announced. It seems highly unlikely that the Fianna Fáil link played any part in Claire Hanna's defeat of the DUP's Emma Little-Pengelly in Belfast South – if anything, her opposition to it may have stood to her. Pengelly had been a surprise winner at the previous election. Even so, the scale of Claire Hanna's victory was impressive. Her share of the vote – 57.2 per cent – was the highest for any party candidate, 0.2 per cent ahead of Colum Eastwood himself, who also came from behind in his Foyle constituency in the north-west to unseat Sinn Féin's Elisha McCallion, in what was her party's biggest reverse of the election.

(Sinn Féin and the DUP it has to be said were, by that stage of 2019, three years into their Stormont stand-off, the best canvassers for other parties' votes.)

Back in the Black Box on Saturday morning the audience is a little muted. Masks do not make for easy Q & As. I take the question of affordability outside with me. I buy a sandwich and sit with it on a bench in Eyre Square.

An elderly man and woman sit at the other end, shopping bags at their feet, shaking their heads in a sort of amused perplexity at the mostly young people passing by, as I remember my grandparents doing, as they might in another season and another place shake their heads at the sight of a field of daffodils just bloomed. Imagine: again.

I lean in as close as restrictions allow. I ask them if they don't mind me asking them …

They hear me out.

The man says politely he has always made it his business not to talk politics with people he has only just met. The woman, though (it occurs to me all of a sudden, they might not be married), tells me she thinks she could live to see it happen. I ask her about the cost, that possible 15 per cent drop in living standards.

'Ah, sure, who hasn't bought something they couldn't afford?'

'Aye, but you can't take this back,' the man says, and is delighted with that.

'Would it be OK if I used your name?'

'It would not,' says the man, then jerks his thumb, 'but you can call her Mary Lou.'

And he is even more delighted with that, as is she.

I head from there through the shopping streets down towards the River Corrib and find my way on to Woodquay and into a craft shop whose name – Ah, Sure, Look It – is the quintessential expression of Irish equanimity. One of the pair of women behind the counter is stitching something when I enter. She wears a black mask decorated with gold stars. I browse the wooden salad bowls, the hand-knitted hats and tea cosies, the cards with pictures of socially distanced sheep (Sheep 1: 'It's all a bit ...' Sheep 2: 'Yeah, I know, Seamus ... Weird ...'), the masks of many designs.

'Can I help you at all?' the other woman asks me.

'If you didn't mind me asking a couple of questions about a United Ireland, you could, yes.'

She turns to her colleague in the gold-starred mask. 'Do you want to serve him?'

The woman puts down the stitching. 'Go ahead.'

We chat a bit about a referendum, and about what a vote for reunification might mean.

'Well, I would have that warm, romantic feeling about a thirty-two-county Ireland, all right,' she says, 'and, I mean, with the year that's in it ...' The Covid, that is, and the much-discussed advantages of an all-island response. (Though again, on the island next door, Scotland has been lauded for the independence of its response.) 'But I never really thought about the cost, no.'

Maybe it is because of the conversation up on Eyre Square,

or maybe it is because I was thinking a moment ago about a present for my mum, but I suddenly remember a conversation with my parents about people saying they were going to wait until they could afford to start a family. 'If we had waited until *we* could afford it you would never have been born.'

I ask about the gold starry masks.

'We're all out,' the woman says.

I am having a bit of a bad run with Southern shops.

Only later do I reflect that a warm, romantic feeling without too much of a thought for the actual cost was one of the milder accusations levelled at the voters who 'fell for' Brexit.

Which I suppose if we are at all inclined to be charitable towards one another could cut both ways.

Later in the day, I am doing something else I have not done in more than half a year: sitting at a hotel bar with a couple of the other people taking part in the festival. The partner of one of them is originally from east Belfast. He is happy out of it. Northern Ireland, he says, is a conservative backwater. Unionists need to get over themselves. 'Come on,' he tells me he wants to say to them, 'Join in! We can have the craic!'

As someone who has spent all his adult life running far away – and fast – from anything that styles itself, or invokes, 'the craic', I want to tell him, with me at least, he is pushing an open door shut there.

He cites, as an example of Northern Protestant self-destructive obstinacy, a text exchange, after Leinster earlier in the evening beat Ulster 27-5 in rugby's Pro14 Final … Apparently this Ulster-fan friend had been winding him up in advance. 'So much for all your bragging,' the guy I am with texted him at the end of the match, and a moment later got a text in reply, 'We still have Brexit.'

The place is beyond all hope.

'Steady on,' one of our other friends says, 'Glenn still lives there.'

And it is funny, sitting here at the bar in Galway it really does feel like a there.

Standing in the railway station next morning in the spaced-out (both senses) queue for the 11.00 to Dublin Heuston, I find myself face to face with Éamonn Ceannt, in a slight recess in the wall next to Platform 2. Born in Glenamaddy, I read, about forty miles from Galway city, a Gaelic Leaguer and founder of the Dublin Pipers' Club, before joining the Irish Republican Brotherhood and leading the Volunteers at the South Dublin Union at Easter 1916. In the portrait I am looking at – it looks like the print of an engraving – he is seated holding his pipes. It is, truth be told, a pretty poor likeness, making him appear considerably older than the thirty-four years he had achieved when he was shot by firing squad in Kilmainham Gaol on 0 May 1916. The photograph on which it is based – I find it later – shows a much leaner Ceantt sporting a moustache that could have been grown expressly to put a few much-needed years on him. The backdrop is just that – a studio's painted scenery. It is a strain to make out of what exactly, but I am going for painted tree trunks with a wooden fence before. In the Galway station version this has been swapped for the bare floorboards of what I take to be a prison cell (Ceantt spent his last days in

Kilmainham's cell 88), and a wall whose blankness is relieved only by a crucifix on which Christ's outstretched arms are level with Ceantt's eyes. Ceantt, from the biographical information I have to hand, was devoutly Catholic. Even so, it is hard not to make a connection between this image and Padraig Pearse's belief in the need for – and the 'purifying' effects of – a blood sacrifice; to make a further connection between the Rising and one particular faith.

Next to the recess with Ceantt in it is a wider section of wall bearing three square, green tablets with gold borders and gold lettering: POBLACHT NA hEIREANN in large font on the first, above the seven signatories of the Proclamation (Éamonn Ceantt is second last, between Thomas MacDonagh and Joseph Plunkett), followed by the text of the Proclamation itself, in English only. I would not claim to know that text by heart, but every line when I hear or read it lands with a silent *yes*, and, *of course*.

Today, however, I get no further than the first sentence: 'In the name of God and of the dead generations from which she receives her old tradition of nationhood, Ireland, through us, summons her children to her flag and strikes for her freedom.'

In fact, I get no further than those three words in the middle, 'Ireland, through us …'

I suppose the answering line in the American Declaration of Independence is, 'We … the Representatives of the united States of America' (how a lower case u can throw open a window on a time before our own, a time when there were only States of America, doing their own thing) 'in the Name and by Authority of the good people of these Colonies'; the difference being that the representatives in attendance at the Second Continental Conference were returned there by what constituted then the popular vote. Of course, the American Declaration of Independence manages to claim that all men (sic) are created equal while its authors, presumably without undue concern on the part of the people who sent them there, kept other human beings as slaves.

'Ireland, through us' has been the claim of successive generations of physical force republicans, who have almost made it an article of faith that the fewer they are in number the greater, and purer, is their justification. Who, after all, elected the seven signatories of the Proclamation?

Is it possible to arrive at a position where you say that the means were wrong even if the society achieved a hundred years later has much about it that is admirable and right; that the means and the presumption of the right to use them encoded in those three words have brought down such suffering on so many people's heads?

Would unionists be better able to accept living in an entity that so conspicuously commemorated those executed leaders If there was a recognition, too – perhaps a fourth green tablet on the wall of Galway's Platform 2 – of the wrongs done, not by the misappropriation or misapplication of the Proclamation, but by following its clearly stated example?

(And, yes, the makers of tablets will be working overtime with the recognitions and apologies of all the other places from which we would have been better not to have begun if we had wanted to get to the point just beyond here where we can all live our best lives.)

Two Weeks On and Gone (Again): Mabon

Birr is far from buttfuck nowhere – in fact, according to Giraldus Cambrensis, an ancient (250 million-year-old) rock, which can still be seen in St John's Place, was the very *umbilicus Hibernicae*: navel of Ireland – but it says something about the extent of my ignorance (and, judging from the blank expressions of the friends I told I was going there, not just my own), or the orientation of my upbringing – the 'midlands' for me is Derby, Dudley, Wolverhampton, Birmingham, Coventry – that it is not somewhere I can ever remember having heard of until, in the third week of September, with the Covid curve beginning to creep upwards again, and with Donegal on the verge of a lockdown, I decide on one more trip before more widespread restrictions are introduced.

I was originally thinking of Lisdoonvarna, in Co. Clare, when I spotted Birr on my MacBook's Maps, right on the border of Offaly and Tipperary. It struck me as in every respect shorter. Not just the fifty-five miles' drive each way, but a seven-letter saving every time I typed the name. Besides, although I have travelled through, I have not yet since I started writing this spent time in those other midlands.

Since I started writing this?

Since as far back as I can remember.

With one thing and another, it is tipping into late afternoon before I hit the road from east Belfast. By the time I reach Newry, a half-hour run along the A1, the BBC Radio Ulster drivetime news programme has already come on. Things have clearly deteriorated while I was running around the house trying to decide what I needed to pack for two nights in Birr. Michelle O'Neill and Arlene Foster, reconciled after their Bobby Storey funeral stand-off, are now saying that travellers from the North should not only avoid Donegal, they should pause before crossing the border at all for any but essential reasons. There is talk, from the other side, of targeted Garda checkpoints. Along with the Chief Medical Officer and the DUP, Sinn Féin, while continuing to say that the island is a single epidemiological unit, is recommending that the north-easternmost counties consider themselves for this weekend to constitute a separate entity.

(I do sometimes feel for the first and the deputy first minister in the middle of all this. How much easier it would be for them both, for us all, if they could speak at all times without passing their sentences through the ideological calculus.)

I pause and debate with myself on the hard shoulder between Newry and the border – I can actually see up ahead the point at which the miles per hour signs become kilometres. I phone home. 'I think work comes under essential travel,' my wife says. 'Can you do the job you were intending to do without travelling?'

A question the 23,000 so-called 'Frontier Workers' – living north, working south, or vice versa – who would usually be on these roads have presumably been asking themselves daily since the pandemic began.

On the basis that I cannot go to Birr without going to Birr I decide to go to Birr.

Besides, if I do not go today, there is a chance I will not be able to go until the New Year to ask the people of Birr whether or not there should be a border for other people to wonder about crossing at moments like this.*

I am not the world's most confident unaccompanied driver at the best of times and tonight the further south I drive there is an added air of something just a few notches below panic to contend with – the opening scenes of *The Purge* float across my mind: get home, get the door locked, before darkness falls and all hell breaks loose – drivers with their fists poised an inch from the horn and not afraid to use it. I have never been so glad to see Offaly, never so glad to see anywhere as Birr (even if I do, with my wrong midlands head on, want to sing 'Ghost Town' as the car enters its deserted streets) and Emmet Square – look, right there, with the big column, bearing nothing but its own weight, couldn't miss it whichever way you came at the town and opening directly off it, the door into Dooly's Grade A hotel, occupying one entire flank of the square.

There has been a hotel, or before that a coaching inn, here since the square was laid out in the middle of the eighteenth century. The arched carriageway that used to lead through to the rear is now incorporated into the main building as the Coach Lounge and running off at a right angle to that is (nowadays at

---

* Garda checkpoints do eventually come into force on 8 February 2021.

least) Melba's nightclub, after Dame Nellie, who once stayed in the hotel and sang from an open sash window on the first floor to crowds gathered in the square below.

She would recognize the place still: the passengers and drivers of the carriages that entered under the arch would recognize it, as they would a good deal of the rest of Birr. Time has not stood still here, but it has not been let run away with itself or with the character of the town.

The smell that greets me as I come in through the porch and into the vestibule – open fire (to the right of the desk), something pleasing in the stew line, a hint of drying laundry – is comfortingly reminiscent of the smell of my Aunt Agnes's house on Leopold Street, at the top of the Shankill Road, c.1967. Only the alcohol tang of the hand sanitizer gives the game and the year away.

Offaly was one of the first counties hit by local lockdown, back in early August when I was in a fog in Tramore. Like all the other hotels and restaurants in town (there are substantially more of the latter than the former), Dooly's had only just opened its doors again when it was forced to shut them a second time. Tonight, three weeks into its re-reopening business is not brisk, although when I am in my room later I hear footsteps on the stairs to the floor above mine, a door opening and closing across the landing: there *are* other guests. The restaurant is closed, but the lounge bar is serving food to patrons sitting at one table in every two, or for large parts of the evening one in every five.

A group of lads come in, have a feed and a laugh with the waitresses, then head on somewhere else. Though not to

Melba's. No one has yet figured out how to do socially distanced nightclubs.

I go to sleep wondering whether the other nine Northerners who on average spend the night in Offaly managed to make it, or whether they are storing up their stays for another night and day, and whether some time when all of this is over you will not be able to move in Birr or anywhere for us, for them, keeping the statistics right.

There are two things I want to visit while I am in Birr, the castle and Crotty Schism church. The second, as it turns out, is on the way to the first and both are – as almost everything else in Birr is – little more than a five-minute walk from Emmet Square, down O'Connell Street and Main Street, in this instance, and right, up Castle Street, at Market Square. Only do not go up Castle Street just yet. Stay with me a minute while I look at the column on Market Square – much shorter than Emmet Square's, of which it is a mirror, but, unlike Emmet's, with a figure on top: Ireland as woman, accompanied by wolfhound and harp and – though it is hard to make out from this angle – a Celtic cross in her right hand. The statue was erected in memory of William Allen, Michael Larkin, and Michael O'Brien, the 'Manchester Martyrs', members of the Fenian Brotherhood executed in 1867 for the murder of a police sergeant in the course of a successful attempt to free two comrades from the van taking them to Manchester's Belle Vue prison. There are more than a dozen monuments in their memory elsewhere on the island, including one in the republican plot of Milltown Cemetery in Belfast, where Bobby Storey's ashes were so recently interred.

I automatically imagine the figure to be Cathleen ní Houlihan, the mythical old woman rejuvenated by the blood of the young men who have given their lives for her, although the National Inventory of Architectural Heritage is specific that she is Éire – Ériu to her kin in the Celtic pantheon – matron goddess of Ireland. (The uncovered head, I later realize, ought to have been a giveaway.)* She has, in purely sculptural terms, a wonderful expression, this particular Éire, proud, unassailable (my wife, looking at the photos I bring back, goes for 'scornful'), although in almost every other regard her being up there is fraught with questions. The great Eavan Boland, poet and thinker, who died aged seventy-five in April 2020, is my touchstone still for how the idealization of Mother Ireland has gone hand in hand with the silencing of actual women's voices. You gotta get them up there and keep them up there outta harm's way!

But I was on my way to church.

The Crotty Schism occurred in the early decades of the nineteenth century and took its name from two cousins, William and Michael, both priests, who established a congregation of their own – the Reformed Church of Birr – after the Catholic hierarchy had, as Michael saw it, done him out of a parish priesthood, to which he felt his parishioners had justly appointed him.

---

* The undoubted Queen of the Cathleens, as seen for decades on Irish banknotes, is Lady Hazel Lavery, painted by her husband, Belfast-born Sir John Lavery, and wearing a long black shawl, although wearing it in a manner that suggests she bought it not long since from a gift shop on the drive to the lakes (Killarney, I am going with) where the portrait was made. She rests her elbow on the harp as though on the open door of a sports car.

A contemporary visitor to Birr, Wriothesley Noel, quoted in a *Midland Tribune* article in 2004, puts the number of parishioners who followed the cousins into their new church at 'about a thousand persons', most of them poor. (The hierarchy refers to them as the 'Birr mob'.) They and the Crottys are in bad need, Wriothesley Noel says, of a new chapel to worship in. At the time of his visit, in 1837, the foundations – '64 feet by 32 feet' – have just been laid on the river side of Castle Street, a couple of hundred yards from Market Square. By the time the building was completed two years later the Reformed Church of Birr was already running out of steam. Some of the secessionists were officially welcomed into the Presbyterian Church, along with Cousin William, but little by little the rest drifted back to the Catholic Church from which they had split. Cousin Michael – 'the archschismatic' – wrote a book, *A Narrative of the Reformation at Birr, in the King's County, Ireland, Of which the Author was the Honoured Instrument*, which bears testimony to the 'fierce persecution' that Wriothesley Noel acknowledges the two men faced, and also to his observation that they perhaps 'want more meekness'.

'Converts,' writes Noel, 'have often a keen temper ... The Messrs Crotty just emerging from the cauldron of popery may feel their blood still boiling in the recollection of it.'

Michael, more meekly, became a Church of England curate in Ripon, North Yorkshire. One of the things that made his blood really boil at the time of the schism was the Catholic Church's insistence that 'all the marriages which we have solemnized for the eight or nine years that we have been at war with Rome were absolutely invalid'. *

I read somewhere online that Birr was more than a little embarrassed by the schism, that the Reformed Church building had been allowed to fall into disrepair, so I am halfway to unsurprised when drawing closer to it – as plain a 64 feet by 32 feet stone-built place of worship as the keenest-tempered convert could wish for (my Plymouth Brethren convert grandfather would have approved mightily) – I see a white Mercedes saloon parked side-on across, and about two feet out from, the doorway. A sign taped to the inside of one of the car's front windows reads, in capitals, 'NO ENTRY, KEEP OUT'.

It could, of course, refer to the car itself: the numberplate tells me in that easy-to-read Southern way – letter denoting county of registration, last two digits of year of manufacture – that it is a 1993, although it does not look as if it has moved for the past several of the twenty-seven intervening years; but there is something too deliberate and determined in the way it is parked to lend that total credence.

You would nearly have to go through both car doors to get at the double wooden doors of the church.

Even more curious is the paler green squiggle, about eighteen inches in length, on the church doors' dark green paint. At the upper end it is maybe two inches wide, at the lower maybe a quarter that. A freak thinners spillage, perhaps, but to me it looks like … well, I do not trust myself entirely. I show my wife when I get home (in the frame right after Scornful Éire).

---

* If you want to see mid-nineteenth-century double use of the triple exclamation mark, turn to page 332 of *A Narrative* …

'Is that a *snake*?' she says.

'That's what I thought as well. It's the door of the Crotty church.'

'A St Patrick reference? Drive them all out?'

'Maybe that explains the Mercedes, too.'

There is a wooden board to the right of the building saying that information on its history can be had from the reception of the Maltings B&B, which stands at the bottom of a steep slope behind the former church, at the edge of the River Camcor.

The door, when I get to the Maltings, is shut and when I follow the instructions on the notice next to the entry phone number pad and dial 4, I get absolutely no response.

I take a walk around. The tract of grass between the B&B and the river is so freshly mown it is plastered to my Docs. The tractor that did the mowing is parked in front of an open shed. I can smell diesel.

I go to the door again and press 4. But, no, nothing.

I wonder did someone see me poking around at the church. I wonder did they see me coming. Or did they have to nip off for a pee. Or did the tractor driver, like Muldoon's Brownlee, just leave.[*]

I tell myself I will try again in the morning and strike out, up the slope and on up the street to the castle that gives it its name.

This year (2020) marks the 400th anniversary of the arrival of the Parsons family, originally from Leicestershire in this corner of what was then King's County, but had previously been a part of the Eile, a lordship or petty kingdom ruled by

* If you don't, you should. Take ten minutes now, treat yourself.

the O'Carrolls, hence, sometimes 'Ely O'Carroll'. To give this a little historical context, in 1641, when the Parsons were still relative newcomers, 59 per cent of land in Ireland was still held by Catholics. By 1714 this had dropped to just 7 per cent.

7.

I mean, fuck.

7.

This (bar the italics, and the fuck) is from the chronology of events at the front of Robert Kee's *Ireland: A History*,* the book of the TV series first broadcast in the winter of 1980–81. To the left of the opening page of Chapter 12, 'Free State to Republic', is a striking photograph of the removal of a statue of Queen Victoria from the centre of Dublin in 1946. There are cranes and pulleys, and a flatbed truck waiting to receive the later-life likeness, which, seated and tipped forward slightly on its rope harness, resembles an invalid or cantankerous elderly relative being carried down the stairs on her way to the home. And there are crowds, behind barriers at the side of the street. This is a big moment. Victoria is not just the ultimate symbol of British Empire, she is, in Maud Gonne's words, the Famine Queen. A famine for which the conditions are coded into those land-holding figures from 1714.

When the statue of Ériu went up on Market Square in 1894, Birr was still Parsonstown, still the town that had grown up around the castle of the family whose head now went by the

---

* Kee lights on 1641 in particular as it was the year of the first widespread rebellion intended to reclaim lands already confiscated.

title of Earl of Rosse. I do not know whether the suggestion, five years later, in 1899, to revert to the ancient name came from inside the castle walls or out, although as the title of the Crottys' Reformed Church suggests, Birr was always there close to the surface. And I was not, by the way, telling the entire truth when I said that everyone in Belfast to whom I said the name Birr looked at me blankly. My colleague at the Seamus Heaney Centre in Queen's University, Rachel Brown, instantly said, 'That's where the giant telescope is.'

The 3rd Earl of Rosse, William Parsons, was a mathematician and astronomer – and an uncle of the founder of the *Irish Times* – who began to build a telescope, nicknamed Leviathan, in the castle demesne within a year of its passing into his hands in the early 1840s. Volume 3 of the *Practical Mechanic and Engineer's Magazine* for 1844 contains, under Miscellanea, a densely written two-column description of its construction, as given to the Belfast Natural History Society earlier in that autumn quarter. The wooden barrel is seventy-two inches wide. With its supporting structure of winches and pulleys and wheels it resembles the kind of medieval siege engine I remember from Saturday afternoon matinees starring Charlton Heston. Actually, it looks like something you could fire a statue of a seated Empress of India out of.

At its unveiling, the Dean of the local Church of Ireland church, St Brendan's, walked through it, 'wearing a top hat and with an umbrella raised above his head,' according to historian and broadcaster Myles Dungan, in a blog to mark the anniversary of the 3rd Earl's death (31 October 1867), 'presumably because he could'.

It remained the largest telescope in the world for the next seventy years. For about half a century, in fact, Birr Castle was what we would now call a globally recognized centre for scientific experiment and invention. The 3rd Earl's wife, born Mary Field, was herself an astronomer and pioneering photographer: a photograph of her niece Mary Ward seated next to a telescope is testimony to both to her own work and to the transmission of the spirit of inquiry to the next generation. William and Mary's eldest surviving son, the 4th Earl, was yet another astronomer; his youngest brother, Sir Algernon Parsons, invented the compound steam turbine.

In their spare time, various of the other thirteen children built a steam-powered automobile.

The castle itself is still a private residence, home today to the 7th Earl, but the grounds are open to the public. Housed in one of the deep outer walls, and introduced by a video featuring both Lord and Lady Rosse, is an exhibition of the scientific and engineering accomplishments of Parsons past, with, in among the other plaques and glosses, a poem alluding to the fact that Leviathan was being built at the same time as the crisis in rural Ireland was coming to a head, although – Myles Dungan again – the Famine instantly rendered the telescope 'inactive' as the 3rd Earl put his astronomical calculations on hold and devoted his time and a substantial part of his fortune to Famine relief locally. (As an MP he had championed Catholic Emancipation.) Parts of Leviathan's outer structure were cannibalized as part of the Great War effort (El Cid would have taken lock stock and giant barrel) before finally in the 1920s the telescope fell into fatal disrepair. One of the castle exhibition staff tells me,

in answer to my question about the castle during the War of
Independence – when the likes of Elizabeth Bowen's Colonel
Bent had their houses burned – that it was not harmed, although
'three young lads' were summarily executed by troops billeted
there.

'They were held overnight in the Keep and shot in the
morning. There's a history there that touches on it,' she
says nodding to a table piled with books for sale, 'but it's not
something they want to promote.'

Her colleague, she tells me, knows more about it. I find him
later, while I am crossing a little stone bridge over the River
Brosna. (A larger, suspension bridge – designed and built by
a nineteenth-century family member – a little way upstream
is closed these days for safety reasons.) The colleague very
considerately, to me at least, breaks off from the guided tour he
is giving another couple of visitors to explain that the summary
executions did not happen during the War of Independence
but during the Civil War that followed. 'The Irish Civic...' he
hesitates, *one of the armies*' (it was the National, or Free State
Army) 'moved in and the Parsons family moved out ... There's
a plaque about it in the Keep.'

So, the Keep, at the end of what has turned into half a
morning's wandering through exhibitions and gardens and
five or six laps of Leviathan, is my last port of call.

The Keep is one of those objects that reveals its etymology
and its function all over again as you approach it, in this instance
across a bridge – fixed now, though you could easily imagine it
being drawn up – and through a pair of heavy iron gates and a
deep archway cut in its crenelated, slit-windowed walls: *what we*

have we will hold right here. And *who* we do not know or *who we suspect* we will hold here, too. As the Three Young Lads were held the night before they were shot.

It takes me a while to locate the plaque, or, rather, engraved stone: William Conroy, Aged 20 Years, Patrick Cunningham, Aged 22 Years, Colum Kelly, Aged 18 Years, Executed Here 26th January 1923.

The woman I spoke to up at the exhibition mentioned possession of a handgun, and a report, almost a century later, in the *Irish Times*, refers to armed robbery, possibly for private gain. Their main offence, though, was almost certainly to have been in custody in Offaly in the month when the order went out from Kevin O'Higgins, Minister for Justice, to execute anti-Treaty prisoners in as many counties as possible, the better – and wider – to send out the pro-Treaty government's message that the IRA, in which government members themselves had so recently served, would be shown no quarter.

The IRA responded by murdering O'Higgins's father the following month, and then O'Higgins himself, in 1927, four years after the end of the Civil War.

The official end, make that.

It is a walk of half a mile from Dooly's to Birr Castle and back. You can do a couple more miles inside the castle walls, but you cover a lot more ground than that in the course of a single morning. A lot, lot more.

That afternoon I drive the twenty miles to Nenagh, across the county boundary into that part of Tipperary still referred to – six years after the administrative designation was scrapped – as North Tipp. Nenagh is home to another Keep, several hundred years older than Birr's, from the decades following Diarmaid Mac Murchadha's fateful request for help in regaining his crown. A mid-sized midland market town by (fairly attractive) numbers, it is also the birthplace of Fr Alec Reid, who as a Redemptorist priest in Belfast in the late 1980s acted as a go-between for Gerry Adams and SDLP leader John Hume in secret meetings that helped kickstart the peace process.

I manage to park just down from Nenagh Garda station on Kickham Street, named after Charles, founding member and former president of the Irish Republican Brotherhood, forerunner of the IRA, and author of *Knocknagow, or The Homes of Tipperary*, pronounced by Seán Ó Faoláin in 1941, sixty-odd years after its publication, as 'the best-seller that any Irish novelist ever produced'.[27] A success Ó Faoláin attributes in no small part to the long shadow cast by the Famine. 'Written by a fenian who had been in jail, with the whole land question running through it, *Knocknagow* came in the precise moment that demanded such a book.'

There is another monument on a traffic island at the top of the street, twenty yards on, where the roads fork into Ashe Road and O'Rahilly Street, named, I am surmising, for Thomas Ashe and Michael Joseph or just 'The' O'Rahilly, the former, like Kickham, a president of the IRB, who died on Hunger Strike in 1917, the latter a founder of the Irish Volunteers, mortally wounded outside the GPO in Easter 1916.* The monument is in

---

* Like I say, I am surmising, but The's sister, An-(you think I am making this up?)-no, has, by Irish republican reckoning, a fair claim to a street name of her own, having helped establish Cumann na mBan, loosely the Women's Volunteers.

the form of an almost perfect cube of limestone, four steps up from street level, with a robed and bearded figure on top, who I mistake at first for St Patrick, but who is in fact (the crown, I should have noticed, and paid more attention to the orb and sceptre) Christ.

The text on the marble tablets on the front and sides is entirely in Irish, in an ancient Celticky script that defies my attempts at recognition, never mind translation, although the dates are clear enough: the Easter Rising and the years encompassing the War of Independence and the Civil War, though a few beyond that, too, running into the later 1920s.

The rear, though, carries the names, in the ancient script again, but this time (in brackets) in Roman script, too, of the 1981 Maze Prison Hunger Strikers, paid for by (brackets again) Irish Northern Aid USA, or to use the abbreviated name by which it is more usually referred to, Noraid. Founded in 1969, Noraid was, throughout the 1980s in particular, closely identified with the Provisional IRA – Noraid members would claim inaccurately, with the possible exception of those who went to jail for gunrunning.

There is a consistency, I suppose, in memorializing the ten men who died in the Maze on a monument facing a street named for a man who died in Mountjoy Prison in the same way and for the same reason sixty-odd years before, but the question is whether it should be implied that there is continuity between the two, an unbroken line of legitimacy.

Three women have been standing, all the time I have walking around the monument, on the corner of a street running off Kickham along the other side of the Garda station. I ask them as

I draw level now if they are from the town. One is. I ask about the monument. She tells me she never really looks at it. The back page, as it were, the Noraided 1981 Hunger Strike tablet, is entirely news to her. One of her friends says that all these things belong in museums where they can be properly explained. 'I don't know now,' the third woman says, 'they do mean a lot to some people.' I tell them what I am about with this book. The Nenagh resident tells me, without hesitation, she favours unity and would be prepared to bear the cost in higher taxes, especially if it meant a fully funded National Health Service for the whole island: she lived for a time in Edinburgh and had the benefits there of free healthcare.

I ask about the cultural implications. Would they imagine that there might have to be a conversation at the very least about some of the place names and monuments, about how Ireland presented itself to the whole of itself?

'Well, if you think, Scotland manages still to be Scotland,' one of the friends says, picking up perhaps on Edinburgh earlier.

'Maybe that's not the best example,' says the other.

Which is the precise moment that the Limerick bus turns into Kickham Street and I realize that the reason they have been standing there all this time is that two of them are about to get on it.

'I just hope it's peaceful, whatever happens,' the woman left behind says. And she is not the only person that I talk to who does.

On the road back from Nenagh I have the radio tuned to RTÉ Sport and reports from the semi-finals, or in some cases (because everything this year is out of whack and sync) the *finals*, of the GAA county club championships. It is a while before I realize that one of the games is in Birr, in St Brendan's Park, about – well, like I say, everything is – a five-minute walk from Dooly's. I drive as fast as the traffic allows, park up in the forecourt of a filling-station-cum-restaurant-cum-multiplex on the far side of the road from the ground and run across just as the crowd – I want to say 'limited to two hundred', but these days two hundred has the look of thousands – are coming out and dispersing: game over.

I am still kicking myself at having missed the match and the opportunity for chats (some percentage of two hundred of them) when I head out that evening for a drink and plump for Green Street, off the north-west corner of Emmet Square. About fifty yards up on the left-hand side is a little, white-painted cottage with a foot-wide band of green at the bottom and orange windowsills, and a picture in one of the windows of Sinn Féin TD Brian Stanley, whose office this is. Laois-Offaly returns five TDs, Brian Stanley being the only Sinn Féin member, although Carol Nolan, who stood in the 2020 election as an Independent and who also has an office in Birr, was a Sinn Féin TD, too, until she split from the party over its stance on abortion.

The bar next door to the office, the Chestnut ('Estd 1823', says the sign above the lintel), is not yet open, not that it would matter if it was. The manager is standing at the door. The early 'sittings' are all booked out, she tells me. 'If you're here about ten, though, I might still be able to find you a table.'

I cross to the other side of the street instead and the bar facing, Kelly's.

I observe the new pub etiquette: mask up, sign in, sanitize, then wait to be allocated a seat well away from anyone with whom I do not already share a house. After a little persuasion, the barman lets me move from the first table he has shown me to, towards the rear and the passage through to the toilets, to a high table for two at one end of the counter, close to the front door, where I can at least see the rest of the bar, even if my nearest neighbour is now the TV. Little Mix are auditioning singers for a boy band they are putting together to go on tour with them. Oh my God they all say. Oh. My. God.

I have picked up in the course of the day the *Nenagh Guardian* and the *Clare Champion*, two substantial looking – and feeling – local newspapers (the *Champion* is still a broadsheet) and have brought them with me in the canvas bag that also has my notebook, my pen, my phone charger, my own personal hand sanitizer and, now that I am seated again, my mask.

I set my pint on the bar to my left and spread the papers out on the table in front of me. Then a moment later, at the barman's insistence, lift my pint from the bar (he cleans the place where it was the moment it is gone) and put it on the table along with the papers.

The *Champion* carries below its masthead a photo of a man wearing an anorak and holding up three medals, and next to it the words 'Fallen Soldiers: North Clare Remembers Rineen Ambush of 1920, p. 3 Living'.

I find the Living section, find p. 3, and find the man with medals again. He is Colm Hennessy, whose grandfather, Commandant Seamus Hennessy, was in charge of the 4th Battalion Mid Clare Brigade of the IRA, which took part in the ambush referred to on the front page. He is in the company now of relatives of other men who took part in the ambush, on 22 September 1920, and relatives, too, of some of the people who were murdered in reprisals later that day by Auxiliaries and Black and Tans on the towns of Lahinch, Ennistymon and Milltown Malbay. The centenary celebrations were necessarily, given Covid restrictions, smaller than the ninetieth anniversary, but Owen Ryan of the *Champion* reports that the commemoration committee 'raised the Irish flag at the site where the IRA engaged with the enemy, killing six RIC men'. I ponder that sentence for a minute.

At the beginning of the year there was uproar when, as part of the 'Decade of Centenaries' – encompassing the Home Rule Crisis, the Great War, Easter Rising, War of Independence, Partition, Civil War – the then Fine Gael government announced, and very quickly scrapped, a commemoration of the Royal Irish Constabulary and the Dublin Metropolitan Police. As even some of the more sympathetic commentators observed, it is difficult for many Irish people to separate the RIC from the 'Auxies' – those British army veterans serving with the Auxiliary Division of the RIC – and the Black and Tans, who wreaked such havoc in those years, and not just in Lahinch, Ennistymon and Milltown Malbay. One of the six victims of the Rineen ambush was indeed a Black and Tan. But the other five …? There is something so definitive about the use in that Living article of 'enemy'.

The manager slips sideways into the seat facing me and asks am I watching the Little Mix show, or can he turn over? Turn over, I say. He says something else – to the TV, I think, but then turns to me and says it again. 'Much news in the *Clare Champion*?'

'Only to me,' I say. In the revised version. 'Actually …' I do say, but he has turned away again and finished switching to RTÉ2, where another GAA game is in progress. The yellow and black stripes are beating the blue shirts and white shorts 0-4 to 0-0 when we join.* Well, I join. The manager leaves. A moment later, a man in a light blue sweater arrives and pulls the chair another foot out from the table.

'Do you mind?' he asks. I don't at all. He sits.

I ask him who is playing.

'Crosserlough and the Kingscourt Stars: Cavan Club Championship Final.'

He looks up at the TV where Crosserlough – the yellow and blacks – have just added another point. He turns back to me. 'Here thirty-three years and still a Cavan man.' Cavan is two counties away, seventy-five miles, but he says it as though we were sitting in a bar in Wollongong.

'Was it work brought you here?' I ask.

He shakes his head. 'Women.'

I let that sit.

We watch a while mostly in silence as Crosserlough streak further ahead before Kingscourt belatedly start to put a few points on the board. Crosserlough, my companion tells me in a rare lull in play, won seven titles back to back in the 1960s

---

* Gaelic games are the only place I know where a team can end with nil squared. The figure to the left of the hyphen represents goals, which are scored under the crossbar and are worth three points, the figure on the right the individual points scored by putting the ball over the bar and between the uprights. Thus, in a game that finishes 3-0 to 0-10, the team that did not score any actual goals wins.

and the turn of the Seventies but have had a leaner time of it since: no wins in forty-eight years. This particular group of players, though, has come up together through the junior championships.

I was only intending to have one pint – I have a dinner reservation back at Dooly's – but decide to hang on, to see how the game goes, and for the intermittent chat.

During the half-time interval (Crosserlough, despite that Kingscourt rally, look to be cruising at the break), I ask him about the size of the crowd at the televised match. 'I'd say there's more than two hundred in there all right,' he says. He knows the ground, Breffni Park, very well, how each section's capacity adds up to its maximum, which is 32,000.

'About the same as Casement Park,' I say. Casement Park is the Belfast Home of Antrim GAA. Casement Park, I realize as I say it, is *Casement* Park in the same way that the Iarnród Éireann station at Tralee, Co. Kerry, is *Casement* Station. It is one of those things, you have always known it but just stopped hearing it.

'I see the planning permission has been granted,' the man says.

The proposal to expand Casement – in the middle of a residential area of west Belfast – has been a long-running, at times bitter, saga.

'Has it?'

Maybe it is my simple inability to follow the latest ins and outs, but he gives me a longer look then than he has almost from the moment he first sat down.

He asks me what part of Antrim I am from. Nobody has *ever* asked me what part of Antrim I am from.

'Belfast,' I say. 'From the other end of Finaghy Road, in fact, from Casement Park. And I'm ashamed to say I've never been in.'

I *am* ashamed, although I have never been into the Ulster Rugby ground at Ravenhill, about the same distance from where I currently live as Casement is from where I did my growing up. Windsor Park, where Northern Ireland play, is home to my code of choice.*

It would be going too far to say it is a cold shoulder the man gives me, though it is definitely a shoulder. I go to mention East Belfast GAA, but instinctively feel that would get the shoulder up further. A couple of minutes later the barman brings him a plate of food to which he addresses himself with great concentration.

Back in Cavan, the teams are lining up again. Within a short time of the restart, Kingscourt, with a flurry of points and a couple of goals, go, improbably you would have thought earlier, into the lead.

This might be only the second Gaelic Football match I have watched beginning to end, the first being the 2010 All-Ireland final when Down somehow let Cork beat them 0-16 to 0-15, and even then, if I am honest, I sort of wandered in and out of the room while it was on to shout a quick 'Up Down!' This, though, is different. The teams in the All-Ireland are their counties' select. Watching a club championship game strikes me, in comparison, as akin to watching American college basketball over the professional game. I was visiting lecturer in Villanova

---

* 'Windsor' is home, week to week, to Linfield FC, whose blue, white and red colours were at times in their history not so much a kit as a declaration of allegiance. I combined supporting them in my youth with supporting Glasgow Celtic.

University outside Philadelphia the year – 2016 – their college team won the national title for the first time in fifty years. (You think you've had it bad, Crosserlough?) I still rate as my greatest ever sport-spectating experience – I was in the Villanova gym, watching the live feed from Houston on a big screen with a couple of thousand students and staff – the moment Kris Jenkins scored the winning basket as the final buzzer sounded, after North Carolina, who had trailed for most of the match, tied the score at 74-74 with 4.7 seconds on the clock.

Crosserlough vs Kingscourt Stars is not quite as dramatic, but Kingscourt, at 2-12 to 2-11 ahead, have an opportunity to score a clinching point in the closing seconds, miss, and concede possession to Crosserlough who go up (or down, my Breffni geography is weak) to the other end and themselves score the point that takes the final to a replay.

Holy moly.

I finish my pint. The man and I exchange glances. In the whole bar it has really only been the two of us watching. It is the result we both wanted (or, rather, the one, with seconds remaining and Kingscourt looking as though they were about to score again, that we would have taken), and yet I leave there thinking that he sees us as being on different sides.

STOP PRESS: 3 October Crosserlough win the replay by thirteen points to eight. First Cavan County Championship since 1972. Back in Belfast, I raise a glass. Two days later the GAA suspends all club matches across the island over concern at numbers attending matches and post-match celebrations.

While we are paused ... In the final days of November, on the centenary of another IRA ambush, at Kilmichael in Co.

Cork, in which seventeen Auxiliaries died, Brian Stanley, the Sinn Féin TD and chair of the Dáil's Public Accounts Committee, whose constituency office faces Kelly's Bar on Green Street, tweets, 'Kilmichael (1920) and Narrow Water (1979) the 2 IRA operations that taught the elect of the British army and the establishment the cost of occupying Ireland. Pity for everyone they were such slow learners'.

Narrow Water refers to the double bomb attack that killed sixteen members of the Parachute Regiment and two Queen's Own Highlanders, near Warrenpoint, Co. Down, on the same August day as the murder of Lord Mountbatten and three other people – an eighty-three-year-old woman and two teenage boys – on his boat off Mullaghmore, just across Donegal Bay from Bundoran. As at Kilmichael, six decades before, the troops killed at Narrow Water were travelling in two lorries, although the largest number of casualties in the later incident were caused by a bomb detonated as the helicopter that had arrived to help the wounded tried to take off again.

The tweet causes considerable outrage, with calls for Sinn Féin to take action over what the *Irish Times* calls a 'glorification' of an 'IRA massacre'. Stanley's own party leader calls the tweet 'ill-judged': 'It was an attempt,' she says, 'to draw a historical parallel between the Auxiliaries and the Parachute Regiment, but that's neither here nor there.'

I thought that was the entire here and there of it.

She goes on, 'I think people will understand that very many of us, right across political life and beyond, marked and recognised the ambush at the weekend. Brian's mistake, and it was ill judged and he is very regretful for it, was an attempt to draw historical comparison between something that happened in the '20s and something that happened in the '70s.'

Or, as she phrases it in an RTÉ radio interview a few days later, 'ambushes in the course of the War of Independence and beyond', an intriguing formulation that appears to (at the very least) leave the door open for a future recalibration where the IRA's campaign north of the border after 1969 is a seamless extension of 1919–21 campaign. *The Anti-Crown*, season 4 or 5, with a different cast but the same roles.

The *Irish Examiner* in the same edition that reports the reaction to Brian Stanley's – now deleted – tweet carries an account of the Kilmichael ambush by Meda Ryan, author of a book on Tom Barry, who commanded the IRA that day. This report shows photos of previous anniversaries, including, from 1966, a re-enactment by the Irish army, and from May 1974 a model of the ambush site on display in one of the Cork County Libraries, with Tom Barry himself showing the County Librarian what was what back in the ambush day.

The author expends a considerable number of words on the question of whether some of the Auxiliaries were shot after trying to surrender. The answer seems to be yes, but only after two of the IRA flying column involved had themselves been shot and fatally wounded by Auxiliary revolver fire after a previous 'false surrender'.

'Soon the death of Volunteers, and the Auxies' deceitful use of revolvers after calling and accepting surrender, became widely known.'

What is not mentioned is that this incident involved Auxiliaries travelling in the second lorry and that by the time it happened as many as nine of the soldiers travelling in the first were already dead, or that – according to the testimony of some of those who took part – some of them had been finished off with rifle butts and bayonets. Ryan opts for '[t]his encounter was short, sharp' – maybe the bayonets are lurking in there after all – 'and bloody', seeming by now to have forgotten her earlier suggestion that the IRA plan was that the Auxiliaries were to be 'apprehended'.

The final line eschews the 'all deaths are regrettable' tone of recent times in completely omitting the seventeen dead 'Auxies' (some bludgeoned, some bayonetted, one, who ran away, captured and shot with his own gun). 'For the rest of his life, Tom Barry regretted he never warned his Volunteers of the old "bogus surrender" war-trick that cost the lives of two of his comrades.'

So, again, I am asking myself – in all seriousness asking myself – fifty years from now, in a thirty-two-county Ireland, which is more likely, that accounts of Kilmichael will have come down a notch from the Meda Ryan *Hotspur*-comic schtick, or that Narrow Water will have been transmuted from 'massacre' to 'operation' or 'ambuscade'?

It is pretty clear that the Provisional IRA's intention at Narrow Water was to kill as many soldiers as possible: nearly a ton of explosives in two separate bombs is a stark statement of that.

What Tom Barry's flying column intended to do with eighteen apprehended Auxiliaries is anybody's guess, but sixty-four other people who came into the hands of the IRA in Cork during the War of Independence were shot and 'disappeared'.

The aim was surely, one way or the other, to wipe them out.

In that they succeeded; but treading a little more carefully there might help just as much in shrinking the ground in which Brian-Stanley-like tweets can flourish as calls, after the fact, for resignations.

In the aftermath of the Kilmichael centenary affair, another tweet comes to light, from 2017, in which Brian Stanley appears to make a disparaging reference to recently elected Taoiseach Leo Varadkar's sexuality. One student member of Sinn Féin's youth wing, Ógra Sinn Féin, takes exception and says so in her own Twitter feed, whereupon she is visited by older Sinn Féin members and told she should remove her comments and learn the meaning of democratic centralism, whereupon *she* … resigns.

This would hold true for any political party looking for your vote, but I will say it again: next time you come to cast yours, anywhere on this island, don't say you didn't know.

Back in Birr, after dinner at Dooly's, I return, just before ten, to Green Street and the Chestnut. The woman I took for the manager when I saw her outside earlier is in fact the owner, Clodagh Fay, and she has been as good as her word, reserving a high-back stool next to one of the front windows for me, with a ledge built into the frame to rest my glass on. A five-branched brass candle tree, three feet high and fully lit, stands at a corner of the counter out to the beer gardens. (Clodagh tells me all the tables out there that can be full are full, but she invites me to go out and have a look. I do. The gardens, like the insides, are beautifully done, and fun – one minute I am thinking the mid-Sixties Carnaby Street of Granny Takes a Trip, the next Mitteleuropa interwar cabaret.) The Chestnut is a wet pub: no food served. Clodagh only opened her doors on Monday of this week for the first time since March. It has been a hard half-year, but she has used it to adapt the premises to changed times, with an extravagant ceiling to floor curtain that can be drawn to section off the front part of the bar on nights when numbers are low and the atmosphere would otherwise be lost entirely. She tells me all this in between bringing me my pint, taking the names of customers who have come in after me and showing two members of her bar staff how to mix the perfect Moo Moo. She has had the bar since the late 1990s when she was in her early twenties. It is, to an extent I have rarely seen, a reflection and projection of her. I would love to talk to her more – about how her vision not just of the bar, but of its place in, well, this place, the island, has changed in the last nearly quarter-century – but it is her first Saturday night open in six months and more, she has enough to be contending with already, and besides it is already getting close to – that saddest of all bar words – Time.

Just as Clodagh herself is calling it, a man comes in. The Chestnut's is a young clientele. I am a good fifteen years older than anyone I have seen, looking around the bar, or on my tour of the beer gardens. I would give this man another maybe ten again, fully white-haired, where I could at a certain angle and in a forgiving light still pass for fair. He orders a Power's and ice and waits for it – the only person in the whole bar standing – at the corner of the counter next to the candelabrum.

He makes a couple of quick, darting movements out from this corner: trying to see round the rest of the room, I think to begin, then revise that to 'trying to make sure that I have had no reason to say I have not seen him'.

Eventually, me not having taken the hint, he comes over.

We are of a generation, the two of us, he says (neither the angle nor the light, clearly, being what I hoped they were), setting down his Power's and ice on the little ledge in the window frame facing mine, that could not see a person sitting in a bar on their own without coming over to talk.

'You're not from here,' he adds, before I have even got a word out.

'I'm not indeed.'

He nods, a sort of place-holding nod: right, so, we'll come back to that.

His name, he tells me, is Bernard, and he is a son of the family who owned this bar for nearly three-quarters of its 197 years, right up to the end of the 1980s. He fills me in on a bit of the history. When he was a child, one half of the building, and the business, was a grocery store. Going back even further, to 1888, this was where one of the teams in the first ever All-Ireland hurling final got togged out (it is turning into a very GAA day) before the match 'on the site of the big Tesco'.

'"Are you collecting points?"' I say.

'What's that?'

'I was just thinking, Tesco's... points... never mind.'*

Bernard left Birr in the early Seventies: he was a younger son, so had no hope of inheriting the family business. Reading between the lines, which he leaves double-, or treble-spaced for

---

* In fact, the teams could have done with collecting points from somewhere. It finished Tipperary 1-1 Galway nil-squared: not just the first All-Ireland hurling final, but the lowest scoring in All-Ireland history.

that express purpose, whoever did inherit did not do the job that he himself would have. Reading between the lines in fact, if he had had the bar it would never have passed to whoever it passed to before it passed to Clodagh and we would have been talking here tonight across the bar counter. But that is so much water under the bridge.

He worked in bars in London then in Barclays, then, on the advice of his boss who thought he was wasted behind the counter of a bank, in a casino in Mayfair. He knows figures, you see. He tells me a story about a hard sum his class had been set for homework one time. His father brought him down into the bar-cum-grocery and gave him a practical demonstration of how to solve it. The next day the Brother who taught them wrote the answer on the blackboard. Thirty-one pupils had the same answer. Bernard's alone was different. The Brother gave him 'three on each hand' for getting it wrong. Bernard, however, insisted he was right and went through the Brother's working out on the board up to the point where *he* went astray, along with the rest of the class.

'The Brother's face when he realized ...' he says, still relishing it.

So, of course, he asked whether the other thirty-one were going to get three on each hand now as well.

'Sit down,' the Brother said, and that, Bernard thought, was the end of it. A week or so later, though, Bernard's father told him to go and put on his best clothes and took him to Dublin for the day as a reward for standing his ground.

So, figures, like I say, he knows, and when, in answer to his question, at the end of this long introduction, I tell him what has brought me to Birr, he tells me straight off that a United Ireland will never happen, for the now familiar reason that the South cannot afford it. He does, though, have an interesting spin on it: the two greatest con men ever were Ian Paisley and Martin McGuinness, 'walking down that staircase, smiling', a reference to the first outing, in spring 2007, of the then leader of the DUP and the leader of Sinn Féin in the Northern Ireland Assembly, and former Chief of Staff of the IRA, in their 'Chuckle Brothers' OFMDFM double act, descending from the first floor of Parliament Buildings to meet the cameras waiting in the lobby.

The North, he says, has screwed the English Exchequer for years, and since the Good Friday Agreement it has been screwing money out of the South, too.

Reconciliation, I think he is saying, did not need to come at the financial cost that it did, perhaps because the divisions were never as real or as deep as they seemed. And he gives me an example from his time in London, 1974, pre-casino, pre-Barclays, when he served Gerry Fitt, a founding member of the SDLP, who was buying a round for a table that included Glenn Barr, a Derry-born loyalist closely identified with the UDA. This was the year of the first failed Northern Ireland power-sharing government, in which Gerry Fitt was a minister, brought down by an Ulster Workers' strike of whose Central Coordinating Committee Glenn Barr was the chair.

What Gerry Fitt and Glenn Barr did have in common, apart from being Northern Irish in London, People from Here Over There, was that they came from a background of trade unionism and labour politics, although it has long been recognized as one of our greatest tragedies that such cross-community interests have, historically, added up to diddly-squat in the polls.

I ask my new companion about popular opinion in Birr, given that the TD with an office next door is Sinn Féin and the one with the office down on Main Street only split from that party over abortion. 'Well, now, Mary Lou is playing to the gallery,' he says as though that answers everything. 'Nobody is going to lose votes around here by talking up an easy end to Partition.' Not that he has any affection for unionism, or the state that it created north of the border. 'This fella has six votes and that one has none, and all that bankrolled by' – that term again – 'the British Exchequer?' A shake of the head: how can that be right? Armagh, he says in the next breath, was the worst thing, no justification at all. I am a bit out of practice – who isn't? – with pubs. I have forgotten how conversations can go in seconds from baby steps to strides in seven-league boots. I *think* he might mean Omagh, where the Continuity IRA killed twenty-eight people in August 1998, the year of the Good Friday Agreement, but he goes on to talk about civil rights, and I wonder then if, just maybe, he is referring to John Gallagher, the tenth victim of the Troubles, shot and killed by B Specials in the aftermath of a Northern Ireland Civil Rights Association meeting in Armagh city twenty-nine Augusts and 3,588 deaths before Omagh.

If we were in a world where shaking hands was still a thing, we would have shaken hands warmly. As it is, we leave the Chestnut together, me to Dooly's, him to see if there is one last Power's to be had in one or other of the bars along O'Connell Street or Main Street.

As we part at Emmet Square, he wishes me luck.

I want to tell him that for tonight at least he was a large part of it.

I see him again early next morning. I have walked down St John's Place to pay my respects to the umbilicus, the Seffin, or Seefin Stone as it is known,* in the grounds of John's Hall, a fine, austere, neoclassical former school, now the Birr Heritage Centre.

(I am going to stick my neck out here and say that St John's Place is the most beautiful stretch of street in all of Ireland.)

He is walking fast and in the other direction from me, towards the centre of town. We do no more than nod. He looks, I think, surprised to see me. I finish my photographs – of the stone, which lives up to one nineteenth-century description of it as a 'huge rude mass of limestone', of the hall, of the gun, also in the grounds, captured at Sevastopol in the Crimean War – and run after him. There is almost no one else abroad this hour of the day. When I am within hailing distance, I ask how he is this morning. He flinches before he turns. Not very well, he says. He looks more than surprised to see me this second time, he looks alarmed, and in no mood to carry on the conversation a moment longer. I tell him that in all our chat last night, I had lost hold of the very first thing he gave me, his forename. He gives me it again: Bernard. Then turns and carries on walking, fast. Clearly being of a generation that you cannot see a person sitting on their own in a bar does not extend into the morning after.

---

* The 'fin' here is Fionn mac Cumhail – Finn McCool, as I knew him when I was a kid – who, legend has it, made the strange slash marks on the surface of the 'Suigh', or See, which is to say Seat. Maybe he was just trying to get a bit more comfortable.

Before checking out of Dooly's, I go back to the Crotty Schism church for one last try. I am pretty sure, looking at the front elevation, that there is a small upper window open that was not open yesterday, and a circular light fitting on the other side of the glass that was not lit then and is now. And there is definitely a boiler on somewhere inside, to judge by the gouts of steam rising up from behind the board that says 'information at reception'. The door of the Maltings B&B is locked again. I lift the entry phone without expectations, when, to my amazement, on the fifth ring – as I am about to replace the receiver – a woman picks up. But, 'We're away,' she says in answer to my question about where I can find out more about the Crotty church. Away I take that to mean in its new staycation sense, where you can be away without ever leaving the place that for the past six months has been your workplace as well as your home. And who am I to suggest to her that she is in fact right there? 'I'm only answering the phone because it's ringing,' she says, reasonably enough. She suggests I come back on Monday. I tell her I am leaving in an hour. 'Oh,' she says and, 'Well.' And that is all. I ask her before she hangs up about the open window, the circular light inside and the gouts of boiler steam.

'Are there people in there?'

'Yes,' she says.

'Living?' I ask, but she has gone.

On my way up the slope again I walk around the rear of the church. There is a newish-looking wooden fence, six or seven feet high, a couple of gates to match, with concrete steps leading up to them, though it still looks more like back than front, and it is still not entirely clear to me how the gates open from the outside.

Maybe, though, all the no entry sign on the Merc out front meant to say was 'use the other side'.

And the snake? Maybe that is a cunning code: remember to bring a ladder.

The last thing I do before leaving Birr is photograph that uninhabited column that has been staring me in the face since the moment I drove into town, dedicated, like the square that shares its name, to Robert Emmet, the United Irish movement leader executed in 1803. 'Renamed in 1922', I read on the brass plaque at its base, alongside the words from Emmet's speech from the dock (that claim, such is the multiplicity of versions that have circulated in the centuries since, has to come with a 'probably'): 'When my country takes her place among the nations of the earth, then, and not till then, let my epitaph be written.'

There is another line in the speech about his tomb being uninscribed, which seems to fit with a column without a statue at the top. It is, given all the Christs and Érius and flag-wavers and fist-wavers raised on pedestals the length and breadth of the island, an admirable reticence. In fact, maybe it should be adopted as *the* new national monument, like the Fourth Plinth of Trafalgar Square, only left entirely to the individual imagination: look up there and see whoever you choose filling the space.*

---

* There *is* a bronze figure of Emmet in Dublin's St Stephen's Green – where he was actually born – a copy of an original, by Irish-born sculptor Jerome Connor, in Washington DC. The original was completed in 1916, the copy presented fifty years later 'to the people of Ireland' by the Robert Emmet Statue Committee of the United States of America. It is a handsome thing (there is another copy in Golden Gate Park, San Francisco). But I still prefer the Birr People's Unpeopled Column.

Actually, photographing the column is the *second* last thing I do before leaving. About a quarter of a mile out along the N52, heading for Tullamore, I pass a sign, on my left, proclaiming that the world's first – I am past too fast to see what exactly – happened here. I need no more reasons to justify my trip, should I encounter a 'targeted Garda checkpoint' as I attempt to cross back over the border; no more reasons to make me wonder anew at my ignorance of the town in advance, but I indicate right anyway at the next available side street and swing back round.

The sign is to the side of the pavement in front of St Brendan's Church of Ireland church (there is, besides the GAA grounds, a St Brendan's Catholic Church, too: Birr is very definitely St B's hood), or should I say, at the rear of St Brendan's C. of I. That is because the front, as I see when I turn into the street up the side of the church to park, faces down an avenue – Oxmantown Mall – to an alternative entrance to Birr Castle Demesne, of which it is, so to speak, the spiritual extension.

The 'world's first' proclaimed by the sign, by the way, is automobile fatality. Mary Ward, whose photograph I was looking at yesterday in the science exhibition, a cousin of the Rosses, was thrown from that steam-powered vehicle the children of the 3rd Earl had built, as it rounded the corner of the Mall towards the castle, and died, almost instantly, beneath its wheels. The year was 1869.

Morning service is just ending, the congregation coming out in ones and twos. I do not know whether I have arrived at the tail end of the decanting, or whether they are simply not all that great in numbers. A white-haired man, in a blue sports jacket and grey trousers, stands at the curving pavement's edge, shifting a black briefcase from hand to hand and talking to a woman who moves away as I approach. (Everyone is wearing face coverings these days, of course, but I am conscious all the way through writing this book that I am a masked man walking up to people I do not know from Eve or Adam.) Approach too closely, as it turns out: the man stops me with a raised hand and asks me to take a step back, into the road, before repeating my opening question.

'Might you have a minute to talk?'

'It depends on what you want to talk about,' he says, which is fair enough.

I am aware of other people in conversation a few feet to my left, two women, two men, about the same age as the man with the briefcase, who tells me now in return for mine his name, Michael Hanna. While we talk, or while I talk and he listens to my opening pitch, another, smaller man comes out. Michael Hanna tells this man what it is I am interested in. I am starting to regret having stopped the car. I feel the need to tell them that my brother-in-law is a Dublin episcopalian and that I am, by upbringing at least, a Belfast presbyterian. The smaller man – his name, which I have to ask him to repeat, as I can tell, from his expression, people have asked him his whole life through, is Salters Stirling – tells me, and tells me he is telling me in the same spirit, that he is a Belfast presbyterian, too. When I ask him where in Belfast he grew up, he replies, 'Forth River House, Ballygomartin Road.'

The 'House' is new to me, but I know the road – forking off the Woodvale at the top of the Shankill – very, very well. It and the streets running off it, up the side of Black Mountain, are part of my DNA.

'My mum grew up on Rutherglen Street,' I say.

Salters Stirling smiles. 'Then they paid ground rent to us: that was our land.'

He and my mum even went to the same primary school, named like his family home after the river that passes through there on its way to join the Blackstaff and at length the Lagan just before it opens into Belfast Lough. Although as my mum points out when I report all this (phoning her as soon as I get back into the car), he was three years younger, she doubts she would have noticed him. It matters much, three years, when you are seven.

Now that we have established our ground, Salters Stirling tells me that he and Michael Hanna could introduce me to 'Protestants of modest means', a social group, he says, that many in the South do not think exists, who have first-hand experience of verbal and physical abuse. Their congregation includes many people from a farm labouring background, 'as well,' he says, gesturing to the spot just beyond my left shoulder where they now are not, 'as Lord and Lady Rosse there'. I should have recognized them from the welcoming video yesterday on the ground floor of the science exhibition. 'A lot of those congregants will remember how Protestant children used to have to walk home from school on one side of the street while being barracked by Catholic children on the other side.' I do not get the feeling he is talking about last week or the week before, but he is not talking about decades and decades ago either.

Michael Hanna says that because there was no real vicious bloodletting in the South around the time of Partition – 'West Cork,' Salters Stirling interjects; Michael Hanna gives him that. Because there was, West Cork aside, no real vicious bloodletting in the South, many there persuaded themselves that there was no real problem either with sectarianism. 'It helped that we were too small a minority to be a threat.' Protestants, even so, 'learned to keep their heads well down.'

When Salters Stirling first arrived, fifty-three ... no (a quick recalculation), *sixty*-three years ago, Birr people still referred to the main square as Cumberland, after George III's younger brother Prince William, Duke of the same, also known as the Butcher of Culloden. Birr is not the only town to have banished him: a statue of him, astride a horse, in central London was taken down at the end of the 1860s, a bare century after it went up. Salters Stirling does not at all regret the name's passing, rather he is trying to demonstrate how, since then, a sort of broadly agreed national narrative seems to have taken hold.

Both he and Michael Hanna think that, in relation to this, the vast majority in the South have not even begun to consider what the accommodation of a million Protestants – the larger number of whom still feel themselves to be British – will mean for the look and feel of the island as a whole.

'Parity of esteem in Northern Ireland,' Salters Stirling says, referring to one of the key planks of the Good Friday Agreement, 'has brought about a bi-cultural identity. That hasn't happened here yet.'

He notes, with regret, that the same 'story-telling' tapestry does not exist in the non-Catholic community, either North or

South. Protestants, in other words, are not as good at selling, as well as telling, themselves. Partly this is because, as he sees it, in the South especially, the opportunity has been squeezed out, and partly it is because of a marked absence of those who might have been able to provide it. He mentions the premature death of David Ervine, former UVF prisoner turned leader of the Progressive Unionist Party, and mentions too – the second time in a little over twelve hours I have heard his name, though admittedly in very different contexts – Glenn Barr.

Michael Hanna has been listening carefully. 'Identity changes slowly,' he says now. He found a letter of his grandfather's not so long ago, dating from just after the Treaty, which was full of longing for a return to Ireland's shores of imperial Britain. Michael, on the other hand, considers himself to be nothing but Irish. This chimes with something Salters Stirling said in passing earlier about Bord Failte, the Irish Tourist Board, wanting to promote Birr and Birr Castle in particular as a centre of Anglo-Irish culture. 'Lord Rosse was furious. "I'm not Anglo anything. I'm Irish."'

'That's a hundred years,' Michael Hanna says, of his grandfather and him. The problem at the moment is that, with Brexit and calls for a border poll both, demand for change is moving too fast: faster maybe than anyone can, in the end, safely manage. (And I do, yes, for a split-second, think of Mary Ward, caught up under the wheels of the steam-powered automobile her cousins had built.) A benign interpretation of Mary Lou McDonald's playing to the gallery, as Bernard from the Chestnut styled it, is that it she is caught like David Cameron in the early 2010s, trying to satisfy a constituency within the party, or the wider movement, with the promise of a vote, one day, soon*ish*. Or maybe she more closely resembles the DUP in the North, cosying up to the tough-talkers, supporting a referendum that they never expected to win and the consequences of which they had barely even begun to think through.

We have been standing at this stage for a good half-hour. We are the last people left on Oxmantown Mall. I apologize that I have kept them so long. Salters Stirling, though, offers me one final story. *His* grandfather, William, was a friend of Samuel Cunningham, the owner of Fernhill, a neighbouring big house in the Ballygomartin area. The UVF used the house and its outbuildings to store guns brought in in 1913 to resist Home Rule, and it was in Fernhill, by now a council-owned 'People's Museum', that the later version of the UVF, along with the UDA and Red Hand Commando, announced their ceasefire in October 1998.

Samuel Cunningham himself was a unionist senator in the post-Partition Stormont Upper Chamber, resigning just before his death in 1946. He and William Stirling would walk, 'while they were still able', down from Ballygomartin to the Irish Temperance League Coffee shop in the Markets area of Belfast city centre. They would often have a conversation, Salters Stirling tells me, that went like this:

'Sam?'

'Yes, William?'

'You cannot govern without the consent of the governed.'

And that, Salters Stirling says, is the way he was brought up. The maxim applied then to the North; it will apply, in the event of any future constitutional change, to the South. Then he breaks into a smile of genuine delight. 'It's an exciting time. I am glad I lived to see it.'

I am glad – whatever I may have thought half an hour ago – that I stopped the car to go and read the Mary Ward billboard.

I am glad I came to Birr.

Four days after I leave – the return journey a breeze; Friday night's air of panic dispersed – Mary Lou McDonald, and it is Mary Lou herself, is again calling for the British government to set in motion legislation for a border poll.

If she *is* playing to the gallery, the gallery is getting good value: referring to the London government's Internal Market Bill, and the secretary of state for Northern Ireland's admission that it broke international law, she quips 'perfidious Albion just got perfidiouser'.

In an interview with the *Guardian*'s Ireland correspondent, she says that 'the promise of a new, progressive, inclusive Ireland, with an NHS-style health service would win over enough voters' to the yes side of the reunification debate. As for unionists, a united Ireland must offer them 'the kinds of protection and assurances they need', which *might* include the continued existence of an assembly at Stormont.

That thought seems to detach itself from the rest of the interview. It feels like the first fallen leaf of autumn to signal a possible change.

★ ★ ★

Loose (Autumn) Leaves

1.

Thursday, 8 October, they are still completing the play-offs for the finals of soccer's Euro 2020, which ought to have been all done and dusted, with England bitterly regretting a missed penalty/poor refereeing decision/sly tug of the shirt or handball, by the middle of July. I am sitting working, sometime after ten, when I check in on the scores on the *Irish Times* website. 'Ireland lose in penalty shoot-out ... Ireland's Euro 2020 hopes are over.' But, no, wait ... look closer: 'Slovakia [who won that penalty shoot-out] will meet Northern Ireland in the Euro 2020 playoff final on November 12th.' Bring on the subs! '*Most of* Ireland's Euro 2020 hopes are over ...'

Unless of course they want to throw their lot in with us.

Samhain

The Gaia website tells me this, the cusp of October and November, is a moment to hit pause. Which is handy. As of the middle of this month, Northern Ireland is in the middle of 'a range of significant time-bound interventions to curb the spread of Covid-19'. Circuit break, to you and me. Earlier in the week that ended with the new restrictions here, the FFG(&G) government in the South announced its first budget, including some serious euros for the Shared Island Unit – half a billion of them over five years – to foster better cross-border relations and develop new infrastructure and education projects. The Unit also got its own website, which begins a couple of days before Halloween scrupulously to record every major newspaper comment for and against the Unit's own agenda, and on the not entirely unrelated and still ongoing Brexit negotiations. One of its first posts is an article by Michael Russell in *The National*, a Scottish pro-independence newspaper,[28] on the dangers of even a 'Low' Brexit deal and, as a sidebar, on the failure of Boris Johnson and his government to provide anything as useful as Micheál Martin and his have with the Shared Island Unit, for all that its critics say it does not go far enough, and for all that, presumably, Michael Russell's paper would advocate a Unit dedicated to sharing an island in the act of moving further apart constitutionally rather than closer together.

That same day – 26 October – the website carries an article on the findings of a Lucid Talk poll, which, to judge from the headline, 'NHS could be crucial in bid to maintain the Union', bears out what I have been hearing over the previous nine months, although the article itself, by Suzanne Breen of the *Belfast Telegraph*, is perhaps a little less dramatic. The poll, in fact, suggests that seven out of ten people in the North would (split almost equally) vote for or against reunification regardless of the health provision in place, with just over a quarter saying that the NHS, or the offer of an equivalent, would sway them.

The Unit's re-boot includes, too, a series of Shared Island Dialogues, to commence later in the autumn, designed, according to the brief, 'to foster constructive and inclusive civic dialogue on all aspects of a shared future on the island'. These proposed dialogues fall some way short of the Citizens' Assembly that is being called for by another contributor to the referendum debate, the Ireland's Future Group – or just Ireland's Future – which announced itself, almost exactly a year ago, at the start of November 2019 with an open letter signed by 1,088 members of civic society, north and – in fact, mainly – south. Their most recent, and detailed, paper, 'The Conversation on Ireland's Future: A Principled Framework for Change', calls on 'participants in the public debate, and in public life, to stop using the "lazy" language of division' in relation to constitutional change and the referendums that would be required to bring it about.[29] They want to 'normalise' – their inverted commas – the debate and say that the Shared Island Unit 'must not run away from the government-resourced work required to prepare for a united Ireland' – their lower case u, too.

Interestingly, the paper takes up the idea of the Stormont Assembly carrying on into a post-referendum future: 'The [Good Friday] Agreement does not contemplate the abolition of the Assembly or the Executive following reunification. These institutions remain operable in a united Ireland and would, presumably, continue unless and until alternative institutions are approved.'

Some might prefer something more solid than presumption, though I think that when 6 and 26 are next 1 – history is too long for it to be for ever an 'if (though too long as well for there not to be other reconfigurations in store beyond that) – a regional assembly will form a part of the equation.

I know a good many people who are active in Ireland's Future and there is much that I admire in their publications and interventions. They do not, though, appear to imagine the possibility that a referendum could be called at any point in the nearer future and not come out in favour of reunification, which, given the expressed desire to reassure unionists and encourage them to engage in debate, is surely something of a missed opportunity. History, as I say, might prove – sooner rather than later – that they were right to be so confident, but rather than just counting down the clock to the next referendum, perhaps they could explore how an island that had voted *not* to unite might continue to live and work in peace. And perhaps acknowledge, too, that to imagine that is not divisive either, or reactionary. To prepare for only one outcome does seem to assume that there is only one outcome you are interested in seeing much less trying to make work. Referring, as another of its documents does, to this place as 'the abandoned reminder of past sins of British-Irish relations', does not suggest any possibility of ever being reconciled to a Northern Ireland within the United Kingdom.*

While I am still trying to find out how – and where – to sign up for the Shared Island Dialogues, I see a tweet to the world at large from Conor Houston – he of Houston Solutions and Connected Citizens and the Bring One Young World to Belfast Committee – saying that he has had the honour to chair a dialogue between young people from across the island, and that he is 'humbled and inspired by their desire for genuine inclusiveness, commitment to understanding each other & having an ambitious & informed debate about the future'.[30]

I hum a little bit, I ha. Then I pick up my phone and call him.

And it is as I expected: it was all done under the Chatham House Rule, whereby people can express opinions without fear (and it sometimes is genuine fear) of them being repeated and attributed. So, Conor is not at liberty to go into the precise details of what humbled and inspired him the day before, although he is able to tell me that he thinks the invitation, from the Taoiseach's

---

*   #Think32 – a Facebook and Twitter entity – offers a similar sort of platform to the Shared Island Unit's website, though with more of an Ireland's Future sense of urgency. The hashtag, by the way, is important here. Without it you might easily find yourself on the website of an Australian company offering thoughtful marketing for growing dental practices. (Though do keep thinking about those 32, too, won't you? I mean, 26 you could maybe manage with, but 6 …?)

Office, to chair may have arisen from that One Young World bid up at Stormont back at the start of February – 'There were DFA [Department of Foreign Affairs] people there that day' – and that some of the young people present then were among the twenty-five participants in yesterday's dialogue. They are, he says, still testing the model a little, the Shared Island crew, but it was – in all honesty – an inspiration. He does give me some of the key themes that the young people discussed in the session, which was called the 'Role of Society and Culture in Shaping a Shared Future'. Climate change was, perhaps unsurprisingly, their number one concern, but with this added logic: if the two parts of the island could work towards a common approach to tackling the climate it would be a sign that they were able to work on other things – things, I take that to mean, more specifically Irish.

Second on their list – again no surprise – is education, followed by health, and then specifically the response to coronavirus, with mental health coming in behind, and finally the implications of Brexit, for border communities in particular.

They were of the mind, too, that the teaching of history needed to be addressed: the 'competing narratives' model – you stick to your history, I'll stick to mine – could not be a get out from an agreed curriculum North and South.

Among the 'marginalized voices' they would like to see better represented in future discussions would like to see it enough that several of them said they would give up their own place at the table – are 'rural communities, ethnic minorities, asylum seekers, unionist views and members of the travelling community'.

That alone is maybe a sobering statement for unionists: you are important, yes, but numerically, from a whole-island perspective you really are not all that. And, of course, even from this small sample, the implication is clear: the dialogues will continue whether you choose to be a part of them or not.

I call one Sunday afternoon to see my mum, with whom I am, as we now think nothing of saying, bubbling, and find my niece's husband Marty in the garage. Back in the 1970s, when we first came to live in this house (came to live here precisely to gain a garage), my dad, a sheet-metal worker by trade, used the garage in the evenings and at weekends as a welding shop where he made railings and gates and banister rails, and by investing most of his free time made a few much-needed pounds on the side. Marty, as it happens, has taken up welding, too, and without a garage of his own is using my mum's, returning it to its previous use, albeit with newer and better equipment. It would, as my mum says, have pleased my dad, not just the welding, but that it was Marty – who always called him Phares – doing it.

Marty in his regular working life is facilities manager at the Ulster Museum. We fall to talking, me at the open garage door, him way down at the back, about work. In the middle of October, just days before the new restrictions kicked in, we crossed over, the two of us, when I was in the museum helping to judge the 139th annual Royal Ulster Academy exhibition. (The RUA started out far more modestly in the 1870s as the Belfast Ramblers' Sketching Club, only arriving at, or claiming for itself, province-wide academy status in 1930 before King

George VI gave it the royal nod twenty years later.)[*] The 139th exhibition was supposed to carry on, like its predecessors as far back as I can remember, for the show is an end-of-year staple here, into the first weeks of the New Year. As things stand, though, it holds the record for the shortest running exhibition in the academy's, the museum's, and quite possibly Irish art's history, opening to the public at 10 a.m. on the third Friday of October, closing at 5 p.m. and, in line with the guidelines that had come into force in the course of the day, not reopening again. And this despite all the museum's meticulous preparations and social-distancing precautions, which had included taking down six dividing walls between its fifth-floor galleries to make a single enormous room with two hundred-odd (crucial hyphen) works on display.

We talk, Marty and I, into and out of the garage, about whether the museum might open again before Christmas. Whether it does or not, Marty tells me, he is already having to plan for the exhibition that comes in after the RUA. He has to get the walls back up in the gallery for that, all six of them.

'What's the exhibition?'

'Partition.'

The word hangs a moment between us.

In the next moment we are both laughing ... six walls ... Partition ...

And the moment after that again, we have stopped. Funny

---

[*] The president shows me her chain of office with the names all the way around it of past presidents, right back to 1930 and Sir John Lavery, husband and painter of Hazel, the uber Cathleen.

or not, Marty still has to get those walls up before Partition goes live on 5 January.

I think of my dad again, welding into the night, completing an order for a neighbour – a three-foot-high side gate, maybe, surmounted by scrolls. Phares would have knocked something up for you, Marty, if he was here and you were still stuck come the New Year.

The UK Internal Market Bill passes its first reading in the House of Commons and is sent to the House of Lords, where it is expected to be filleted before being sent back to the Lower House to have all the fillets replaced. Unless … Unless …

Despite the ongoing and increasingly unhinged rearguard action of the Trump camp, Joe Biden is confirmed as president-elect of the United States in the course of the November weekend before the Lords' debate.

That is Joe 'Northeast Pennsylvania will be written on my heart, but Ireland will be written on my soul' Biden.[*]

RTÉ News plays out on Saturday night with swelling orchestral music underscoring the lines from Seamus Heaney's 'The Cure at Troy' about hope and history rhyming, which Biden quoted more than once in the course of his campaign. The *Irish Times* leads with a headline, 'Biden win should focus British minds on Brexit strategy, says Coveney', above the minister for foreign affairs and defence's assertion that 'Joe Biden is a real friend of Ireland'. Biden, he goes on to say, has

[*] Font size may, of necessity, differ from one to the other.

been shaped entirely by his Irish roots. 'I think this will be a cause for "pause for thought" in Number 10 to ensure that Irish issues are prioritised as we try to close out this phase of the Brexit negotiations.' A couple of days later, and in the same vein, the newspaper's editorial, speaking of British foreign secretary Dominic Raab's attempts previously to persuade the Americans of the UK's intentions with the Single Market Bill, suggests that 'his sympathetic interlocutor is being moved on'.[*31]

In print and online there is an amount of swagger. Ireland has got its big American mate back. The Brits will get what's coming to them now. Joe Biden's characterization of Boris Johnson as a British Trump only adds to the Us-uns versus Them-uns atmosphere. In tone, of course, some of it is not very far removed from the DUP's gloating over Trump's own election, four years ago. So, you know, you might say, they are good value for it, the Brits and the DUP both. *It was never the behaviour we objected to, just the direction of travel.*

And lest you interpret this wrongly, I hear more of decency and dignity in four minutes of Joe Biden's acknowledgement speech than I heard in the four years of his predecessor's time in the White House, than possibly ever passed his predecessor's lips.

Troy Davis of the Stephen F. Austin State University, Texas, makes the interesting point that it was actually the British government which in the 1920s helped the Irish Free State achieve official recognition in the United States: 'a significant

---

* Fintan O'Toole, writing in the same issue, in a register that is not as easy for the ear to catch, sees Biden as 'the second coming of the global Irish Catholic saviour ... not so much Irish as Kennedy-ish.'

milestone,' he writes in the *New Hibernia Review*, 'not only in Irish history, but in the history of the British Commonwealth: the Free State became the first member of the Commonwealth to gain separate diplomatic representation in another country.'[32] It also marked the point at which Irish nationalist leaders began look less to individual Irish Americans for support and more to the US government, Democrats in particular. It is not just Brexit: Biden's election victory is being felt in some quarters as a boost for the prospects of an early referendum.

(Davis makes another point: the majority of Irish Americans supported the 1921 Anglo-Irish Treaty because it gave Ireland the same status as Canada, and Canada was doing all right. How strange, a hundred years on, that it is the UK that is hankering after the status of Canada.)

Back on the Saturday night of Biden's confirmation, meantime, as the RTÉ News credits roll, writer Lisa McGee is tweeting: 'Don't say anything about Derry, Lisa. Just let it be. It's bigger than that. HEANEY WAS FROM COUNTY DERRY AND WAS EDUCATED IN DERRY CITY. Sorry.'

I feel a little how I feel watching images of the 'United Kingdom' that go no further west than Hereford, no further north than Carlisle, that do not even dream of anything over the water that they could possibly have left out. The 26 would hate to think it, but they can at times be a bit, well, *England-y* in how they look at the 6.

In one of the most frequently played, and shared, archive clips in recent days, a reporter calls out to Joe Biden asking him for a quick word for the BBC. 'The BBC?' Biden says. 'I'm Irish.'

He is a great one for the quips, Joe.

Another one doing the rounds is from his time as vice-president to Barack Obama, welcoming Fine Gael's Enda Kenny to the White House for the annual St Patrick's Day presentation by Taoiseach to president of a bowl of shamrock. Facing the cameras, and apparently forgetting the symbolism of the three-striped flag over his left shoulder, he says, 'anyone wearing orange is not welcome here'. It *is* a quip and God-or-whatever-means-the-good (to borrow MacNeice's formula) help us all to be less quick to take offence, although to judge by the online response there are many who positively revel in the sentiment.

That 'shamrock ceremony' has in fact played an important role down the years in bringing together people from all religious backgrounds and political allegiances here in the North.

In the course of that same spring of 2016 that I spent watching Villanova win the college basketball championship, the US consul general to Belfast, Dan Lawton, who along with Paula Hawkins, his wife, had been a great supporter of the arts in the city, got Ali and me on the shamrock ceremony guest list. Any notions we had that we might be going to spend quality time with the president – or the vice-president – were dispelled when we arrived at the White House that afternoon to find three lines, scores deep, waiting to pass through the security tent. I recognized a fair number of faces in the lines either side of ours, politicians, community or charity representatives: nodding acquaintances some of them in Belfast, but here, three thousand miles from home, exchangers with Ali and me of shy smiles. 'Look at us all, in our excitement.'

I do not know which of the lines Gerry Adams was in, but when he got up to the search area he was taken aside by security

THE LAST IRISH QUESTION

service personnel who kept him standing for an hour and a half while they checked his identity. This, to say again, was under the Obama administration, with Joe Biden as VP, and at a time when Gerry Adams was still president of Sinn Féin, not a year like 2005, say, when invitations were withdrawn following the murder by members of the Provisional IRA a few weeks earlier of Robert McCartney outside a Belfast bar.* Prior to the 2011 ceremony, indeed, under the same Obama–Biden administration, Gerry Adams had spoken, with typical modesty, about the 'keen interest [in Washington] in the outcome of the recent [Irish] general election, Sinn Féin's success in it and in my election to the Louth and East Meath constituency'.

And, to say again, too, being taken aside by security is my own recurring nightmare (see Dublin Airport Terminal 2): anyone, anywhere, having their identity checked, or queried, has my instinctive sympathy. Eventually, the security check still not complete and word having reached him that President Obama had begun his remarks inside, Mr Adams turned on his heel and left.

'Sinn Féin,' he said, with ears of thickest cloth, 'will not be made to sit at the back of the bus by anybody.'

Not so much a case of making common cause with others as assuming their hurt and grievances as your own.

As it happens, Sinn Féin was well represented inside the

---

* It is customary to say that Robert McCartney was beaten and stabbed to death. Those verbs, though, come nowhere close to conveying the truly appalling injuries that the gang of nine armed with sewer rods and knives lifted from behind the bar inflicted on him. 'This is IRA business,' they told customers in the bar. 'Nobody saw anything.'

White House that day. Martin McGuinness was there, as was Mary Lou McDonald, who was singled out for mention in his remarks by Enda Kenny. Not only that, Gerry Adams himself had been present at the earlier Speaker's Lunch, with a mere ninety invitees, including the president (and Richard Gere with whom Adams posed for photographs), which, if the multiple hundreds in attendance at the shamrock ceremony constitutes a bus, is a bit like Sinn Féin having already been invited to share an Uber.

'Administrative input error' was the typically bland reason given by the Secret Service for that March 2016 embarrassment, which sounds like Secret Service speak for what, thanks to the BBC's *Little Britain*, is commonly known as 'computer says no': the system trumping the evidence of the naked eye. It should not happen. You would like to think it could not, but security the world over tends to be not just blind and deaf to evidence, but utterly po-faced with it. Ask Sir Paul McCartney, turned away the month before from a 2016 Grammy VIP After Party, and heard to remark to his companions, who included Beck and a Foo Fighter, 'How VIP do we gotta get? We need another hit, guys! We need another hit!'*

Reading back over the manuscript of this book one final time, in April 2021, I am pulled up again by that 'back of the bus' remark. At the end of March, the Public Prosecution Service finally released its report into the events surrounding Bobby

---

* Note to Gerry Adams: by 'hit' Sir Paul had in mind something in the vein of 'Let it Be' … or even 'Coming Up', in the video for which he appears at one point dressed as Ron Mael of Sparks, dressed as Éamon de Valera.

Storey's funeral in June 2020. Despite the recommendations of the PSNI, who had interviewed twenty-four members of Sinn Féin, the PPS has concluded that no prosecutions would follow, not least because the police themselves had been in discussion with the funeral organizers in the days leading up to the burial.

Among the all-too-familiar voices on the Radio Ulster phone-ins is one I have not heard before. Lilian Seenoi-Barr is director of programmes with the North West Migrants Forum and was one of the organizers of a Black Lives Matter protest in Derry also in June 2020. My own daughters were at a BLM demonstration the same day in Belfast. Police issued sixty-eight fines on the spot for infringement of Covid-19 restrictions. The Policing Board, which has oversight of the PSNI, later found that 'protesters who raised their rights were told the [health] regulations were the law ... none of the [police bodycam] clips appeared to consider the attempts by the protesters to obey social distancing guidance'.

Referring to the PPS's Bobby Storey report, Lilian Seenoi-Barr says, tellingly, 'I am not surprised, but I am very disturbed by the differential treatment. The very least we expected in a liberal country that supposedly respected the rule of law [is] that we are all going to be treated equally within the law. It is very clear that there are people who are above the law and people who must follow the law.'

Maybe, when it comes to that particular bus, all Sinn Féin has ever wanted is to be in the driving seat, with all the best seats saved for its mates and fellow travellers.

But I am skipping here over one crisis to get to another. In the middle of November, the Northern Ireland Executive

SAMHAIN

spends four days proving to the world that it could not organize a piss-up in a brewery, or even the date from which a piss-up might – or ought to – be allowed to happen.

As the end of the two-week coronavirus circuit break approaches – a circuit break into which some elements of the first minister's party were clearly dragged kicking and screaming – the DUP uses one of those bits of the Good Friday Agreement that most people were unaware ever existed to block proposals for the extension of partial lockdown measures by a further fortnight. The device is an Executive-only equivalent of the much-abused and widely disparaged Petition of Concern, which enables unionists or nationalists to demand that an issue, or piece of legislation, be subject to a cross-community vote of the entire ninety-member Assembly, with a majority of each 'bloc' required to carry it. At Executive level, a cross-community vote can be triggered by any three ministers acting in concert. The DUP, as the largest single party, has three ministers (meaning it does not need the support of anyone else), to Sinn Féin's two – though each also has a junior minister and, of course, in all but name, a joint-first minister – with the Ulster Unionist Party, the SDLP and Alliance all on one minister each. Commentators and a great many voters, to judge by the online and on-air contributors, are outraged at the abuse of a measure designed to protect minority rights, especially when, as in this instance, it relates to a public health issue – the biggest public health issue Northern Ireland has faced in the hundred years of its existence – and relates, too, to a proposal put forward by another Unionist, UUP health minister Robin Swann. Except, as with the Petition of Concern, the Good Friday Agreement is a little coy about

211

what the Executive three-member measure is intended to do. If it does not say what it is really for, is the DUP line, who is to say it cannot be for this?

The DUP meantime accuses Sinn Féin of reneging on an agreement reached between the two parties the weekend before. (Be not fooled by the five-party line-up: government here is the rule of two.) Michelle O'Neill, they say, has been leaned on by Mary Lou McDonald, who did not want the party to support the lifting of restrictions in one jurisdiction while simultaneously arguing for their imposition or extension in the other, the mantra being where at all possible to act as though the island is one political, as well as epidemiological, unit. Michelle O'Neill, who was chairing the Executive meeting at which Robin Swann's proposal was tabled, did not, Arlene Foster says, attempt to arrive at a consensus, but instead pushed for a vote, leaving the DUP with no option …

A classic piece of Northern Irish 'now look at what you went and made me do-ery'.

It is a farce, of course, an embarrassment, but – or maybe I mean *and* – one that might well throw up questions for any future all-Ireland political entity. Will there need to be, as well as reassuring words, checks and safeguards built into the parliamentary system – weighted majorities, maybe, to protect the rights of the new minority, and any future minorities – and, if so, how will the legislators of tomorrow prevent those too from being abused?

I can see politicians from up here, to be frank, being a pain in the hole, and I am not just thinking about the ones with Unionist currently in their party name.

And why should anyone outside the current border put up with the like of that?

For the same reason that all of us inside it have had to put up with it for the past twenty-plus years: the alternative is worse.

That is, if you think the alternative is 'a return to violence' and not a better approach to politics.

History, even recent history, can offer plenty of examples of countries breaking up, but not too many examples of them getting back together. In my lifetime I can think only of North and South Vietnam and East and West Germany. Of course, Ireland does have a bit of a head start on each of these. It is highly unlikely, for a start, that a future Dublin-centred government would impose a change of name on Belfast, as the Hanoi government did on Saigon, now officially Ho Chi Minh city. (Though Saigon – still preferred by many who live there – was itself a nineteenth-century coinage.) We have had over twenty years of 'Strand Two' cooperation – to use the Good Friday Agreement term for North–South relations – to say nothing of a half-century's shared membership of the European Union, which the Northern Ireland Protocol ensures has not yet been completely dismantled; we have, bar some differences of policy – in the scheme of things very slight – a common economic model. We do not, it is true, have a common currency, but the disparity in living standards already noted is not as great as between, say, East and West Germany. (The poor in the 26, sadly, are every bit as badly off as the poor in the 6.) The change if and when it comes will not be as sudden as a wall coming down. In fact, in areas where walls are a feature of everyday life here in the North, in Belfast in particular, there may well be a demand from those who live closest to them not to touch a single brick in the short and quite possibly medium term.

Even if they are not exported to other parts of the island, even if the terms of reference have been turned on their head or torn up altogether ('loyal' to what now? 'triumphalist' how?), the chances are that some of the old enmities will retain the capacity to sow discord and from time to time flare up into violence.

And what, leading on from that, about policing? There is already ample evidence that hostility towards the police is growing in working-class Protestant areas, and not much sign of a reduction of it in working-class Catholic areas. Policing – like politics – should never be a zero-sum game, but there is at the moment a distinctly nil-squared feel abroad.

The Police Service of Northern Ireland would, presumably, have to be incorporated into An Garda Síochána. Presumably, too, files and records that belonged to the former would now be the property of the latter, unless of course Dublin and London had come to a blush-saving arrangement. The storming of the Stasi headquarters it would not be, but it is hard to imagine, prior arrangements notwithstanding, that some things of interest and perhaps concern would not come to light.

Lost for the better part of a day, as I mull over such questions, in Germany and Vietnam, I stumble on the term Đổi Mới, meaning Renovation, and referring in this context to the policies adopted by the Vietnamese government from the mid-1980s on, after a difficult first decade of reunification, in pursuit of a more market-based economy, with predictable winners (the urban already well-to-do) and losers (the rural poor). Trying to fix the term in my head, and cognisant of the several diacritical marks, I go to one of those how-to-pronounce sites ... and hear coming back at me something that sounds uncannily close to my Southern relatives and friends trying to tell me how *I* sound then I say words containing the -ow diphthong. As in hoi noi broin coi.

And I think that might not be a bad name for the stock-taking that needs to be done before we do anything here, whether that is preparing for reunification or for the fact that the current constitutional arrangement is with us for another while:

How Now?

It is perhaps under the influence, too, of thoughts such as these that I find myself in the early stages of this disputed circuit break extension (there will one day be a single word for that) sitting down with my fourteen-year-old daughter to watch *Good Bye, Lenin!*, Wolfgang Becker's film released in 2003, but set in 1990, telling the story of a woman – a proud citizen of the German Democratic Republic who wakes from a heart attack-induced coma in the aftermath of the fall of the Berlin Wall, and of the lengths her son goes to to convince her that nothing has changed.

Afterwards, we entertain ourselves for nearly as long as the film itself lasted with thoughts of a version relocated from Berlin to Belfast – *Good Bye, Carson!* – and what we would do to maintain the fiction that the 'ideal Northern Irish world' remained untouched. If you would like to turn to the back of this book, you will find an entry form for a competition to suggest the equivalent of the Spreewald Gherkins that Alex, the son, struggles to find for his mother on the newly *Wessi*-ed supermarket shelves. Or there again, my editor may have done his job and told me to wise the fuck up.

Two thoughts I am fairly sure he and I will agree should be left in: first, it is vital that the citizens of any state can see themselves reflected somewhere in it; and, second, what is known in Germany as 'Ostalgie' – nostalgia for the old East – is not so much a desire for a return to a former state (or State) as a reluctance to jettison everything associated with it, or to see and hear it disparaged.

Two thoughts … and an observation: I double-check – Lenin in the statue being taken down in Becker's film (I will not spoil the plot by telling you when) offers the viewer an open hand. Carson on his pedestal outside the Parliament Buildings at Stormont is caught in full oratorical flow, his right arm raised and bent, his hand grasping at thin air.

* * *

Loose (Autumn) Leaves

2.

Thursday, 12 November. Ireland's Euro 2020 hopes really are over: Northern Ireland have been beaten 2-1 after extra-time at Windsor Park by the same Slovakia team who earlier in the autumn dumped out 'Most of'. The defeat, it has to be said, was on the cards from the moment, yesterday, that the BBC Football website ran a major article on Jonny Evans: 'Northern

Ireland's Best Ever Defender?' Which pretty much guaranteed that not only would Northern Ireland lose but that Slovakia's first goal would come from a miscommunication between Evans and one of his midfielders, their second would be with an assist from his right buttock, and that in the final seconds of extra-time, unmarked six yards from the opposition's goal, he would steer a header gently into the Slovakian goalkeeper's arms. Though the answer to the BBC website question is still 'yes'. By some distance.

Sorry, Most of Ireland fans, if you did indeed throw your lot in with us. *What on earth were you thinking?**

* * *

In the final week of November, the *Irish Times* reports on the publication of the interim report by the Working Group on Unification Referendums on the Island of Ireland, through the Constitution Unit of University College London[33] (if I had another week, I would give you both acronyms) that finds that voting on Irish unity without a back-up plan poses grave risks. For a moment I am transported back to the late 1970s, my mates and I in our school holidays, working as road sweepers: leaving the depot each morning, full of purpose, then after running our brushes up and down just a few streets parking the cart in an alleyway while we went and found a café for a long, late

---

* What on earth was I thinking? Ireland's – Most Of's *and* Rest Of's – Men's Euro 2020 hopes over, yes, but not so the Euro 2022 Women's Championship, for which Northern Ireland have qualified – their first time ever in a major tournament final.

breakfast. Among the Working Group's other less than startling findings is that 'if the Oireachtas legislated for unification while Westminster did not, Northern Ireland would become disputed territory … [and that] it would be highly desirable to avoid this eventuality'. In other news, a study has found that getting into the bath while hugging your electric heater could cause your hair to frizz …

I get round to reading the actual report, rather than just the *Irish Times* report on the report, the next day. And what can I say, if I had not already given you enough reason to suppose it, I am a complete slabber: the Working Group has considered everything, and in great detail. And this is only interim.

One of its most significant findings comes in the penultimate page of the report proper: 'The rules for referendum and election campaigns are badly out of date in both the UK and Ireland, and urgently need to be strengthened. This would be particularly important for referendums on a question as momentous as the question of unification. Voters must be protected from misinformation and have access to high-quality information.' Higher quality, you get the feeling they mean, than slogans on the sides of buses. 'Campaign finance regulations must be robust enough to ensure fairness between the two sides across the two referendums.' Here again, it is difficult to see past the Brexit referendum and accusations that Vote Leave bolstered its nationwide campaign by channelling money through the DUP, which took out an ad in the *Metro* newspaper (not available in Northern Ireland) worth over a quarter of a million pounds. Whether campaign finance regulations will do any better than previous investigations in answering the question – repeatedly posed – of whether Sinn Féin has profited at elections from the proceeds of the 2004 Northern Bank robbery is anyone's guess.

'The process as a whole,' say the Interim Report's authors in conclusion, 'must be fair, and its administration rigorously impartial.'

To which we can all surely only say, Amen.

Yet again, health provision emerges, from the report, as the single greatest issue for voters, with 51.7 per cent of respondents in the data the Working Group is working *off* saying that the system in the South would discourage them from casting a vote in favour of reunification and fewer than 9 per cent saying it would encourage them. The two biggest factors for respondents inclined to vote 'yes' are the strength of the Irish economy (30.9 per cent), and continued, or renewed, membership of the EU (28.7 per cent). On the question of same-sex marriage, it is more or less a dead heat: 19 per cent saying the issue would discourage them from voting for reunification and 19.4 per cent saying it would encourage them. (In truth, given that same-sex marriage is, at long last, legal on both sides of the border I am not entirely sure what those percentages tell us, unless that there is a lingering suspicion that the DUP will find a way, even now, to thwart the legislation in the North.) It is, however, worth noting – as the Working Group does – that the vast majority of respondents not only identified as nationalist (62 to 18 per cent), but were also male (69 per cent) and university-educated (67.5 per cent). Oh, and at least 95 per cent white, with another 4½ per cent providing no information.

One respondent who identifies as unionist expresses the concern that even in the event of a 'no to reunification' outcome,

Sinn Féin in particular will keep coming back until it gets the result that it wants. The Good Friday Agreement, as noted at the very start of this book, reduced the minimum period between referendums from the ten years set out in the 1973 Northern Ireland Constitution Act (introduced in the aftermath of the proroguing of the 'Home Rule' Stormont government) to just seven. Once you have had one, in other words, it is easier to have or to argue for another.

And even if you think that is unnecessarily jaundiced, it is a fact of these referendums – and the respondent is probably right that we should think of them as plural – that they only end, and then definitively, with a yes: there will be no seven-year re-run after that. In a sense then the whole idea of a referendum is weighted in favour of those who back reunification. The 'nos' can win as many times as they like, but the first time they lose, they lose for good and all. The best that unionists can hope for is that they can keep making the case, over and over and over. It ought to at the very least put them on their mettle – get out there, be positive, express yourselves, win the crowd over.

As it is, I suspect the other dressing room is feeling a bit like the Manchester United dressing room before the game with Tottenham Hotspur where Alex Ferguson gave the shortest team talk in history: 'Lads: it's Spurs.'

'It's the unionists.' Give them enough time, they will beat themselves.*

---

* Though note, unionists, 4 October 2020, Manchester United 1 Spurs 6 (and maybe draw a veil quickly over the corresponding fixture the following April).

The night I finish the Interim Report – the last Friday night in November – is the night of the annual *Late Late Toy Show*, which, for anyone who has never seen it, is a three-hour takeover of the RTÉ's premier chat show by children helping the presenter – for the past dozen years Ryan Tubridy – test-drive the best of the festive season's toys and games, the whole interspersed with musical numbers by young performers and the kinds of tales of everyday fortitude and heroism that make you wonder what, seriously, you have or have ever had to complain about. For a lot of people sitting down to watch, year after year, it is, more than the city centre lights going on, more than Advent Sunday, the real start of Christmas, and not just in Ireland: the *Toy Show* is starting to go online-global.

It remains, though, a bit of a headscratcher to many Up Here. I try to find the viewing figures for RTÉ in the North, but when I click on a promising looking link 'All-Ireland viewing figures for RTÉ' it turns out to be the figures for *the* All Ireland GAA inter-county championships, though I can tell you that the figures for the Gaelic Football and Hurling finals combined come nowhere close to the 1.54 million viewers who tuned in for the last *Late Late Toy Show* for which I have figures (2019). My kids watch it – and look forward to it weeks in advance – because my wife grew up watching it. Their friends, for the most part, have never even heard of it. One friend of mine, long since relocated to London, confesses that nothing makes her feel more Northern than the social media nostalgia-storm the show stirs up among *her* Southern Irish friend groups.

Early on in this year's specially-adapted-to-Covid show a brother and sister from Cork introduce one of their puppets – lavender face, lilac hair – as 'Polly ___' the next word is a little unclear, but it begins with a *p* and an *r* and ends in an *n*, *t*. 'Protestant?' asks Tubridy, incredulously, before the word has had time to settle in anyone else's brain. '*President*,' says the little girl, but too late: Polly Protestant (or Polly *the* Protestant, as social media seems to prefer) is born.

And how – to use the old Northern Irish gag – do you know she is? Because she looks like one.

If I had had the wit or the wherewithal, I would have rushed out a whole family of them: *Take the fear out of reunification for your children with The Protestants* …

As to that feeling of Northern-ness my friend mentioned. I like Trinity College Dublin academic Rosie Lavan's tactical deployment of the comma in her *Seamus Heaney and Society* monograph (I was doing an event with her earlier in the week of *The Late Late Toy Show*), where she refers to her subject as a 'Northern, Irish poet'.[34] I suppose it would work just as well with 'citizen' for an interval of whatever duration.

And then suddenly duration is the word that is on everyone's lips. On 9 December, in the first sign that Brexit trade negotiations might not have been going quite as badly as has been reported all through the autumn and in now to winter, Michael Gove, as co-chair of the EU–UK Partnership Council, gets to his feet in the House of Commons to add detail to the headline agreement reached the day before with his EU counterpart, Maroš Šefčovič, on the implementation of the Northern Ireland Protocol. The controversial and – no 'limited' or 'specific' about it – illegal clauses in the United Kingdom Internal Market Bill, which is to say, numbers 44, 45, and 47, voted down by the House of Lords, will not now be reintroduced.

That sound you hear in the background is the government's electronic egg timer going off, the hardboiled setting having clearly been nudged to soft.

Over on the *Slugger O'Toole* website, regular commentator Brian O'Neill is in no doubt whatsoever: we now have a border in the Irish Sea setting the island on a path to an economic unity. 'And all this just in time for Northern Ireland's 100th birthday. Will Northern Ireland see 150 years or even 120 years? Place your bets: the wheel is spinning.'

Mary Lou McDonald in her interview with the *Guardian*'s Owen Jones has already suggested it will not even see 110: reunification will happen before 'the decade of opportunity', as she styles the 2020s, is out. Crime writer Val McDermid comes in even lower, giving Partition, in the context, too, of a second Scottish referendum on independence, another five years at best: 'The notion of having a border up the Irish Sea and pretending that somehow it's okay and it doesn't change anything, it's manifest nonsense.'

Whatever your take on the Protocol, or Brexit as a whole, Gove's statement is an exercise in disingenuousness. 'British sausages,' he says through a British sausage-sized smirk, 'will continue to make their way to Belfast and Ballymena', to which a couple of members (I believe that is the polite word) on the Conservative benches actually say, 'hear, hear'.

It takes several opposition MPs' questions for him to fess up to what lies on the far side of the three-month 'grace period' that has just been agreed: certain products will almost inevitably have to be sourced thereafter from within the island of Ireland, or elsewhere in the European Union.

So, come the end of March, in fact quite possibly not-here, not-here, British sausages.

At least the export licences that Boris Johnson promised could be binned *have been binned altogether*, except, says Gove, with an extra kink of that British-bangers-to-Ballymena smirk, for endangered species and war diamonds ... or they have 'for now', according to BBC Northern Ireland's business and economics editor, who points out that all anyone has to go on at present is a one-page summary and Gove's Commons statement, the latter, he manages to suggest in his BBC-ish way, not altogether reliable. 'I still think this could be one that comes back ...' And indeed, within twenty-four hours, he is reporting that while details are *still* hard to come by, licences could apply to half a million transactions a year, which either means a surprising number of Irrawaddy dolphins or ...

Actually, the endangered animal and illegal diamond trade is nothing to joke about. It is very simple: Gove takes us all for mugs, and not just the DUP, whom he and his have repeatedly gulled, as commentators are lining up to remind them. My favourite out of the many jibes goes to David McWilliams, who describes the DUP as 'the party that never misses an opportunity to miss an opportunity'.

Former UUP leader, Reg – then Sir Reg, now Lord – Empey, meanwhile, calls the initial acceptance of an Irish Sea border (back when Johnson convinced the DUP they would retain a veto over it) as the 'biggest strategic mistake that unionism has made

since Partition in 1921'. By which I take it he does not mean
that Partition itself was a big strategic mistake, although truth
to tell his predecessor many times removed, Lord (previously
Sir and previouslier plain Edward) Carson, would probably not
have argued with him if he did.

Of course, there is – just – a chance that this could all turn
out well for Northern Ireland, that the new arrangements,
while not quite creating the Hong Kong in the Irish Sea that
some enthusiasts envisaged after the 2016 referendum (their
enthusiasm often hidden beneath a veneer of despair that Brexit
was happening at all), would at least allow it to box clever and
make the most of being able to feint one moment to the EU
side, the next to the UK. Were there to be tangible benefits
from that, would the dynamic change again? Might Northern
Ireland in time, instead of being the thing that divided the rest
of the island and the island next door, become the very thing
that brought them closer together? Might Ireland – all thirty-
two counties of it – be more settled by maintaining a little bit
of difference between the twenty-six and the six?

I remember an elderly woman in Forkhill in South Armagh
telling me the year after the 2016 referendum that, when border
checks were in place, she would *only* shop in Dundalk, on the
southern side of those checks, 'just to be contrary'. As soon
as the checks went so did her desire to go there. She shopped
in Newry now, even though it was a bit further away. She
was a nationalist, but she was Northern, after all. (Northern,
nationalist, as Rosie Lavan might have it.) Besides, she seemed
to imply, what would the Border Counties be without a little
lingering sense of otherness either side, but the north midlands?

Without that extra psychic energy, that special weight and significance that they have acquired, would they become less obvious destinations in their own right and, more than ever, simply places passed on the way to somewhere bigger?

Many see the UK's decision to scrap the Internal Market Bill's mid-40s clauses and compromise with the EU on the Protocol as an example of the Biden effect in action. Those clauses were conceived of in the Trump era. Even in the event of a No Deal Brexit – the prospect of which is not yet entirely banished – the British can tell the president-elect that they have taken care of Ireland. So, you know, what about that trade deal we were talking to you about …?

And, of course, Biden is coming at the issue of Brexit and its implications from a very particular angle: he is not just Irish, he is border Irish, his family having emigrated from Carlingford, Co. Louth, down the road a stretch from Newry, and on the other side of Carlingford Lough from Northern Ireland's second largest port (in its twenty-ninth largest town), Warrenpoint.

Ballina, on the other side of the island, in Co. Mayo, does have a claim on him, too,* but Carlingford residents demonstrated their connection – literally – the November Sunday after his victory with a parade for 'Cousin Joe' through the streets of the town, led by the Carlingford Pipe Band, who popped one of their glengarry caps on the head of a hardboard cut-out of the president-elect. And he visited himself, back in 2016, while still

---

* One of the Ballina connection flew to the States during the campaign to encourage Irish American support. 'I know he's very in touch with our struggles here in Ireland,' she said.

the vice-president, searching for ancestors in the local graveyard and stopping into a whitewashed pub, once owned, he was pretty sure, by a not-too-distant relative.

In one of those alignments for which I would not be surprised there was somewhere an ancient clay tablet, the Saturday after the Protocol heads of agreement – 12 December – turns out to be not only the first day after Lockdown Mark 2 in the North, but also under new adjustments to Level 3 restrictions in the South, the day when inter-county travel is again permitted for work purposes and – intriguingly – for golfers, resident in one county but registered at a club in another. It is also a beautiful, wintery, sunny morning in Belfast *and* – the ancients would never have predicted this – in Newry, and fifteen miles further down the road in Carlingford. I decide on a whim that that is where I am going to spend my day. I have my homemade folded-sheets-of-A4 workbooks; I have a golf umbrella in the car boot. I think if anyone stops me to ask, or if the weather breaks, I am well covered.

(There are, as it happens, a lot of Guards about, but it is speed they are interested in, unless those are a new species of infrared thermometer, capable of penetrating windscreens, that they are holding up as I pass with that anxious – and I fear all-too-Northern – glance down at the clock.)

The few times I can remember driving to   rather than through – the northern part of Co. Louth I crossed the border on the A1, Dublin-bound, then came off at the Ravensdale exit and doubled back. Everyone tells me, though, it is quicker going via Newry, just as long as you avoid the town centre. So, I go this morning via Newry, and I manage not to avoid the town centre and finally in my exasperation give up and get back out onto the A1 – the N1 the moment I cross the border – and leave again at the Ravensdale turnoff (a handful of miles from Faughart, birthplace of St Brigid) and what, in Tourist Board white on brown, is listed as the Carlingford Ferry Scenic Route.

They are not kidding. To the left of the road, the ground rises steeply and ruggedly; to the right, between the trees and hedges and the (only occasional) houses, glimpses are afforded of the Carlingford Lough estuary, glittering this morning. It is one of those roads you would not care if it never ended. When it does, at last, coming in at a right angle to the R176, I turn left, so that I am approaching Carlingford town from the south side, the western side of the Lough, narrowing all the time, until cars and even people can be made out in (I'm going with) Rostrevor, on the eastern, which is also the Northern, shore.

The border itself runs right up the middle. I love the thought of it ebbing with the tide a couple of times a day, of smugglers' charts with Low Border times ringed in red.

The skyline on the approach to the town is dominated by Slieve Foy, one of those mountains that have not bothered too much dressing up the fact that they are great lumps of rock forced up aeons past by subterranean forces, and a magnet this morning for the only patch of cloud in the wide blue sky. Between the lough on one side, indeed, and the mountain on the other, this really does feel, in a way that much of the rest of the 300-mile wiggly line does not, like border country. The road through the town back to Newry by way of Omeath passes through a tunnel cut, roughly, into solid and picturesquely dripping rock.

Without it, in centuries long gone, your best, indeed your only, bet for – relatively – easy north–south travel was to track inland to the Moyry Pass, the so-called Gap of the North, where in 1600 English forces under Lord Mountjoy fought out a months-long, hundreds-dead and fairly emblematic draw with the army of Hugh O'Neill.

On the top of the tunnel is a road – I am mildly surprised *not* to find chains attached that could pull it up at short notice – connecting the town proper to the remains of King John's Castle, built by Hugh De Lacy in the very first years of sustained English, or Anglo-Norman, presence in Ireland, and renamed after a visit by the monarch in 1210. Actually, I am not sure 'built' is the word I want there. The castle looks almost to have been sculpted out of the bedrock, or perhaps after getting on for a thousand years to have begun to merge back into it.

Nick Coffey, a retired RTÉ political correspondent with connections to the town, told the *Irish Times* in autumn 1998, 'When you get out of your car in Carlingford now, you can smell the greed in the air.' Since the Tourist Board declared it a heritage town a decade before, 'every little nook and cranny in the place is spoken for and prices are way beyond the reach of native sons and daughters'. A lot of the property, the article seems to suggest, in this town of barely a thousand, was being bought by people from the North.

I sniff the air, when I get out of my car, across the street from the Garda station, and walk down an entry that brings me to a quay with narrow steps curving up from it to the castle, but the only smells I am getting are those I associate with a low tide, boat fuel and warm winter sunshine.

Just ahead of me on the steps up to the castle is a woman with her primary-school age daughter and son. They make room to let me pass at the top: no one was ever going to take King John's Castle coming from the quay side. I take a turn around the remains, pausing to read the panels detailing the castle's history, and to take in that (no other word for it) commanding view. Actually, I do not know how anyone could ever have taken the castle from *any* side. When I come back round to the top of the steps about a quarter of an hour later, the woman is sitting in the sun while her children clamber over the rocks behind her. From comments her son makes about it not being as slippery as last week, I conclude that this is something of a Saturday morning ritual.

I ask her if she would mind talking for a moment and start to explain what I am about. She interrupts me at mention of Brexit and tells me she is not actually Irish, and at once I hear the north-east of England in her accent. So much, I think, for my Saturday-morning-ritual theory. But then she qualifies it again: she is not actually Irish, but she has been living here for the past twelve years. Her husband is from Carlingford – a blow-back-in, or briefly blown-out, rather than a complete blow-in.

Unlike a great many English people who do not even live on the island, she has not yet got round to applying for Irish citizenship, although she is thinking about it pretty seriously now. Her mother, who is still in the (English) north-east, is very concerned about the latest noises emanating from the Brexit negotiations, with predictions that No Deal could see UK residents restricted to stays of no more than ninety days in EU states. 'I mean, she is in good health now,' the woman says, 'but maybe some time in the future ...' She trails off but bounces back a moment later with a general exasperation. 'And then there's all the queues.' At the ports and airports, she means. Who, whatever their age, needs the hassle of them?

She thinks reunification could only be a good thing in the long run, although there is a lot about the North as it currently is that she admires. The schools for a start. 'We had been thinking about sending these two to school in Newry' – post-primary, that is – 'but we changed our minds after Brexit.' It will be Dundalk now, she tells me, or 'Cooley', the latter said as though it was the name of a town or a village rather than the whole peninsula. (The Cooley Kickhams GAA team play – in green, gold and white – at Fr McEvoy Park, in Monkstown, a place best known for being halfway to a lot of other places.) She knows people, though, who have bought houses on the Newry side of the border, just to have an address there in termtime. 'As it,' she says, 'the schools weren't going to know.'

She smiles. 'It's a bit complicated around here.'

Complicated enough that she would rather I did not use her name. She would not want to be seen to be criticizing anyone's choices. They were all trying to do their best by their families.

Later on, I get talking to a woman in the vintage shop on River Lane, which descends steeply from the foothills of Slieve Foy into Market Square, the watercourse for which it is named (river maybe bigs it up) open along one side of the lane until it meets the square at the corner of Des Savage's Food Market, where the Carlingford Christmas tree stands. The woman – Marina – is a civil servant in Belfast Monday to Friday, but comes down every Saturday, when restrictions allow, to help out in the shop, which is run on a cooperative basis with her sister, who lives in Carlingford, and a couple of friends.

She is sceptical about the suggestion that people are buying houses north of the border to send their kids to school there. It is the kind of thing you hear said, but it is always a friend of a friend: she has never met anybody who actually has.

I get the feeling she cannot imagine anyone wanting to leave here for any reason.

'As soon as you come over that hill' – this is another route I missed, bypassing Newry, but coming off before the Ravensdale exit – 'you breathe easier.'

No matter how many times she has done the journey, she finds herself sometimes still stopping the car at that point to let it sink in, not just the view, the feeling, too.

I ask whether that is getting away from the North specifically or just the city, whether you might not feel the change of pace – and air – that she mentions if you had driven up from Dublin, or if you headed out of Belfast in the other direction, up the north Antrim coast. She allows that that might be so and agrees with me there is a bit of Cushendall or Cushendun about Carlingford, but, still, she maintains, there is something very particular here.

Not that she expects people back home to heed her. To her mind one of the greatest barriers to a United Ireland is that some people in the North just do not want to know – and never will want to know – the rest of the island. It clearly pains her, not on the constitutional level, but for what it says about our lack of curiosity.

I think again of the statistic that says more people from Northern Ireland visit the Border Counties than come from the entire twenty-six counties to any part of Northern Ireland, and wonder whether the lack of curiosity is not two-way.

Between talking to the woman at King John's Castle and talking to Marina, I stopped for a chat with a young couple I saw earlier down on the quay. They, wouldn't you know, are not from Carlingford either, but have taken the opportunity, this first weekend the restrictions allow for it, to travel over from Cavan. They tell me they were not born, either of them, when the Troubles ended. The young man tells me his father will not hear any talk of a United Ireland: there is peace now, leave it be. There is nothing to be gained by a referendum, only more trouble.

A few days after Christmas 1972, the UVF left a car bomb in the village of Belturbet, a couple of miles south of the border with Fermanagh, and close to where his father farms. A teenage boy and girl were killed. Working backwards, from the age of the young man I am talking to, I am guessing those teenagers murdered in 1972 were contemporaries of his father's. Friends possibly. I am guessing, too, the father looks at his son and his girlfriend and thinks, not them, not again.

The young man, though, tells me he thinks it might well take something like another war to bring reunification about in the end, which takes me aback more than a bit. He cannot see that anyone in the North would willingly want to join the South, given the disparity in the health services in particular.

'The fifty quid to see a doctor,' I say.

'Aye,' he says, 'and that's just to see them.'

The young woman actually works in healthcare. 'I'm just about to qualify as a nurse.' In the past, she says, a lot of people in her position would have gone across the water to England to do a year there, for the experience, but Brexit is changing that, making them warier. I ask whether any of them would have come north. She shakes her head. 'Not unless they had a family connection there already.'

Their friends do talk about a United Ireland now and then, more so lately 'with Covid', but in fact Covid or the response to it makes the prospect of reunification happening any time soon seem very remote indeed. 'I mean, if we can't even work together on that ...' She shakes her head again.

And is it OK if I use their names?

They look at one another then at me. Their smiles are apologetic.

'Not to worry,' I say.

On the recommendation of Marina in the Village Vintage Shop, I head across to the Village Hotel (there is a lot of Village in the town), also known as McDevitt's, for lunch. While I stand at reception sanitizing to my elbows, a member of the hotel's bar staff takes my details for the purposes of track and trace. I have just given my – Northern – mobile number when she stops. 'Can you confirm that you are a resident of Co. Louth?'

'I'm not,' I say, and she instantly puts a line through my name. 'I'm sorry, I'm not allowed to serve you.'

I am about to plead my folded paper workbooks, my golfing umbrella, but it is clear that I am in the wrong. I apologize (while somewhere in the back of my mind wondering how the young couple from Cavan are faring for food while they are here) and head instead round to an alfresco place I noticed when I was parking my car, just on up the road another lot of yards from the Garda station.

The Wildwood Food Box is an adapted horse trailer, pulled up at one end of the forecourt of a long, low warehouse (is my best guess). A blackboard on the pavement side proclaims everything wholesome and made this morning. There are, scattered about the forecourt, tables and chairs that appear to have only recently met, and a large paraffin stove, around which, when I get there, are gathered a number of men who look as though they will never again be able to get enough heat into them, standing with mountain bikes that have actually seen a mountain lately, in fact have brought a fair bit of it back with them on their tyres and mudguards, to say nothing of the riders' own legs.

It is a while before I twig that the building in whose forecourt the Food Box is parked has been repurposed as a bike hire and repair shop. Another thing I note: the specialist walking boot, or shoe, is the footwear of choice in these parts. Sea-level Carlingford is maybe five hundred yards wide. After that, it is all, very quickly, uphill.

I have just taken my coffee and vegan sausage roll over to a chair, set, shyly, side-on to a table it clearly thinks too good for it, when a man comes along the street with *his* primary school age son and daughter. Hot chocolates with all the toppings for them, a coffee for him, and a chat with the Wildwood owners, whom he clearly knows … about Brexit. Or more particularly about the effect of a No Deal outcome on the price of beef and flour. The latter, he thinks, is going to get a hell of a lot more expensive. As for the former, 'we'll just need to slow down the rate of slaughter for a while'.

As Saturday morning talk goes you could hardly describe it as small.

I beg his pardon for eavesdropping but ask him if he could explain what he means about the rate of slaughter.

'Well, there are seven million head of cattle on the island, and they are slaughtering thirty-five thousand a week ...' Two hundred weeks, I think, and they would all be gone, apart from any babies, which might have grown and ... what age do they start to have babies of their own? I have the gist – Irish self-sufficiency – but have lost the actual numbers thread. I opt instead for the 'general disruption' line of inquiry. How bad does he think things are likely to get here if Britain *crashes* out?

'Very.' There is the loss of the land bridge to Europe for a start.

I mention the new ferry services, announced earlier in the week from Rosslare, in Co. Waterford, straight to France. Mention, too, that brand-new Northern Ireland Protocol agreement.

'There's what you read in the papers and what you hear on the ground, and somewhere in between is the truth,' he says, and only just stops short of tapping the side of his nose.

'Does that go for talk of a border poll, too?'

'People are getting carried away,' he says. 'If there is going to be a United Ireland within my lifetime it will have to be with consent.' From the way he lands on this last word I do not get the impression he intends by it 50 per cent + 1 of all eligible voters in Northern Ireland, but unionists first and foremost. 'Anyone who thinks otherwise is living in Cloud Cuckoo Land.'

I tell him it might be the most populous county in Ireland.

'Brexit could as easily drive a wedge,' he says then. 'It could give unionists the heebie-jeebies all on its own.'

Sinn Féin, to his mind, are exactly the same as Boris Johnson. Brexit was the horse that Johnson decided to ride into power, which is all in the end that he is interested in. For Brexit, read referendum. And, as with the Tories and Brexit, Sinn Féin might end up getting it before they know what to do with it.

He is not from Carlingford either, but west Co. Offaly. I tell him I was in Birr not so long ago.

'I'd say they saw things a bit differently there,' he says.

I ask him, as I ask everyone I talk to, whether, when I come to write this up, I can use his name. He thinks for a moment – I can hear it coming, or at least the first bit. 'Better not,' he says. 'I'm not well liked.'

And everyone within earshot laughs.

I have been wondering why I have not been able to find, in a town with only half a dozen streets of any size, the whitewashed pub I saw Joe Biden pop into in that clip from his 2016 visit. Now, as I stand on Newry Street writing onto my quadruple-folded sheet of A4 the words of the Not Well-Liked Man, a white Citroën Berlingo van passes me: *President of America Joe Biden*, reads the legend on the side, complete with stars and stripes, tricolour and EU flag. *Welcome Home to Whitestown* ... and in case you missed it the first time, a variation across the double rear doors: *From Whitestown Co. Louth ... To the White House, Washington!*

Which is when I remember that though Carlingford town has claimed him, the president-elect's people are more (or less) accurately from the Carlingford *area*. I also remember passing a sign for Whitestown earlier, after turning off the road marked Carlingford Ferry Scenic Route.

And then the strangest of strange things happens. As I come out of the town (did I need to say I ran back to the car? I ran back to the car) on to the R176, I find I am being preceded – escorted, it feels like – by the Carlingford Pipe Band, the same band that led the victory parade for Cousin Joe at the start of last month. Parked cars line the road on either side. People take photographs and clap. For about two hundred yards, there is just the band and me. I essay a couple of waves to the left and right – it feels like the civil thing to do – in between calling out of my wound-down window to ask onlookers what exactly is going on. It turns out I have chanced upon the end of a ceremony to mark the unveiling of a Christmas-special roadside hoarding: Let Every Heart a Manger Be. When the band at last falls out, the pipe-major tips me a small salute. I had been half hoping for a glengarry cap, same as Joe, but the salute is such a courteous gesture, I tip him one in return.

A little further on, Mary Lou is in a hedge, at the forking of two roads, saying flatly, 'Irish Unity makes sense, let's talk about it', which I assure her I am, after my own fashion, doing right this minute.

Whitestown is allegedly 4km off the main road in the direction of the Lough. I would not have put money on there being anything like 4km between the main road and the Lough, or 4km of straight road at any rate. I spend the next half-hour looking for anything remotely town-like, following a promising bit of (even narrower) road with a scattering of houses on it for a few hundred yards, doubling back then when they amount to nothing, following another stub, and another, and another. Only when I get home do I discover that all those possible bits were *it*, that Whitestown is a prime example of a clachan – an 'informal' arrangement of a village.

I do, at least, in my back-and-forthing, find the whitewashed pub, Lily Finnegan's. (And I remember now that Biden's Whitestown people were Finnegans.) It, too, gets a mention in that 1998 piece which speaks of greed in the Carlingford air, although the focus is more on the buildings opposite, derelict and fallen in back then, but since fully restored and – a doubt on the part of the 1998 *Irish Times* writer – sympathetically at that. Whether they are inhabited by people from the area – a further doubt of his – is another matter. There is no one around to ask today, or no one who is not clearly walking the tell-tale boots, the thousand-yard stare – to somewhere beyond.

Lily Finnegan's itself has a model in the window of Lily Finnegan's, which reminds me of what someone next to us in the queue for the shamrock ceremony said about the White House being much smaller than they had imagined, more like a model of the real thing. The pub this afternoon is shut, so I do not have the opportunity of investigating whether the model of the pub has another model of the pub in its front window – and here I know for sure I am back in *Third Policeman* territory, and the boxes within boxes that drive Flann O'Brien's narrator to the edge of madness.

Scrub 'do not have the opportunity of investigating': am spared the inevitability of discovering.

In fact, I am finding this whole, wide, uniformly flat area oddly unsettling. I feel very far removed from everything, and not, as they say, in a good way.* A signpost at a T junction (on the other side of the crossbar of the T, the sea) reads 'Whitestown Scenic Loop' and quickly in one direction becomes a less-than track under my wheels, going apparently nowhere. And then the car itself is apparently going nowhere. I get out to make sure I have not got stuck. The sun by now is starting to sink behind me; even the scattered houses a winding kilometre or two away are being swallowed one by one. And then I see it, see them, the sun's rays catching the water aslant, and for a moment, rather than shrinking the horizon seems to widen, and widen, and widen … And yes, I think, yes, *yes*! You really could contemplate taking on the whole of the free world from here.

I blame the pipe band escort as much as the sea view. I get back in the car, reverse, at the third attempt to the downstroke of the T.

Coming out onto the main road again, headed north, I see Slieve Foy has changed into its night-cloud cap, salmon-pink.

I drive back slowly through Carlingford (and not just because the Guards are still out taking the temperature of the traffic), passing under the bridge across to King John's Castle, and on out along the road to Newry, the Lough, to my right, narrowing and narrowing, losing its identity and ceding its name to – what else? – Narrow Water, site of the 1979 IRA massacre that Offaly

---

* In *The Third Policeman* this would be the moment when the breeze would bring the sound of marching feet … or foots: the army of one-legged men on the move, spelling curtains.

and Laois TD Brian Stanley is sorry now that he tweeted about. The bombers must have kept watch from somewhere in the high ground off to my left as I come through the village of Omeath (think Carlingford in capsule form), waiting for the moment the first lorryload of paratroopers passed the stationary trailer of hay bales in which their bomb was hidden. The gate lodge where the survivors of the first explosion took refuge – the gate lodge where the second, even more deadly, bomb had been planted – led to Narrow Water Castle, or Keep, a descendant of another Hugh de Lacy fortification, built only a few years after King John's Castle. Some of the soldiers fired back across the water – possibly mistaking the sound of ammunition igniting in the flames from the first bomb for shots directed at them – and killed Michael Hudson, who was over from England on a fishing holiday and who had come down to the shore at Omeath village with his cousin to see what on earth was happening on the other side. Michael Hudson, as it happened, was the son of one of the Queen's coachmen and lived in the Royal Mews, in the grounds of Buckingham Palace. That he should have died on a day when the Queen's uncle-in-law, Lord Mountbatten, was killed on the other side of the island off the coast of Sligo would merit the words 'awful' and 'coincidence' if they did not distract from the simple fact that it was appalling that he should have died at all.

The water keeps on narrowing, becoming the Newry River, or Canal – I am never sure where one ends and the other begins any more than I am able to tell at what point exactly on this drive I crossed over from South to North – and then I am on the outskirts of Newry itself, and there is the road I missed earlier today on my way here, rising at a steep diagonal that takes me out above the town on to the A1, and within forty minutes I am back in Belfast.

I keep thinking about that thing Marina in the Village Vintage Shop said, that a lot of people in the North just do not want to know the rest of the island. It strikes me that as well as cutting both ways not wanting to know maybe runs sideways, too. Time and again these days I see evidence of adherents to one side of the referendum debate trying to thwart or dismay those on the other.

The week after my trip to Carlingford, the Northern Ireland Office (NIO) launches its campaign to mark* the centenary of the two-thirds Ulster state, 'Our Story in the Making, NI Beyond 100'. It is actually a pretty nifty piece of footwork, managing to invoke the centenary at the same time as leapfrogging right over it.

I see the centenary bent over, holding its ankles, making a back. I remember, from school, how hard some people would land with their two hands, intent on flattening you.

What is not at all nifty is the NIO's decision to release, as a taster for the campaign, a series of images that includes one of Seamus Heaney. It so happens that the controversy this causes comes very close to my own doorstep. The NIO says that permission to use the image was granted by the Seamus Heaney Centre at Queen's University Belfast, where I work. It was not. The Seamus Heaney Centre does not own the portrait in question, which is part of the Queen's University's collection,

---

* This follows an earlier NIO internal campaign to identify a verb midway between 'celebrate' and 'lament'.

and has said so several times to the ad agency working on behalf of the NIO.

For a couple of days, the provenance of the permission becomes as much a part of the story as the campaign itself and the NIO's co-opting of Heaney into it, although it is this latter matter that inevitably comes to dominate the debate. The story provides the *Irish News* with two front-page stories and an editorial across an eight-day period in the run-up to Christmas Eve, a period that might traditionally be a little slow for news, but this year includes dramatically rising coronavirus cases and the last throes of the Brexit negotiations.

First and foremost, this is about doing things right, and about the fact that the NIO simply did not. As for what Seamus Heaney would have thought or felt – and his 'please be advised, my passport's green' line is much repeated, as is the fact that not one unionist politician saw fit to attend his funeral in 2013 – I will defer in this and every instance to those who knew him best, his own family, and maybe suggest that those queuing up to speak (or indeed shout) for him, would do well to take a lead from the family's dignified response.

The way in which the campaign was put together, though – and from the little I was privy to I would say 'at speed' – suggests, if not a carelessness, then at least a failure to think through the consequences fully. To which you might say 1920, 2020, *plus ça change*.

By further polarizing nationalists and unionists, however, or giving nationalists and unionists further opportunity to mark out the distance between them, it does not bode well for the year ahead.

Hold on to your ankles tight, Wee 6 Centenary. There are a lot of heavy hands about to land, and those are only your friends I am talking about.

And then it is Christmas Eve, and, like that, it is done: the Trade Deal whose star in the last few weeks and even days has waned more often than it has waxed lands with a thump: a 1,200-page Christmas miracle, Boris Johnson proclaims. All the best Christmas films, of course – as Johnson knows, having travestied the 'doorstep carol singers' scene from *Love Actually* in a 2019 Tory Party election broadcast – are about Christmas Eve, about 'getting there' against the odds, even if they are odds of your own creation.

For Ursula von der Leyen, the European Commission president, it is a 'good deal ... it is a fair deal, it is a balanced deal.' It is also generally accepted to be a thin deal, focusing mainly on goods, rather than services. The one great big fat fact of it is that, thanks to the Northern Ireland Protocol and that Limited Additional Process on Goods Arriving in Northern Ireland, as Michael Gove would have it, the United Kingdom as it has functioned for the century since Partition will cease to be in one week's time.

Which is not to say that there cannot or will not be a UK Mark 3 that surprises everyone (including, I suspect, Boris Johnson) by working better than Mark 2. (Mark 1, of course, having incorporated the 26 as well as the 6.).

Ursula von der Leyen may have been referring to more than the Brexit negotiations when, closing her statement announcing the deal, she quotes T. S. Eliot's 'Little Gidding':

What we call the beginning is often the end
And to make an end is to make a beginning.

The DUP, who supported Brexit, announce that they will be voting against the deal that sets out the terms for how it will be effected. Labour, who (in the end) opposed Brexit, announce that they will be voting for the deal. For the former, Brexit is still good, but this deal is about as bad as it could be; for the latter, Brexit is still bad, but a deal of any kind is better than no deal, and never mind that this deal would go through whether they voted for it or not.

Opinion in the South seems unevenly split between (at the lower end) genuine sadness at confirmation of the UK's leaving and (at the upper) positive gloating, heaping scorn on the Brits for their attempts to pass off a self-inflicted defeat as a victory.

There are a – very – few voices cautioning against schadenfreude, and about the less than veiled prejudice in some of the commentary, but in the main there seems to be a perception that Ireland has played this all pretty well, increasing its standing on the European and indeed the world stage, and has an opportunity now to profit from its nearest neighbour's self-imposed exile.

In fact, the countries that make up these islands are ending the year like so many teenagers who have taken to their rooms and who are all following different – at times dramatically different – rules and timetables. (That is low, I admit: apologies to teenagers everywhere.) Even those who have been most consistent in their approach – to Covid as well as Brexit – are capable of bewildering changes of direction, like the contestants in Mike Reid's semi-unhinged *Runaround*, a 1970s kids' quiz show, premised on undermining contestants' confidence in their first decision. The opening programme of the 1979 series (it is up there on YouTube) is instructive, though least of all in relation to the game itself.

'If there are any newcomers to this country,' our host says, by way of introduction, 'and I know by the laws these days there aren't many' – I cannot tell whether his smile is one of delight at the fact that there aren't, or the fact he has just got away with criticizing the government's immigration policy on a children's game show – 'but if there's any of them, these are the rules. Now, the kids are asked a question to which there are three possible answers, which are on the board in front of them up there. Now, the idea of the game is that if they know the answer they go to a wrong answer' – a wink – 'and then they run around so they can mislead their friends off the right answer … Now, if they are right, they get a yellow ball, which counts as one point … Now, this is where the game has changed, it used to be a red ball, but because we have gone to great expense, the yellow ball counts as one point, and the outright winner of the game' – you can almost hear Reid losing the will to live, as well as all semblance of grammatical construction: *it has taken him nearly three minutes to get here* – 'the red ball counts as two points! Got the idea?'

Erm … No.

Though I am entertaining myself by adapting those rules with burgundy passport and blue passport for yellow and red ball, and translating Mike Reid's cockney into Boris Johnson's – what is that exactly? 'buffoonery'?

I am by nature, I like to think, an optimist – or maybe that should be, taking a 'Little Gidding' lead, an Elio(p)timist:* things will go on; everything that now is will one day not be, and things as yet undreamt of will arrive and take on the semblance of permanency until they too, unthinkably for the generation then living, pass in their turn into history, and so on and so on and so on.

For the life of me, though, I cannot yet see what the next configuration here might be.

* I have ordered a drawing board. As soon as it arrives, I promise, that will be the first word back on it.

Nollaig/Athbhliain

My sister- and brother-in-law in Dublin have given me *Twilight Together: Portraits of Ireland at Home*, a lockdown project by music photographer Ruth Medjber, who – with the permission of the people inside – took photos of households through their lit front windows. I am reminded of Jonathan's line from earlier in the year about Ireland as it presented at Phoenix Park during Pope John Paul II's visit in 1979: all white and all with the same haircut. It may, of course, be a lockdown thing, but in 2020 the beard, for men, on this evidence, is verging on ubiquitous. Medjber's Ireland is not – in keeping with statistics on population change – anything like as uniformly white, although there are reminders within these pages that it is not yet uniformly accepting of people arriving from other places. One photograph, three-quarters of the way through the book, is of a man called Ben who faces deportation after fourteen years living and working in Ireland. His partner, Bernie, works on behalf of those seven and a half thousand persons in need of international protection (to use the preferred term from that *New Yorker* piece) currently living in Ireland's Direct Provision Centres.

Here in the North, meanwhile, attacks on the homes of persons in need of international protection continue to be an all-too-regular occurrence. Early in the New Year arsonists destroy the building used by the Belfast Multicultural Association.

My wife's Christmas reading is a book, which she is reviewing, by Simone Wesner of the Department of Film, Media & Cultural Studies at the University of London, Birkbeck, on the fate of visual artists in Saxony (from 1949–1990 part of the German Democratic Republic) before, during and after German reunification, a book that one previous reviewer, Evelyn Preuss, believes should be of interest to 'historians, political scientists, art historians, German and Eastern European Studies scholars, as well as transition researchers'.[35] I am not sure whether this last describes me, but I find myself, as Ali relays it to me, morbidly interested in its tale of misunderstanding, marginalization and self-censorship. Thirty years on from the events of 1989–90 – the fall of the Berlin Wall to reunification – former GDR artists find themselves accused of hypocrisy or even complicity for operating under, and accepting financial support from, the old regime. They have difficulty in expressing, or having accepted as valid, feelings other than complete antipathy for a place – and a system, in its broadest sense: a way of negotiating your way from one end of the day to the other – that many of them were born into and grew to adulthood in. Back in the early 2000s, I wrote an essay for an exhibition about an East Berlin bar called Luxus – in English, Luxury – which had established itself, with minimal redecoration and zero attempt at upkeep, in a former kosher butcher shop. The owner had done time under the GDR regime for the almost definitive East German crime of 'shirking'. A starker contrast to Alex's mother in *Good Bye, Lenin!* it would be hard to imagine. And yet, and yet. Ask

him about what had happened since ... He makes a face, or
he made one then. The East Berlin he knew was disappearing
without trace and the people who had kept themselves, often
at great personal cost, at a critical angle to the old are lumped
in with it for not rushing with open arms to embrace the new.

The opposite of *that*, I concluded, is not necessarily *this*.

The second last day of the year is also the eighty-third
anniversary of that constitution I have been sleeping with
under my pillow all these months coming into effect. (It was
voted through five months earlier, in July 1937.) There have to
date been thirty-eight amendments, technically thirty-two: the
twelfth, the twenty-second, twenty-fourth, twenty-fifth, thirty-
second *and* thirty-fifth amendments were all rejected, although
the twenty-sixth, ratifying the Nice Treaty, was pretty much a
re-run of the unsuccessful twenty-fourth; the thirty-sixth on the
other hand repeals another amendment, the eighth, in relation
to Article 40 of the original document, thereby ensuring that
provision be made in law for the regulation of termination of
pregnancy. The rejected twelfth and the successful thirteenth
and fourteenth, adopted the same day, also related to abortion.
Taken altogether, in fact, there have been only slightly fewer
amendments and attempted amendments relating to abortion
than to the European Union: five to seven. The nineteenth
amendment, meanwhile, endorsed by referendum on 3 June
1998, in parallel with the vote north of the border on the Belfast
Agreement, recognizes that 'a united Ireland shall be brought
about only by peaceful means with the consent of a majority
of the people, democratically expressed, in both jurisdictions
in the island'.

There have, tellingly, been as many amendments put forward in the twenty-two years since 1998 as there were in the preceding sixty-one years, which strongly suggests a generation, or two, remaking a state in their own image. Other amendments surely await. Or – I think of the hotels of my childhood, venues for wedding receptions and once-in-a-decade family reunions: grand houses, progressively added to and modified, outhouses brought in by way of long flat-roofed corridors – maybe there is just one, the amendment that says let us move on to a whole new edifice.

Imbolc's Back

The United Kingdom of Great Britain and Northern Ireland duly left the European Union on 1 January 2021. And on 1 January 2021 Northern Ireland duly remained part of the European Single Market.

The EU and the UK have agreed a three-month 'grace period' to allow businesses time to adjust to the new measures – agreed only days before they were otherwise due to come into effect and to allow the British government time to do little fiddly things like, you know, build the customs posts at Northern Ireland's ports that were always, always, always going to be part of the outworking of the Protocol and work on which ought properly to have begun at the start of the transition period last Biddy's Day.

The first shopping day after the new arrangements kick in, I take a walk, late afternoon, to my local wholefood shop, whose owner, Michael, an ardent Remainer, once told me how conflicted he felt, listening to the sentiments of his Leave-voting customers. 'They aren't stupid, Glenn.'

Standing a couple of feet in from the front door, before the table and DIY Perspex screen Michael installed when the first lockdown lifted last May, I ask the young woman serving today for my usual kilo bag of rolled oats.

'I'm sorry,' she says. 'We can't get them because of Brexit.' I laugh. She doesn't.

Wholesalers across the water were reluctant in the weeks before Christmas – before the *Love Actually* trade deal was reached – to fulfil orders. She is hoping that they can be persuaded now. The grace period is fine for the supermarkets but offers far less protection for small traders like them.

I am almost tempted to leave a line blank for anyone who has already thought it to insert: 'They aren't stupid … really?'

Why would anyone vote to hurt themselves, or their neighbours, in this way or not at least have wondered whether such hurt might be a consequence of what they voted for?

Which might sound like a big question to be asking over a bag of rolled oats. Except it is not, as it turns out, just a bag of oats, and even the supermarkets are not as well protected as we, and possibly they, had expected. As the month progresses there are more and more gaps on the shelves as suppliers in Great Britain struggle to get to grips with the goods-to-Northern-Ireland paperwork (because as the Protocol legislation repeatedly makes clear, unfettered access to markets is entirely one-directional) or try to decide whether it is worth their while getting to grips with it at all. (John Lewis, Made.com among others decide it is not.) Michael Gove, not smirking now, says there were always going to be difficulties to begin with and that – picking up a phrase that Health Secretary Matt Hancock left lying around after his most recent Covid-19 briefing – things are likely to get worse before they get better.

In one of those only-in-this-country moments, at the start of the second full week of the year, Sinn Féin, sounding more upbeat than Michael Gove, claim that, in fact, supplies are already almost back to normal – a case of 'what they say they see is what you don't get': every shop you go into, there are clear signs to the contrary. (A couple of months later, Northern Ireland's chief pharmaceutical officer warns that, as the BBC reports, without mitigation, the supply of medicines and medical devices into Northern Ireland would also be considered a 'very high risk area', with up to 98% of medicines and medical supplies currently coming in through Great Britain.)[36] The DUP, meanwhile, continue to rail against the Protocol – withholding their support when the new trade deal is brought before the House of Commons – their representatives, doing the rounds of radio and television studios, resembling so many clockwork tin toys, wound to within a single turn of busted, hopping on the spot, or falling on their sides, their legs and their wheels still moving.

Of course, Northern Ireland from its very inception enjoyed special status within the UK (I mean, not *every* part of the Union was allowed to deny upwards of 35 per cent of its population any hope of entering into government), and of course, of course, of course, *of course*, in recent decades in particular it has been so heavily subsidised as to appear effectively propped up. But this current state of affairs feels even more precarious. Less Propped-up than Pop-up.

And then just when you think things cannot possibly get more *messed* up …

29 January 2021. For several hours late yesterday afternoon and evening there was, technically speaking, a hard border on the island of Ireland, put there not by the United Kingdom

but by the European Union, rattled by the UK's having stolen a march on vaccinating against Covid-19, and trying to cut off what the European Commission saw as a backdoor route through Northern Ireland for further supplies from factories in Europe. Without warning to Westminster, the Commission invoked Article 16 of the Protocol, which reads (paragraph 1): 'If the application of this Protocol leads to serious economic, societal or environmental difficulties that are likely to persist, or to diversion of trade, the Union or the United Kingdom may unilaterally take appropriate safeguard measures.' Without warning to Westminster, *and* without warning to Dublin and apparently without any regard for what the effects might be within Northern Ireland.

The EU looked, in those hours, to have done to the Irish government what the Conservatives had done repeatedly to the DUP, played them for mugs: this was never really about you; this was only ever about the bigger *us*.

And although the decision was reversed before midnight, you did not have to be a Democratic Unionist to suspect the Commission of double standards. In fact, Sinn Féin were just as vocal as the DUP in their condemnation, which, as one unnamed EU official said, was a measure of just how badly the Commission had blundered. Anyone looking for another measure could do worse than read the editorial in the *Observer*,[37] no friend of the Tories, and resolutely pro-European: 'The vaccine crisis has shown the EU at its worst. By contrast, it has shown Britain at its best,' it says, singling out for praise the Johnson government's early purchasing decisions *and* the efficient management of the rollout under the directorship of Kate Bingham, a venture capitalist with no prior vaccine experience, married to a Conservative minister: precisely the sort of appointee the paper would week in, week out – and with reason – train its sights on.

It gets harder with every day of these locked-down TV-fuelled times not to translate current affairs into character-driven television drama – and I have been trying: really, really I have been trying (and trying to ignore, too, that as 2020 gives way to 2021 it is *The Great*, based on the intrigue-ridden life of Catherine II of Russia, that is setting the tone), but you would have to say, in returning-television-series* terms the EU Article 16 announcement was a smart start-of-new-season move, especially after that generous and dignified speech by Ursula von der Leyen at the end of the last season: *didn't see that one coming … what do all the principals do now?* In any other terms you would say it was completely fucking stupid.

Quite apart from anything else, it gives renewed impetus to the DUP's demands (in part answer to that question in the previous paragraph) for the Protocol to be junked: the EU acted unilaterally, why not now the UK? The party announces that it will be launching a challenge to the legality of the Protocol in the High Court and will in the meantime be refusing to participate in North–South bodies set up under the terms of the Good Friday Agreement. As ever in politics here – and perhaps politics anywhere – you have to look at what else is happening at any given time, which in relation to unionism in the present moment means the rise in support for the TUV – Traditional

* I am going with *Break-ups & Make-ups* as a working title.

Unionist Voice. Never was the singular more apt: the party has largely been a vehicle – think Smart car – for Jim Allister.

By early February the anti-Protocol rhetoric has been succeeded by … well, it is hard to tell what exactly: graffiti appears in the port town of Larne, which is interpreted as threatening staff carrying out checks on freight coming into Northern Ireland from Great Britain. The DUP-dominated Mid and East Antrim Borough Council, covering Larne, withdraws its staff temporarily, claiming that unspecified individuals have been taking a note of car registrations. Within days, though, the facilities are open again and the staff back at work after the police say there has been no 'credible threat', and unions deny that they had ever gone to the council with concerns about car registrations being taken in the first place.

At the same time as all that is – or is not – going on, there is a very definite and deliberate act of loyalist paramilitary intimidation in east Belfast. In the middle of a Tuesday afternoon – and within full view of the main road – up to sixty masked members of the UVF ignore the small number of police deployed to … stand and watch them, it looks like, while they make their way to a community centre, which distributes food parcels to vulnerable families, and in which a number of people, including women with young children, have taken refuge. (All those worries I was having when I approached people in the street to talk, thinking to myself, 'I'm a masked man' …? I need not have worried. You still know *masked men* when you see them.) The television news reports suggest that among those taking refuge are members of the family of Ian Ogle, whom the UVF beat and stabbed to death on a nearby street at the start of 2019.

The centre closes its doors in the aftermath of the incident, citing threats to staff and users. On cue, a group that speaks for the UVF and other loyalist paramilitaries says there have been no threats ... It is becoming something of a motif.

Arrests do follow, including of the man regularly spoken of as the leader of the UVF in the east of the city. At time of (finishing) writing, charges are still pending.

All of this is sadly consistent with a report before Christmas by the Independent Reporting Commission (IRC), set up to monitor what progress is being made towards ending paramilitary activity. The short answer, in this the third year of reporting, being 'not much':

'[F]or Northern Ireland as a whole,' the report concludes, 'the continued existence of paramilitarism in our view constitutes a "clear and present danger" on an ongoing basis.'[38]

There are, soberingly, scarily, no fewer than twelve paramilitary organizations currently operating in Northern Ireland, more than there were in 1998 at the time of the Good Friday Agreement. It is no sort of stretch to say that all the republican ones will also be operating, or have some sort of presence, in the South. Some of them can be truly described as 'micro'; others ... not so.*

Although those members regularly engaged in paramilitary activities – beatings, intimidation, racketeering, murder – might number in the hundreds, the two main loyalist organizations,

---

* One of those, the New IRA, which maimed PC Peadar Heffron and murdered journalist and activist Lyra McKee, in April attempts to murder another PSNI officer and her three-year-old daughter with a bomb attached to a container of flammable liquid.

the UVF and the UDA, can between them call on up to 12,500 (mostly) men. That is almost 6,000 more than the PSNI, 2,000 more than the combined Defence Forces of Ireland, army, air corps and navy (including reserves), and only a little over 2,000 behind the Garda Síochána. And we have not begun to count the republicans.

You have got to ask of the successive governments who have countenanced this, what the fuck were you thinking?

Twelve months on from the start of the coronavirus outbreak there are already calls for public inquiries into the British government's response. I have never in the nearly quarter of a century since 1998 heard anyone ask for a proper reflection on the handling of the 'peace' here. There seems to have been a universal acceptance that to confront the paramilitaries was to risk a 'return to violence'. In ways that it never was at the height of the conflict, their presence has been normalized. This is our 'learning to live with Covid'. And as with Covid it is the poorest who have suffered and who continue to suffer most.

And two days on from writing *that* I read that the Loyalist Communities Council, an umbrella group that includes representatives of the UVF and the UDA,* is temporarily withdrawing its support for the Good Friday Agreement in protest at the Protocol.

Seriously … just what the fuck?

*

---

* Would that it was only umbrellas they toted.

On 10 March, ahead of the second successive St Patrick's Day in lockdown, half-page ads appear in several newspapers in the US appealing to the Irish government to promote and plan for (capital-)Unity and calling, too, on the American government and public representatives to urge the British government to set the date for 'the' Unity Referendum (capitals again). The ads are paid for by Friends of Sinn Féin, a registered agent of Sinn Féin itself in the USA. They carry the endorsement and the emblems of five other organizations including the Ancient Order of Hibernians, which is as exclusively Catholic as the Orange Order is Protestant. ('Five other Irish-American organizations co-signed our letter,' the Friends of Sinn Féin homepage says, 'and we are proud to stand with them for Irish Unity.') The cost of a *New York Times* ad alone is $90,000. Whether the total cost amounts to the quarter of a million quid the DUP spent on its *Metro* Vote Leave ad, I could not say, but you would imagine it must come pretty close. And while you might argue that there is a difference between appealing to voters and appealing to governments, it is still a clear example of a political party using a media outlet in a country where it does not stand for election to seek to influence policy in the place where it does and an example, too, surely, of what the Working Group on Unification Referendums on the Island of Ireland had in mind when it stressed that campaign finance regulations needed to be robust enough to ensure fairness between the two sides. And all this at a time when the atmosphere in Northern Ireland is already tense due to the difficulties in the implementation of the Protocol and loyalist reaction to it. It is hard in this context to see how reassured anyone anxious or fearful about the outcome

THE LAST IRISH QUESTION

of a referendum would be by the line that a United Ireland 'will be a welcoming home for all', especially when it is preceded by the bald assertion, 'The Unionist (Pro-Union with Britain) electoral majority in the North is gone.'

The ad's sign-off, 'With your support we can be the first generation of Americans to visit a free and United Ireland', has me scrabbling back through my notes for a speech – there it is, 2 January, and apologies, not a speech, a *tweet* – by Kevin J. Boyle, who sits on the Democrat side of the Pennsylvania House of Representatives: 'In 2020 we saw the passing of an Irish patriot for the ages. Born in 1956 into state of systematic British and Unionist oppression, Bobby Storey dedicated his life to fighting that injustice. While Bobby left before his time, his cause of *a free and united Ireland* is coming.'

There is much in those forty-nine words to unpack, but let us just pause for a second at the five I have italicized in the final clause. The 'free' clearly maps back onto the 'British and Unionist oppression'. Northern Ireland – in Kevin J. Boyle's view and in the Friends of Sinn Féin's – equals 'Unfree Ireland'. Which makes the million or so people who identify with its Britishness … what? Victims of false consciousness? Dupes? Quislings? *

Or maybe just wary, many of them, that for every reassurance that they have nothing to fear in an Ireland of Equals they are served up a reminder that for a certain strain of republicanism they are and always will be the bad guys here.

---

* Friends of Sinn Féin conveniently/wilfully overlook the fact that while a majority no longer vote for parties with Unionist in their name a sizeable number of those who vote Alliance – fast becoming the third largest party – are at the very least open to Northern Ireland remaining in the United Kingdom.

I am wholly unsurprised when I discover, after visiting their website, that the free and united sentence in the Friends of Sinn Féin ad is lightly adapted from a quotation, earlier in the year, from Gerry Adams.

And, you know, if Gerry says it, it must be so.

The week after St Patrick's Day, RTÉ gives over an hour and a half of primetime television to a special *Claire Byrne Live* on the question – and it is posed as a question: the largest character on the studio backdrop throughout is the question mark itself – of a United Ireland.

First up are Mary Lou McDonald and Leo Varadkar. This is Sinn Féin, through its current party president, in that aforementioned 'nobody has anything to fear' mode. Mary Lou says she does not expect a referendum tomorrow or next week – which does make you wonder why her party's friends in the US went and spent all that money urging that a date be set – but adds that it would be a dereliction to 'fail to feel the winds of history and change moving around us'. For all her emphasis on conversation, however, this is still, as she says at one point, the 'endgame'. Again, we will talk to you about any outcome as long as it is this one.

Leo manages to not agree while agreeing, or maybe the agreeing precedes the not, which increasingly seems to be the corner Fine Gael and Fianna Fáil have painted themselves into, by virtue of Sinn Féin having taken up position right next to the door they all say they want to walk through eventually. There will be a United Ireland and he hopes to see a United Ireland but not the way Sinn Féin are going about it. We have first to make sure all the strands of the Good Friday Agreement are working properly, the Assembly at Stormont, the North–South institutions, and the East–West relationships, between Ireland and Britain. He asks what things the (Southern) Irish people would be prepared to change in order to accommodate a million people – Northern unionists – who are at the very least uncertain about what a United Ireland would look like and mean. He offers up his own job title – Tánaiste – and throws in the Taoiseach's: both of these derive from Celtic chieftains. Would they be appropriate in this New Ireland? Claire Byrne mentions the anthem – 'Amhrán na bhFiann', composed originally in English as 'A Soldier's Song' – and the flag. On the latter both Varadkar and McDonald are nimble of foot. All things ought to be on the table, but symbols are not in any case the main concern for the majority of people and besides the flag already unites the orange and the green. Or occasionally still, as they do not say, the gold and the green.

The DUP MP for East Londonderry, Gregory Campbell, is brought into the conversation remotely to say what anyone who knows the DUP and Gregory Campbell in particular would expect him to say, though with perhaps not *quite* as much sneering as usual,* that a United Ireland is not going to happen. (It would be remiss of me not to say that he uses the same 'Cloud Cuckoo Land' as the Not Well-Liked man I spoke to in Carlingford.) He does push a new line – a riposte perhaps to that 'no Unionist majority' stat that Sinn Féin is so fond of – that Northern Ireland now consists of three minorities: unionist, nationalist and those who see themselves as neither,

---

* This is, with Gregory, extremely relative.

what several of the other contributors to the debate are in the habit of referring to as the Middle Ground. The focus, he insists, ought to be on ensuring that Northern Ireland works for all three of those.

As for unionists like him being open to persuasion ... Listen to these three words, he says, 'We are British.'

And that, with a bit of come back and up-summing from the Tánaiste and the Sinn Féin president, is it for Act/Part 1.

The stage is reset during the break to accommodate a 'range of voices', the first of them belonging to Andrew Trimble, a former Ireland rugby international and a Northern Protestant living in the South. His generation – he is thirty-six – do not want binary, green or orange. They are the moderate ones, the growing (that term) Middle Ground: the white, I guess, although that does tend to suggest that there is no moderation in the other two colours or that you cannot get white with a hint of either one.'

'If the majority is moderate,' says the advocate of the devil in the voice of Claire Byrne, 'it should be easy to effect change.'

Trimble is followed by singer Niamh McElduff from Tyrone who talks about the Irish language and Gaelic Football – 'we like to play our football at Croke Park, why shouldn't we have our politicians in Leinster House?' – and quotes former Tyrone player Peter Canavan as saying while he was trying to win an All-Ireland friends of his were trying to free it. Then comes first lawyer and commentator Sarah Creighton – I think I am

---

* I looked long, I looked hard, on your behalf, and it appears that Farrow & Ball are the only paint company offering both an orangey white and a greeny.

remembering this in order – and second Jamie Bryson, who is roughly Andrew Trimble's generation, and whose interview is preceded by a quote to the effect that he would rather choke on his own blood than live in a United Ireland. 'A rhetorical flourish,' he tells Claire Byrne now, before going on to say that, while he does not agree with it or condone it, it would be foolish to think that there would not be people who would use violence to resist reunification in the same way that there were people who had used violence all these years to resist the Union with Great Britain.

The next contributor, Joe Brolly, 'analyst and former [Gaelic] footballer' as he is billed, makes a point of lauding the transformation that has already been wrought – 'We have had a spectacularly successful peace process, for me, the most successful peace process the world has seen; I mean, you look at how quickly the violence has been switched off …' – before turning to the failings of the DUP: Gregory Campbell's version of Northern Ireland is 'Fantasy Land' (I dream of it and 'Cloud Cuckoo Land' drawn against one another in a World Cup qualifier), and as for his party's contempt for the Irish language, Gaelic games, its homophobia and its racism …

Claire Byrne cuts him off. Gregory is not here to defend himself. Joe Brolly looks utterly astonished. Defend himself against what?

There is a further studio discussion between broadcaster Dearbhail McDonald ('comfortably Irish British'), historian Diarmaid Ferriter, and former Fine Gael Taoiseach John Bruton, who quotes John Hume on the need to think of uniting people, not territory, and points out that Northern Irish wages will need to be brought up to Southern levels in the event that unity is achieved: on average (if I got my figures right earlier) €8,000–10,000.

When the lights come up after the second interval they are on a single chair facing Claire Byrne's, occupied by the current Taoiseach, Micheál Martin, his natural hesitancy making him appear not so much headliner as (to leap to another arena altogether) tailender. He, too, sidesteps a delivery about the flag and the anthem. Those are the symbols rather than the substance that people are really interested in. He talks of the Good Friday Agreement's emphasis on parity of esteem and says that must be carried over into the government structures of a new Ireland and repeats John Hume's line about uniting people.* There is a slight smile when, in answer to a question about the cost of Northern Ireland, 'the unwanted child' in Diarmaid Ferriter's words, he says, 'hence the importance of the British-Irish relationship to underpin the evolution of a shared island'. I *think* that might be code for Britain is going to have to underwrite the costs for a while after unification. Any ardent Brexiteers who saw cutting Northern Ireland adrift as a price worth paying for taking back control of budgets as well as borders, in other words, are going to have to accept that on top of EU 'divorce settlement' payments there will now be maintenance to pay.

And that is the curtain, or stumps.

* Intriguingly, later in the spring when he takes over as leader of the UUP, Doug Beattie begins introducing the term 'Union of People' into his interviews with the press.

And maybe at the end of the evening the line that sticks with me is a line of Seán Lemass's, as rendered by Diarmaid Ferriter, on the occasion that he advised his cabinet to stop using the Free State-era term 'the Six Counties' when speaking of Northern Ireland. It was time they learned to accept the fact of it and time to recognize the distinctiveness of it, whatever the future constitutional arrangement might be:

'Gentlemen [and of course they were all then], there will always be a Northern Ireland.'

This season is serving up an episode a week. We have barely had time to digest the *Claire Byrne Live* debate – and that 'most successful peace process in history' comment – when, in the final week of March, Northern Ireland's Public Prosecution Service (PPS) announces that no prosecutions will be brought as a result of Bobby Storey's funeral last June, despite recommendations by the PSNI that some of the twenty-four Sinn Féin politicians from South and North both who were present and subsequently interviewed by police be charged. In the view of the PPS the 'fact that large crowds gathered to watch did not make participation unreasonable in circumstances where efforts had been made to limit those formally participating to 30 persons'. Nowhere in its judgement does it say anything about the scores of men in white shirts and black ties who walked behind the cortège, who frankly for me as a citizen were always of rather more concern than the fifty or thirty or whatever the number was that Pearse Doherty could not remember he was a part of in the cortège, nor does it make clear how summoning those people to attend, down to how they dressed, squares with making efforts to limit those formally participating. Nor indeed does it specify who the 'stewarding company' was that the organizers employed, though I am going to take a wild, wild guess here …

That third IRC report before Christmas was less reticent about what passed before the viewing public's eyes back in June. It specifically mentioned as a cause for greater debate and focus funerals and commemorations, for which it suggests the catch-all term 'Memorialisation of the Past':

'There have been several occasions during the year where echoes of the paramilitary past were brought starkly into the present by means of events such as funerals or the public displays at various times of flags and emblems depicting paramilitary figures or events … these events and incidents have the capacity to damage trust and confidence between communities.'

I would question – given their earlier assertion of 'clear and present danger' – whether it was only echoes of the past brought into the present we were witnessing at such times. *This has been with us all the way. This – as much as the new film studios and tech start-ups and boutique hotels and Titanic Experiences – is what life looks like here and has looked like here for the past twenty-three years.* The report's conclusions, though, would seem to me to have implications for any form of shared island, and to call into question some of those assertions on the Claire Byrne United Ireland (?) special about symbols.

We have in mind events/occasions such as funerals, anniversaries, murals, flags, emblems, memorial plinths, remembrance areas, street names, club names etc. This

THE LAST IRISH QUESTION

is by no means an exhaustive list and these examples are mentioned simply by way of illustration. The common denominator is the connection in some way to paramilitarism, and past paramilitary figures and events. In light of the continuing controversy around these issues, what we are suggesting is greater debate and focus on the whole area, so that whenever such events, people or moments are being commemorated – memorialised – account is taken of the potential wider impact in the context of what the Fresh Start Agreement calls the "continued transformation of our society."

The Public Prosecution Service's decision is based in part on a perceived lack of clarity in the regulations in force on the day of Bobby Storey's funeral, despite some of the twenty-four Sinn Féin politicians questioned having helped frame them, and in part on the fact that, as previously stated, the organizers had had discussions in advance with the police about arrangements, either of which, the PPS's team of senior prosecutors assisted by Senior Counsel concluded, could constitute a 'reasonable excuse defence'.

The DUP responds to the second part of this reasoning by calling for the Chief Constable to resign, ignoring both the fact that his service had recommended prosecutions, and that their party had contributed to the lack of clarity element of that reasonable excuse.

The other unionist parties follow suit, although in the matter of the DUP and the TUV it is not always apparent who is following who.

And then on the evening of Good Friday rioting breaks out in the Sandy Row and Donegall Road area, right on the southern edge of the city centre, and bordering what was once referred to as the 'golden mile' of restaurants and bars. For several hours, rioters – a couple carrying Union Jacks – hurl petrol bombs, bricks and masonry at police Land Rovers and riot shields.

Finding myself in the city centre the following evening – at 7 p.m., on an Easter holiday, not the busiest, even before you factor in the closure, due to global pandemic, of almost the entire retail and hospitality sectors – I am, simply put, completely unnerved. I weigh up which of the buses I can take, headed east, that will be least likely to be hijacked. I let two, almost empty, double-deckers depart – one going via the Newtownards Road, one going via the Albertbridge Road – and opt instead for a Glider, one of Belfast's new-generation purple concertina long buses, on the basis that, with their only having come into service since the last serious unrest five or six years ago, no one will have figured out yet how to bring them down.

In fact, the road (Albertbridge) is perfectly quiet. I almost blush behind my mask at my earlier panic. Shortly after I get home, though, my younger daughter shows me a clip that is circulating on social media of cars being hijacked and set alight at a roundabout at Newtownabbey, a couple of miles to the north of the city centre. This being in the fiefdom of the South East Antrim UDA, which operates outside the 'command structure' of the rest of UDA, and the South East Antrim UDA ('a criminal cartel that have wrapped themselves in a flag', in the words of one former senior police officer) currently being under heavy pressure from the PSNI, we might add to disquiet over the Northern Ireland

Protocol, existential fears stirred up by calls for a border poll, and the PPS decision over the Bobby Storey funeral, a very specific desire here simply to create a bit of a distraction.

The burning bus comes two nights later on the Shankill Road: a petrol bomb tossed through the front door while the driver is still inside. (The driver escapes, but no thanks to the petrol bombers.) The rioting by this time has followed a time-honoured pattern, spreading sideways out from the Shankill towards, and finally across, the peace line with the nationalist Springfield Road. Many of those arrested are in their early or mid-teens. Even the older ones were scarcely more than infants when the Good Friday Agreement was signed twenty-three Aprils ago.

I am talking to a producer from one of the main Radio 4 news programmes. 'We all thought it was settled,' she says, and I think that the gauzy curtain I have spoken of, hanging in the mid-distance when I look, or sometimes even think, South, is for people across the water looking, or thinking, over here more like a metal shutter.

Belatedly politicians of all shades talk of the need to take the heat out of the situation (the two largest parties are past masters at calling for the heat to be taken out, having just whacked up the thermostat themselves), though it takes the best part of a week for their words to have any perceptible effect.

Actually, it takes the best part of a week and the death, the Friday following Good Friday, of Prince Philip. The disturbances are not switched off exactly, but they do over the next couple of days lessen then cease. Michelle O'Neill, acknowledging the role played by the Queen and Prince Philip in their visit to the Republic and in meeting Martin McGuinness in Belfast, offers her condolences. 'On behalf of all of the people of Northern Ireland, [Sinn Féin] send love and best wishes to Her Majesty the Queen and to all of the royal family.'

Arlene Foster acknowledges and welcomes that and other conciliatory comments. In a special sitting of the Assembly marked by civility and courtesy on all sides, she says, 'I think the unity of spirit has been evident so let us all harness and channel that spirit moving ahead as the Assembly and Executive work through the very real and significant challenges that face us.'

Oh, Arlene. If only you knew.

It is, in the end, gay conversion therapy that does for her, or at least that sets the boulder rolling down the hill. For a change in recent times, Northern Ireland is ahead of the Republic, which is only at the stage of commissioning a scoping paper, and Britain, where the word is that plans will be brought forward 'shortly', in debating a motion – introduced by two Ulster Unionist MLAs – calling for conversion therapy in all its forms to be banned. A DUP amendment allowing for continued religious interventions is defeated and the UUP motion is carried by 59 votes to 24. The twenty-four are all DUP, plus Jim Allister. But the DUP has twenty-eight MLAs. Arlene Foster – though she voted for the amendment – is among the five (including two fellow Executive ministers) who abstain from the main vote.

At the start of the last week of April four letters from local councillors begin to circulate expressing dissatisfaction with the party leadership and calling for a return to traditional Christian values. Within days, the letters have been signed by as many as twenty-three of the twenty-eight MLAs. Exactly the same number as voted against the motion to ban conversion therapy. Four of the party's eight Westminster MPs sign, too.

Before the week is out Arlene Foster is – if not quite gone – then going, announcing her resignation as party leader at the end of May, as first minister of Northern Ireland at the end of June and from the DUP on the same day.*

Ironically, one of the charges I have heard laid against her is that she was not sufficiently outraged by an online tribute made by the Cavan and Monaghan branch of Sinn Féin to Seamus McElwain, killed by the SAS in 1986, suspected of up to ten killings himself in the Fermanagh border area, and believed to be the man who in 1979 shot and almost killed Arlene Foster's own father at the family farm in Roslea.

I can only think this is what Matt Carthy, Sinn Féin TD for Cavan and Monaghan, has in mind when he says in the twenty-minute video that Seamus McElwain 'took the war to the British'. He repeats the unionist-majority-is-gone line. The delivery of 'the republic', he says, is at last within reach. This is a man who sits in the parliament of the United Nations member state officially described as the Republic of Ireland. The final frame is the Irish flag fluttering, full screen, while 'Amhrán na bhFiann' is sung. There is little here to suggest that the party that might form the next government in the South and emerge as the largest party in the North has any intention of looking

---

* Some reports suggest more than four letters – letters, in fact, from over half the DUP's eighteen local associations – others just the one. A month on from her resignation Arlene Foster claims to have seen none and openly questions whether they, or it, ever existed.

critically or generously at either the symbols or the substance of the concerns of those for whom Britain is not an alien, occupying nation, but a word they sometimes use for home.

I am typing these words on the last day of April. Beltane again tomorrow. Two days after that again Northern Ireland reaches its centenary.

The smart money is on Edwin Poots, the current minister for agriculture, environment and rural affairs, assuming the party leadership. (As minister he backed the withdrawal of staff from the new customs facilities at the start of February.) There is much debate about whether he is as hardline as he appears to the outside world: instances of his political pragmatism and ability to think, and act, on an all-island basis are cited.

One thing is certain, he will rewrite the history books.

Starting with that date of Robert Kee's at the very start of this one: there never was an 8000 BC. The world by Edwin Poots's reckoning is only 6,000 years old. Northern Ireland has been here for a pretty impressive 1.67 per cent of it.

(Poots duly won – beating Sir Jeffrey Donaldson by a single vote – and indicated that he would nominate Paul Givan as first minister. Sinn Féin used the requirement that they nominate, or renominate, Michelle O'Neill as deputy first minster – or else cause a collapse of the Assembly and an election that the DUP wanted even less than they did – to force the DUP's hand finally on the Irish language. That is, to force the British government's hand. The party sought and got a written guarantee from the Secretary of State that if legislation promised in New Decade, New Approach had not been passed by the Assembly before October, Westminster itself would legislate. Poots and Givan were the only DUP members present at the late-night talks of which this was the outcome. Just after noon the next day the two men walked out of an extraordinary meeting of DUP MLAs and MPs and into the Assembly chamber where Poots nominated and Givan accepted, despite the fact that they had just been outvoted 24-4 by their own party colleagues. Within hours, and just twenty-one days after being confirmed as leader, Poots was gone. Even by his reckoning of time, he had been leader for the blink of an eye.)

It is easy, nearly too easy, to laugh, or – to go back again to the very opening pages – to agree with Norman Davies that Protestant Ulster is a retarded time capsule. But it would be a huge mistake to think that most DUP voters – as opposed to party members (who number only in the hundreds) – are outraged by failure to support conversion therapy or vote for them because of their views on the Creation.

They vote for them in the main, or have voted up to now, because they think they are the best guarantors of the Union with Great Britain. If those voters are looking elsewhere now, or just not voting at all, it is because of the mess the DUP has made of Brexit, it is because of the Northern Ireland Protocol, the border in the Irish Sea, and because of the fear that all these taken together make a referendum on a United Ireland more likely.

Meanwhile, the latest opinion poll commissioned by BBC NI's *Spotlight* programme suggests that a majority in Northern Ireland, if voting tomorrow, would opt to stay in the United Kingdom. A slimmer majority see Northern Ireland still in the UK in ten years' time, but that majority becomes a minority when looking ahead twenty-five years.

More people in the North would like to see the Northern Ireland Protocol scrapped than kept, but an even greater number, the same percentage – 56 – as voted Remain in the 2016 referendum, want us to stay in the EU.

With a 2½ per cent margin of error, we could hardly be more evenly poised. Except in one area: more than three-quarters see a possibility of further violence whatever the outcome. 'Brexit with guns' is the term I hear. You can call that the lazy language of division, but the harder job is to get all our politicians to stop speaking it – all the time, that is – in order that those who vote for them will stop thinking it. That includes crowing over the passing of a Unionist majority as well as threatening to withdraw from institutions or start a campaign of civil disobedience.

Of course, you would like to think that ten, and certainly twenty-five years from now, we would have dealt with the problem of and the problems underlying – paramilitarism, but then twenty-three years ago, when we went to the polls, we thought that we would have done that long before now.

I am listening to another interview with Lilian Seenoi-Barr, the programmes director at the North West Migrants Forum who was so completely unsurprised, at the start of April, by the difference in how police handled Bobby Storey's funeral and Black Lives Matter protests. Speaking a few weeks later on the Community Relations Council's 'Forward Together' podcast,[39] she says she does not believe that the Good Friday Agreement brought peace to Northern Ireland: it stopped violence on the streets. There is no peace here, or if there is it is, as she says, a negative peace.

The absence of violence has been used very particularly to promote this place, but it is not until you actually live here that you realize that there has been very little progress. Our legislators and our legislative assembly still operate within the binary of sectarianism. 'The policies we develop are to advantage the "two traditions" in the North, and then we will think about this "other" community.'

And while there is only negative peace, there is always the risk of violence coming back. She identifies, without passing any judgement, the Protocol 'and even the rhetoric of an Irish border poll' as unsettling people and requiring not just sensitivity but a complete overhaul of political leadership and process.

'We don't talk to each other,' she says, 'we shout at each other and whoever shouts loudest is the one who gets heard.'

Maybe before they talk any more about exporting the Stormont model some of those in there shouting the loudest would do well to listen to the voices of people from within this 'one community, many traditions' (Lilian Seenoi-Barr again) whom it has so clearly failed.

I rejoice in Lilian Seenoi-Barr's choice to make her life here, to be, in her words, a British, Irish, Kenyan, Masai mum here (she does not add activist, but I rejoice in and am grateful for that, too), and at the same time I sympathize with anyone who concludes that these are not at all the conditions in which they are prepared to make *their* life.

Early in the New Year, long before the latest violence, but with the signs everywhere that it might not be far away, my younger daughter told me she was thinking she wanted to follow her sister and go away when she finishes school.

It was winter, we were in lockdown, again, which might have helped account for both our moods, but her frustration, her disillusionment, was real, and palpable.

I sat her down across the kitchen table from me. I told her I loved her very, very much, even more than I loved this place, which is, helplessly, a lot. 'But, please,' I said, 'the first chance you get, leave, and apart from visiting your mum and me, think long and hard before ever coming back.'

Endnotes

1 *Irish Times* pre-election editorial, 7 February 2020.
2 Fintan O'Toole on entirely sensible vote: *Irish Times*, 22 February 2020.
3 Mary Lou McDonald post-Covid interview, *Sunday Times*, 26 April 2020.
4 Michael Gove 'limited additional process on goods arriving in Northern Ireland', *Guardian*, 20 May 2020.
5 Average Earnings *Belfast Telegraph*, 9 January 2014.
6 Ireland's global clout, *The Economist*, 18 July 2020.
7 David McWilliams 'Three Decisions' quoted in *Irish Times*, 13 July 2020.
8 Northern Ireland views on the South 1965 YouTube, 26 January 2021.
9 Kelly Sullivan, 'Elizabeth Bowen and 1916: An Architecture of Suspense', *Modernism/Modernity*, 3 February 2020.
10 Colm Tóibín's review of Paddy & Mr Punch, *London Review of Books*, 18 November 1993.
11 White horse in fanlight, *Evening Herald* article quoted in *Come Here to Me* website, 20 May 2019.
12 Mary Burke 'disremembered' abuse, 'Disremembrance': Joyce and Irish Protestant Institutions, Irish-American Cultural Institute, Vol. 55, Numbers 1 & 2, Spring/Summer 2020.

13 Advertising and Eucharistic Congress Barry Shepherd, 'Infectious piousness' – Advertising and the Eucharistic Congress, 1932' *The Irish Story* website 30 August 2017.

14 Lughnasa Court Case, *Donegal Live*, 18 January 2020.

15 Rosita Boland, 'Twenty-four Hours in Bundoran', *Irish Times*, 1 August 2020.

16 Anna Nolan, *Irish Independent*, 4 August 2020.

17 Tampax letter 1, *Irish Independent*, 30 July 2020, Tampax letter2, *Irish Independent*, 21 January 2013.

18 DUP Irish Language Commitment, FactCheckNI, 30 January 2017.

19 Michael Clifford on Fr Paul Connell, *Irish Examiner*, 30 April 2016.

20 Mick Fealty on Workplace Relations Commission decision, *Slugger O'Toole*, 24 December 2020.

21 Thomas Joseph Woodgate memorial, RTÉ News, 13 October 2020.

22 Ireland's Direct Provision, *New Yorker*, 4 June 2019.

23 *Irish Statesman*, 3 October 1925.

24 Lemass on Seanad, quoted in F. S. L. Lyons, *Modern Ireland* (London, 1971) p. 537.

25 Danny Hughes on GAA, *Irish News*, 28 February 2018.

26 Colum Eastwood 50 & Frank McNally century of estrangement, *Irish Times*, 11 September 2020.

27 Seán Ó Faoláin on Knocknagow, *Irish Times*, 7 October, 2013.

28 Michael Russell on Low Deal, *The National*, 25 October 2020.

29 'The Conversation on Ireland's Future: A Principled Framework for Change', published by Ireland's Future, 3 December 2020.

30 Conor Houston, Twitter, 26 November 2020.

31 Raab's sympathetic interlocutor moved on, *Irish Times*, 10 November 2011.

32 Free State diplomatic recognition, Troy D. Davis, 'Irish Americans and the Treaty, the View from the Irish Free State', *New Hibernia Review / Iris Éireannach Nua*, Vol. 18, No. 2 (SAMHREADH/SUMMER 2014).

33 Working Group on Unification Referendums on the Island of Ireland: Interim Report, November 2020.

34 Heaney's Northern comma, Rosie Lavan, *Seamus Heaney and Society*, (Oxford, 2020) p. 139.

35 Evelyn Preuss on Simone Wesner, *Artists' Voices in Cultural Policy* (London, 2018), *Studies in 20th & 21st Century Literature (STTCL)*, Vol. 44 (1).

36 Chief Pharmaceutical Officer on medicine supply chain, *BBC NI*, 15 April 2021.

37 Article 16 editorial, *Observer*, 31 January 2021.

38 Independent Reporting Commission, Third Report, 17 November 2020.

39 Lilian Seenol-Barr, 'Forward Together' podcast (Holywell Trust), Episode 5, Season 3, 13 May 2021

Wise the fuck up.